The Culinary Institute of America
BREAKFASTS &

ALSO BY THE CULINARY INSTITUTE OF AMERICA

The Culinary Institute of America's Gourmet Meals in Minutes • Book of Soups

Baking at Home with The Culinary Institute of America

BRUNCHES

Over 175 New Recipes from the
World's Premier Culinary College

Photography by Ben Fink

LEBHAR-FRIEDMAN BOOKS

NEW YORK · CHICAGO · LOS ANGELES · LONDON · PARIS · TOKYO

THE CULINARY INSTITUTE OF AMERICA

Vice-President, Continuing Education	Mark Erickson
Director of Marketing and New Product Development	Sue Cussen
Director of Intellectual Property	Nathalie Fischer
Editorial Project Manager	Mary Donovan
Editorial Assistants	Margaret Otterstrom, Rachel Toomey
Marketing Project Assistant	Amy Townsend
Recipe Testers	Veronica Arcoraci, Alexis Jette-Borggaard, Lisa Lahey

The Culinary Institute of America would like to thank chefs Olivier Andreini, Marc Haymon, Bruce Mattel,
and John Reilly for their skilled execution and presentation of the recipes and methods for the photographs.

Special thanks to Villeroy & Boch and to Warren Cutlery of Rhinebeck, New York,
for providing some of the items used in the photography.

LEBHAR-FRIEDMAN BOOKS

A company of Lebhar-Friedman, Inc., 425 Park Avenue, New York, New York 10022

LIBRARY OF CONGRESS CATALOGING-IN-PUBLICATION DATA
Cataloging-in-publication data for this title is on file with the Library of Congress.
ISBN 0-86730-907-5

Art direction, design, and composition by Kevin Hanek
Set in Adobe Minon Pro

Manufactured in Singapore by Imago Worldwide Printing on acid-free paper

CONTENTS

Chapter 5

PANCAKES, WAFFLES & CRÊPES *111*

Chapter 6

EGGS *141*

Chapter 7

GRAINS & LEGUMES *169*

Chapter 9
SOUPS, SALADS
& SMALL BITES *221*

Chapter 8
MEATS, FISH & POTATOES *193*

Chapter One

BREAKFAST & BRUNCH
MISE EN PLACE

*B*REAKFAST AND BRUNCH are perhaps the most intensely "personal" of meals. Breakfast is a hard habit to change, but if you are in the habit of stumbling through the door with just a mug of coffee or tea, you owe it to yourself to try and get into the breakfast habit. We all have favorites, the morning equivalent of the comforting soups and stews we use to get through the winter.

Some of us treat ourselves to foods that are sweeter than we serve at lunch or dinner like muffins, fruit pastries, coffee cakes, cereals topped with sugar, or griddle cakes swimming in syrup. Others like to enjoy something bracingly salty and smoky to start the day—bacon, lox, sausage, or cheeses. Savory hot dishes like hash or home fries contrast against stimulating and tart fruit juices. Some foods are soft and creamy, others are succulent, still others crunchy or chewy.

Getting your kitchen stocked with breakfast foods and the tools that make breakfast a snap are vital if you are going to join the ranks of those who can testify that they work better, play harder, and think more clearly if they've broken their fast with a delicious and sustaining meal.

Breakfast can be as simple or elaborate as your time and appetite dictate. With the right ingredients on hand you can stop letting the day's schedule choose your menu. If you've overslept, you can choose from an array of great options tucked in your fridge or pantry to take along in a brown bag, like homemade scones or a container of your own granola to stir into some yogurt. An unexpected houseguest or two doesn't always have to mean a mad dash to the bakery before everyone wakes up. Even picky eaters can be fed and cosseted without driving the cook crazy.

Ingredients

Many of the ingredients listed below can be kept on hand for relatively long periods of time. Look for tips and strategies throughout the book on how to incorporate seasonal favorites into your breakfast plan, as well as ideas for capturing the fleeting season of perennial breakfast favorites such as strawberries and raspberries .

EGGS

Sometimes, when a cook interviews for a job at a restaurant, the chef will ask the candidate to make an omelet. This simple, unassuming dish can be prepared in literally hundreds of ways and served at almost any time of day, from breakfast through dinner. We've devoted a whole chapter to eggs and described some basic egg cookery techniques. Our recipes call for Grade AA large eggs.

Keep eggs in the refrigerator to keep them wholesome and delicious. If you have access to farm-fresh eggs in your area, by all means try them. The fresher the egg, the better the flavor. You can also find cage-free eggs, eggs enriched with omega-3, eggs from hens fed a vegetarian diet, and certified organic eggs.

In addition to making eggs to enjoy on their own, you'll find eggs as important ingredients in many other dishes. Some recipes call for eggs to be separated.

Applying egg wash Many baked goods are given a rich color and a shiny glaze by brushing them with an egg wash before they go into the oven.

Egg washes are made from whole eggs, a mixture of whole eggs and yolks, or just yolks. Blending a small amount of water, milk, or cream loosens the egg enough so that you can apply a thin glaze.

- *Make egg washes just when you need them.*
- *Use a pastry brush.*
- *Apply a thin coating and brush away any pools that develop on the surface.*
- *If possible, line the pans for egg-washed baked goods with parchment paper; the baked goods will lift away from parchment more easily than from an unlined pan. Cleanup is much simpler, too.*

DAIRY

From a dash of cream or half-and-half to lighten coffee to tart buttermilk in a pancake batter to a smear of cream cheese on a bagel, breakfast dishes call for an array of dairy products. Most will keep for several days in the refrigerator. Milk, cream, yo-

Dairy Pantry

- Milk (Note: Recipes in this book were developed with whole milk; in some cases you may be able to substitute low-fat or skim milk.)
- Buttermilk
- Yogurt (from cow, goat, or sheep milk; whole milk, reduced-fat, and nonfat; soy milk, plain and flavored)
- Cottage cheese (small or large curd, whole milk, 2%, and nonfat)

- Sour cream (whole milk, reduced-fat, or nonfat)
- Crème fraîche
- Heavy or whipping cream
- Half-and-half
- Cream cheese and Neufchâtel (in bars or tubs, also whipped)
- Cheddar (aged cheddars have a sharper flavor)

- Swiss (Gruyère or Emmenthal)
- Manchego
- Monterey Jack
- Parmesan
- Butter (unsalted, salted)
- Goat cheese (fresh and aged)
- Brie
- Blue cheese

gurt, and soft cheeses often have a date on the label. This date indicates the last date that the product is fresh enough for sale.

BREADS AND PASTRIES

Freshly baked breads, muffins, scones, and pastries make a truly remarkable addition to breakfast. In Chapters 3 and 4, we've included instructions for making breakfast breads and pastries, as well as tips for making it possible to produce these breakfast favorites without having to get up in the middle of the night. If you have a good source for baked goods, then by all means, feature them at your morning meals.

Some breakfast favorites are difficult to make at home (bagels and bialys). Good-quality bagels are getting harder and harder to find anywhere, but if you are a fan, it's worth the search. When you find them, buy plenty so that you can have some on hand to eat right away and some to store for later in the freezer.

Most baked goods are best held at room temperature, unless they have a filling made with eggs or other highly perishable ingredients.

Frozen baked goods thaw relatively quickly at room temperature. For individual bagels, muffins, or rolls, allow about 1 to 2 hours (or take them out of the freezer at night and let them thaw overnight). You can refresh thawed baked goods in a warm oven (300° to 325°F) for a few minutes, but don't put them in the microwave! They can turn rubbery.

- *Muffins and quickbreads (see the recipes on pages 38–49)*
- *Coffee cakes (see the recipes on pages 50–56)*
- *Funnel cakes (see the recipe on page 72)*
- *Breads for toasting (see the recipes on pages 79–81)*
- *Challah and brioche (see the recipes on pages 88–89)*
- *Pastries (see the recipes on pages 96–105)*

SPREADS AND SYRUPS

Some classic breakfast standbys—toast, bagels, pancakes, and waffles—cry out for a topping. We've included recipes for some outstanding spreads and flavored syrups. Having a nice supply in a cupboard is a great way to add variety to breakfast.

Jams, jellies, and marmalades will last unopened in a dark, dry cupboard for up to 1 year. In addition to using them as a spread or topping, try them as a filling for a sweet omelet. (If you make your own jams, jellies, or marmalades, be sure to use the guidelines prepared by the FDA for preparing and canning them safely.)

Compotes and relishes you make yourself should always be stored in clean containers, tightly covered, and labeled with the date you made them. They will last for several weeks in the refrigerator.

Flavored (compound) butters can be sweet or savory. We show one option for shaping them on page 123. Or, try serving them in little pots or crocks. Flavored butters freeze well. A good technique for freezing is to roll the butter into a log, wrap well, and add a label with the date. Then simply slice off what you need.

Molasses and honey last for several months in the cupboard, as long as they are tightly capped.

Maple syrup is best stored in the refrigerator where it will last for several months. Wipe any drips away from the sides, bottom, lid, and opening of the jar.

Sauces, including fruit coulis and purees, are simple to make. The recipes we provide can be doubled or tripled to take advantage of seasonal bounty. Store them in the refrigerator for up to 2 weeks or in the freezer for up to 4 months.

Curds are probably the most perishable spreads since they include egg yolks. They don't freeze very well, but you can keep them in the refrigerator for up to 1 week. Purchased fruit curds can be stored unopened in a cupboard for several months. Once opened, refrigerate and use within 2 weeks.

Nut butters (peanut, almond, or cashew) are a great alternative to butter as a spread for toasts or rolls. Freshly ground nut butters may separate as they sit; stir them to recombine just before serving. Keep freshly ground nut butters in the refrigerator. Commercial brands are homogenized so they won't separate; they can be safely stored in a cupboard in all but the hottest weather.

GRAINS AND LEGUMES

These nutritious staples last for months in your cupboard or pantry. Some stores sell grains and legumes as bulk foods.

Some grains, especially whole grains, may be sold in vacuum-sealed jars or pouches. Once the package is open, keep the contents in storage bags or containers that seal tight; they will typically last for at least 6 months and up to 1 year.

Whole grains can go rancid within 2 or 3 months since they still retain the oil-rich bran and germ. To keep them fresh and flavorful for longer periods, store them in your freezer.

A good selection of canned beans makes it easy to create great breakfasts. Be sure to drain and rinse canned beans before you use them.

FRUITS

Keep fresh fruit on hand for breakfast and brunch. You can slice bananas into a bowl of cereal or dish of yogurt, cut wedges of melon or scoop them into balls, or cook fresh or dried fruits into sauces and compotes. Fruit salads are simple to make ahead for breakfast on busy mornings. You can even pack some in a container to take on the road. A heaping bowl of fresh fruit is one of the most attractive and useful centerpieces you can choose for breakfast or brunch.

When berries, peaches, and cherries are in season locally, buy plenty to freeze. Blueberries and cranberries freeze beautifully; simply put them in freezer bags, seal, and store. More delicate berries (raspberries, strawberries, and blackberries)

Grain and Legume Pantry

- Oats (steel-cut, rolled, quick-cooking, and bran)
- Cornmeal (yellow or white; stone ground)
- Wheat (bulgur, germ, bran)
- Rice (including wild rice, Arborio, long-grain)
- Buckwheat (kasha)
- Rye
- Quinoa
- Dried lentils
- Couscous (North African, Israeli)
- Dry pasta and noodles
- Dry or canned beans (black, fava, kidney, chickpea, black-eyed peas)

Fruit and Vegetable Pantry

FRESH FRUITS

- Bananas
- Citrus (grapefruits, oranges, lemons, and lime)
- Apples
- Pears
- Berries
- Melons
- Pineapples
- Kiwis
- Mangos
- Papayas
- Peaches
- Apricots
- Plums
- Cherries
- Figs

FROZEN FRUITS

- Berries (frozen without added sugar or syrup)
- Mango chunks
- Pineapple chunks
- Peach slices

DRIED FRUITS

- Raisins (dark and golden)
- Currants
- Cherries
- Apples
- Cranberries
- Figs and Dates
- Apricots

FRESH VEGETABLES

- Potatoes
- Onions
- Tomatoes
- Mushrooms
- Artichokes
- Peppers and chiles
- Beets
- Asparagus

FROZEN VEGETABLES

- Corn
- Spinach
- Peas
- Broccoli spears

CANNED OR JARRED VEGETABLES

- Chiles (jalapeños, chipotles, green chiles)
- Pumpkin puree
- Tomatoes (paste, diced, whole, pureed, crushed)

DRIED VEGETABLES

- Mushrooms
- Chiles
- Tomatoes

should be spread in a single layer on a sheet pan and frozen (uncovered) until solid. Then transfer the berries to freezer containers or bags. Usually there is no need to thaw frozen berries before adding them to pancakes or muffins.

We've included dried fruit in some recipes. A wide variety of dried fruits can be found in most markets. Stock up on breakfast favorites like raisins, currants, prunes (dried plums), cranberries, and cherries to give a sweet-tart punch to baked goods like sticky buns or scones.

VEGETABLES

Potatoes, onions (including garlic and shallots), and tomatoes are important basic vegetables for the breakfast menu. Store them in a dark, dry, cool cupboard or pantry.

Lettuces, leafy greens, seasonal delicacies (asparagus, new peas, fiddlehead ferns, ramps) and other farm stand finds should be used as soon as possible, but most will last a day or two if they are kept in the refrigerator. Tomatoes can be kept on hand as fresh, sun-dried, and canned.

Salsa has become an indispensable breakfast and brunch item to give plain egg dishes some zip. Making your own is simple with just a few basic ingredients: tomatoes, peppers and/or chiles, scallions, and a dash of lime juice. Frozen vegetables make it simple to add flavor, color, and nutrition to quiches and egg dishes.

HOT BEVERAGES

Whether your preference is a steaming jolt of coffee, a soothing pot of tea, or a cup of frothy chocolate, hot beverages are *de riguer* for most people.

- *Coffee is sold as whole bean and ground. Try to match the grind to your coffee maker for the best results.*
- *Tea is sold loose and in bags.*

- *Drinking chocolates may be powdered (cocoa) or in bars; the better the quality of your chocolate, the smoother and richer your hot chocolate will be.*

COLD BEVERAGES

Juices, juice blends, smoothies, and cocktails are some of the refreshing options we've included in the book. Add a few of these drinks to your menu to give a bit of extra flair.

Fresh squeezed juices (single fruits or blends) can be made using a reamer, a crank-style juicer, or an extractor. Bottled juices and frozen concentrates make it easy to keep juice on hand for busy mornings or hectic weekends. Other beverages to stock for breakfast and brunch include:

- Water (still and sparkling) and seltzer
- Champagne
- Table wine
- Spirits (gin and vodka appear in many brunch cocktails; have brandy and rum on hand for flavoring baked goods and to plump dried fruits for use in baked goods and compotes)

INGREDIENTS FOR BAKED GOODS

Flours can be safely kept for up to 8 months if stored properly. Nuts are rich in oils, which can go rancid after a time. Most nuts can be safely stored for a period of 6 weeks. All flours and nut products should be stored in a cool, dark, and dry place.

- Flours
- Sugars
- Leaveners
- Walnuts
- Pine nuts
- Almonds (including almond paste)
- Peanuts (including peanut butter)
- Pecans

PREPARED ITEMS: FROZEN, JARRED, AND TINNED

Frozen pastry doughs last for months. Let them thaw overnight in the refrigerator for the best flavor and texture once baked. If you enjoy making pastry doughs, make a double batch and then freeze the portion you don't use. Wrap them well and be sure to add a date to the label.

- Puff pastry (in sheets or as shells)
- Phyllo (available in two different sizes; also as phyllo shells or cups)
- Pie shells

MEATS, POULTRY, AND FISH

Adding some meat, poultry, or fish to a breakfast or brunch menu gives the meal more staying power. Keep portion sizes smaller than you might for lunch or dinner. Rich, smoky sausages, bacon, ham, salmon, and trout are classic breakfast meats. At brunch, you can branch out to include whole roasts, which you can carve at the table.

- Bacon and pancetta
- Canadian bacon
- Sausage
- Ham and prosciutto
- Beef or ham steaks
- Shrimp, scallops
- Poultry
- Smoked fish (salmon, trout, sturgeon)

EQUIPMENT

Breakfast and brunch dishes typically call for the same basic equipment any well-stocked kitchen might have on hand. There are a few indispensable items that make breakfast preparation easier: nonstick pans for eggs and crepes, a waffle iron, and of course, a coffee maker and a teakettle.

Equipment List

STOVETOP

- Skillet (spider, frying pan)
- Crêpe pan
- Omelet pan
- Griddle

SMALL APPLIANCES

- Toaster/toaster oven
- Blender
- Food processor
- Waffle iron
- Juicer (reamer, extraction, or crank-style)
- Coffeemaker
- Coffee mill or grinder

- Espresso maker
- Cappuccino machine

MISCELLANEOUS

- Tea kettle
- Teapot
- Tea ball
- Coffeepot
- Coffee filters

BAKING EQUIPMENT/PANS

- Muffin tins
- Loaf tins
- Pie plate
- Tart pan

- Custard cups
- Soufflé dishes
- Biscuit cutters
- Brioche molds
- Baking sheets
- Rolling pins

HAND TOOLS

- Spatula
- Whisk
- Mixing bowls and pitchers
- Measuring spoons and cups
- Citrus reamer and zester
- Timer

- Thermometer
- Box grater
- Colander
- Parchment or wax paper, aluminum foil, plastic wrap
- Storage containers

CUTLERY

- Paring knife
- Chef's knife
- Slicer for meats
- Kitchen fork
- Mandoline
- Serrated knife
- Peeler

SETTING THE TABLE

Taking the time to set the table is a luxury many people don't feel they can afford on busy mornings. Even if the morning is rushed, having handsome mugs and cups, cereal bowls and spoons, and cheerful napkins on the table or counter makes everyone feel better about starting their day.

- Mugs, cups and saucers, plates
- Platters and serving bowls
- Pitchers (including insulated pitchers to keep beverages hot and small pitchers for syrups and sauces)
- Hot plates and chafing dishes for brunch buffets
- Tablecloths and placemats
- Napkins
- Flowers
- Edible displays (fruits, vegetables, or fresh herbs)

BREAKFAST MAY BE one of the most important meals, but it is also one of the most neglected. Since it is a daily meal, it is easy to fall into the simple routines that get us out the door and on with our day quickly. We at the CIA believe that by investing some time in a breakfast or brunch buffet on a weekend or holiday, you can get more flavor and more nutrition into the start of your day on "ordinary" days, too. We hope that you will find some inspiration to take breakfast beyond humdrum in this collection of wonderful morning foods. A Sunday brunch is a wonderful place to start branching out. Here are some observations and ideas about breakfast and brunch buffets:

- *Breakfast should be a fortifying, flavorful, and nutritious start to the day.*

- *Buffets are a great way to introduce your family and friends to something new and still be sure you've got plenty to fill up picky eaters or staunch traditionalists.*

- *You can choose how much or how little you want to do ahead.*

- *You can use a variety of cooking styles coupled with some basic buffet concepts to make both breakfast and brunch more exciting to eat and easy on the cook.*

- *Many breakfast and brunch foods cook so quickly that you can make them "to order."*

- *Breakfast and brunch dishes provide a wonderful means to showcase fruits and vegetables of every season and from every region.*

- *It's a great time to serve luxury items like smoked salmon, prosciutto, and caviar.*

- *Breakfasts and brunches are ideal for family celebrations—holidays, birthdays, anniversaries—especially when the "main event" is just one part of a weekend- or even week-long celebration.*

- *By combining foods that hold and foods that are cooked in a few minutes, you can accommodate everyone's schedule, from sleepyheads who drag from their beds at the last possible moment to "morning people," ready to get up and get moving at the crack of dawn. Or you may have a cross section of dawdlers who linger and travelers who need to get on the road.*

- *The availability of a broad range of dishes from around the world enables you to custom-tailor your breakfast and brunch style.*

A breakfast or brunch buffet is a great way to get together when schedules are otherwise too busy. To get started, think about what your personal "clock" is like as well as the morning styles of whoever might be joining you. Use the buffet approach to get over any resistance you feel. Set things up to make as much of the buffet self-serve as possible and try some of these techniques to get ready the night before:

- *Decide what you'll be serving.*

- *Pick a spot to serve from; leave yourself a little counter space.*

- *Pile the silver and napkins in a lined basket.*

- *Get out bowls or plates.*

- *Set out glasses for juice. A pitcher makes things more elegant, but you can skip it to cut down on cleanup.*

- *Position mugs or cups close to the coffee pot, along with a pitcher for cream or milk and a sugar bowl.*

- *Move the toaster to a convenient spot and put a cutting board, a bread knife, and table knives to spread butter, cream cheese, jam, or peanut butter nearby.*

- *If you plan to make pancakes, waffles, muffins, or biscuits, measure out the dry ingredients into a bowl and cover with plastic. Mix up the wet ingredients and keep them in the refrigerator.*

Some Sample Breakfast & Brunch Menus

"DASHBOARD BREAKFASTS"

Smoothies
Scones (Ham and Cheddar
or Glazed Dried Cherry)
Cheddar and Onion Rye Rolls

HEARTY PRE-GAME OR PRE-SKI

Hot Chocolate
Ham Steaks with Red-Eye Gravy
Garlic Cheddar Grits
Hash Browns

FAMILY WEEKEND

Cardamom-Spiced Coffee
Four-Grain Waffles
Breakfast Sausage
Raisin Cinnamon Bread

LAZY SUNDAY MORNING

Mimosa
Granola and Yogurt Parfait
Eggs en Cocotte
Brioche à Tête
Orange or Chocolate Biscotti

Seasonal Brunches

SPRING

Kir Royale
English Muffins with Strawberries
Couscous Salad with Curried Vegetables
Elephant Ears

SUMMER

Sangria
Huevos Rancheros
Mexican Chorizo
Fresh Fruit Platter

FALL

Hot Mulled Cider
Roast Turkey Breast with Pan Gravy
Chestnut Dressing
Wild Rice and Cranberry Pilaf
Asparagus with Mustard Sauce
Apple-Filled Turnovers

WINTER

Café au Lait
Sticky Buns
Dutch Baby with Spiced Fruit
Macaire Potatoes

Chapter Two

Breakfast &
Brunch Drinks

*S*TEAMING MUGS OF coffee, tea, and hot chocolate are the fuel for many Americans in the morning and throughout the day. Taking the time to find the best coffee, tea, and drinking chocolate means that you can make your own hot breakfast drinks, ones that equal or better the quality you are likely to find at coffee shops, delis, and drive-throughs on the way to work. We've included several recipes for spiced coffees and teas, as well as a great repertoire of cold drinks that can be served as "breakfast in a glass" or can add sparkle and elegance to a wonderful brunch.

Brewing Coffee

The definition of a great cup of coffee is a personal thing, but to be sure that you get the coffee you like, keep three things in mind: the coffee itself, the water, and your pot.

THE COFFEE

Good-quality coffee is more widely available today than ever before. You have the choice of a wide variety of coffees, both whole bean and preground. If possible, sample a variety of beans. There are two types of coffee beans, Arabica and Robusta. Arabica is widely considered far superior to Robusta. If you buy you coffee from bulk dispensers, that is usually the type of bean you are getting. Blends incorporate a number of different varieties and even different roasts to give the coffee a specific aroma and flavor.

Another important element in a coffee's flavor is the roasting process. The darker the roast, the more pronounced and complex the flavor will be. Lighter roasts have a more delicate flavor. Espresso, French, and Italian roasts are the darkest. The beans will have a very dark color with a pronounced sheen since the oils in the beans are driven to the surface as they roast. American roasts are lighter in color and tend to look matte rather than shiny.

Whole beans maintain their quality longer than preground coffee. You can store whole beans in a dark, covered container at room temperature for several days. For longer storage, keep the beans in the freezer.

Grind coffee yourself using a coffee grinder or a coffee mill. It is best to do this right before brewing the coffee. Each type of coffeemaker calls for a specific degree of grind. Drip-style coffeemakers use a fine grind. Express or plunger-style pots call for a slightly coarser grind. If you aren't certain, be sure to look at the instructions that come with your coffeepot.

The standard ratio for coffee calls for one *measure* of coffee, which translates as 1½ to 2 tablespoons of ground coffee for every 6 ounces of water you use. The more coffee you use in relationship to the water, the stronger the brewed coffee will be.

THE POT OR COFFEEMAKER

Most dedicated coffee drinkers have a favorite pot they use. Drip-style coffeemakers hold the coffee in a basket lined with a disposable paper filter, or a reusable gold mesh or nylon filter. Some baskets are cone-shaped, and others have a flat bottom.

Espresso machines are used to brew coffee with pressure. The finely ground, dark-roasted coffee is packed into a basket, and water is forced through the coffee. The result is a thick, intensely flavored little cup of coffee topped with a bit of creamy foam. Espresso is often consumed as "shots." A single shot of espresso is about 1½ ounces. Double espresso is two "shots" and so on. If you love espresso but don't have a pot, simply use triple the amount of coffee you would to make a standard brew.

Clean your pot and the basket well after each use. If you use an electric coffeemaker that holds the water in a reservoir, be sure to clean it with a vinegar-and-water mixture to remove any mineral deposits that the water can leave behind. This will keep your coffeepot functioning properly. It also improves the flavor of your coffee. Follow the instructions that came with your coffeemaker for cleaning.

THE WATER

Most coffeemakers call for cold water. Use bottled or filtered water if your tap water has an unpleasant odor or taste. Your coffeemaker should bring the water to around 190°F for the best extraction. If the water is colder than that, the coffee may taste weak. If it is too hot, the volatile oils that give coffee its rich aroma may be lost.

If you brew coffee with a non-electric coffeemaker, fill your kettle with cold fresh water and bring it to a boil. Turn off the heat and let the water rest for a minute or two so that it can cool from 212°F (the boiling point of water) down to 190°F. Clean your kettle with vinegar and water periodically to remove any buildups left behind by the water.

Lighten your coffee with milk, cream, or half-and-half. If you like sweet coffee, use granulated or raw sugar. For a different flavor, try maple syrup or molasses.

Brewing Tea

Dedicated tea drinkers know that your water should be at the boil, your pot preheated, and your tea selected carefully.

Teas can be black or green. Green tea has a mild flavor and lighter color. Black tea is fermented; the leaves and the brew are darker in color and more intensely flavored. Some teas are flavored with herbs, spices, or citrus. Herbal teas are made from herbs such as mint, chamomile, or ginger.

While some tea drinkers prefer loose teas, others find the convenience of tea bags appealing. Whether you use bags or loose tea, be sure to observe some basic guidelines.

Fill your kettle with fresh, cold water. Use bottled or filtered water if your tap water has an unpleasant odor, or if you have a water softener.

Bring the water to a full boil and then pour some into your pot to preheat it. Once the pot is hot, pour out the water and add the tea. Loose tea is added directly to the pot, but if you prefer, use either tea bags or a tea ball. A tea cozy keeps the pot hot while the tea brews.

Most teas require at least two or three minutes for a proper infusion. Remove tea bags or tea balls once the tea is the strength you like. If you like loose tea, then the leaves will stay in the pot. In that case, you should have a second pot filled with hot water so you can adjust the intensity of your own cup.

Milk, honey, sugar, and lemon wedges are common accompaniments to tea.

Blender Drinks

Blender drinks, often referred to as smoothies, are increasingly popular breakfast options. They are a quick and easy way to incorporate a serving of dairy and some fresh fruit into your day. You can use any fresh fruits you like, including berries, tropical fruits like mango and papaya, peaches, pineapple, or melon. If fresh fruits aren't at their peak, frozen fruits or fruit juices are another option.

Most smoothies include yogurt as their base; choose a good-quality unflavored yogurt. It is up to you whether you prefer to use whole milk, reduced-fat, or soy yogurts. Experiment with goat or sheep's milk yogurt if they are available in your market.

Mulled and Spiced Drinks

Hot, steaming cups of mulled cider or wine chase the chill on cold mornings and make a perfect accompaniment to a fall or winter brunch menu. We've included a few different recipes, including cardamom-spiced coffee and mulled cider.

If you don't want to go to the bother of making a spice sachet, simply strain the mulled or spiced drink through a fine-mesh strainer to remove the herbs before you serve the drinks. Preheat the cups so the drink retains its heat longer.

Café au Lait

MAKES 8 SERVINGS

*T*HE FRENCH have given us this wonderful steamy coffee drink, perfect to enjoy with a buttery brioche or a pastry for breakfast. Serve café au lait in large heated cups, or serve it in "bowls," essentially large cups without a handle.

4 cups brewed coffee, hot

4 cups milk

Ground cinnamon for garnish, optional

1. Keep the coffee hot while you steam or froth the milk.

2. Steam the milk using a milk steamer or bring it to a simmer in a small pan over low heat. Use an immersion or countertop blender to whip the hot milk until frothy if you have simmered it on the stove.

3. Combine equal parts of coffee and hot milk in heated cups. Garnish with a little cinnamon if desired.

Café Latte

MAKES 8 SERVINGS

*T*O MAKE this a double latte, use a double shot of espresso for each serving. Lattes are served in glasses rather than cups or mugs.

8 espresso shots, hot

4 cups milk

Ground cinnamon for garnish, optional

1. Brew the espresso in an espresso pot or use triple the amount of coffee you normally would to brew 16 ounces of coffee. Keep hot.

2. Steam the milk using a milk steamer, or bring it to a simmer in a small pan over low heat and use an immersion or countertop blender to whip the hot milk until frothy.

3. Combine a shot of espresso and ½ cup of hot milk in a heated glass for each serving. Garnish with a little cinnamon if desired.

Cardamom-Spiced Coffee

MAKES 8 SERVINGS

*T*O MAKE a sachet, cut a 7-inch square of cheesecloth. Place the cinnamon sticks, cardamom pods, and allspice berries in the center of the cheesecloth. Gather the cloth around the spices and tie closed with cotton string to make a little package. It makes removing the spices from the milk easier. Another option is to place the spices in a tea ball, breaking the cinnamon sticks into pieces to fit.

One 13½-ounce can sweetened condensed milk

½ cup milk

1 spice sachet of 2 teaspoons cardamom pods, 2 cinnamon sticks, and 4 allspice berries

1⅔ cups ground French roast coffee

1½ quarts water

1. Warm the sweetened condensed milk, milk, and spice sachet over medium-low heat for 10 minutes. Remove the pan from heat and cover. Allow the mixture to steep for 30 minutes. Remove the spice sachet.

2. Brew the coffee using the 1½ quarts water to make a slightly stronger coffee. Add 2 tablespoons of the spiced milk to each cup of coffee or to taste. Serve hot.

Hot Chocolate

MAKES 8 SERVINGS

*F*OR BEST results, place the chocolate mixture in the refrigerator overnight. If you are a serious hot chocolate fan, you can make a double or triple batch and then hold it in the refrigerator for up to 5 days. The mixture develops a smoother texture and richer flavor as it rests. Hot chocolate will develop a skin if it is left to sit too long, so be sure to serve it right away.

24 ounces dark chocolate, finely chopped

1 cup heavy cream

2 quarts whole milk

1. Place chocolate in a heatproof bowl. Bring the cream to a boil and pour over the chocolate. Cover and let rest for 5 minutes. Stir the mixture until completely smooth.

2. Bring the milk to a simmer. Gradually whisk the milk into the chocolate mixture. Cool completely and refrigerate until ready to use.

3. When ready to serve, slowly heat the chocolate mixture over medium-low heat. Serve hot.

Hot Mulled Cider

MAKES 8 SERVINGS

Y OU MAY be able to find pear cider to use instead of the more widely available apple cider. If possible, buy cider that has not been pasteurized for the freshest, fullest apple or pear flavor.

2 quarts cider (unfiltered)

1 cinnamon stick

3 or 4 whole cloves

3 or 4 allspice berries

Zest of 1 orange

8 thin orange slices for garnish

1. Combine all the ingredients except the orange slices in a saucepan. Simmer until the flavor of the spices and orange zest are infused into the cider, about 20 minutes.

2. Strain the cider and serve in heated mugs or glasses. Garnish each portion with an orange slice.

Eggnog

MAKES 8 SERVINGS

A DD A shot of brandy, bourbon, or rum to each portion of eggnog before serving it to the adults, if you wish.

2 cups milk

2 cups heavy cream, divided use

¾ cup sugar, divided use

2 large eggs

½ teaspoon vanilla extract

⅛ teaspoon salt

Ground cinnamon or nutmeg for garnish

1. Heat the milk, 1 cup of the heavy cream, and ½ cup of the sugar in a heavy-gauge saucepan until simmering.

2. While the milk-cream mixture heats, blend the eggs with the remaining ¼ cup sugar, the vanilla, and salt. Gradually add about half of the hot milk-cream mixture to the eggs and then return the egg mixture to the saucepan.

3. Simmer over very low heat until heated to 165° F. Continue to simmer, stirring constantly, for 3 minutes.

4. Strain the eggnog through a wire-mesh sieve into a bowl and cool rapidly in an ice bath. Transfer to a pitcher or jar, cover well, and chill for at least 2 hours and up to 24 hours before serving.

5. When you are ready to serve the eggnog, whip the remaining cup of heavy cream and fold it into the eggnog. Serve in cups or glasses garnished with a dusting of ground cinnamon or nutmeg.

Chai

CHAI IS a popular Indian beverage made from black tea, milk, a sweetener, and spices. Mixtures known as chai masala may include cardamom, cinnamon, ginger, and peppercorns to give the drink its heady aroma. Some sugar or honey is essential to bring out all the flavors.

1½ quarts cool water

12 bags Darjeeling tea

3 cinnamon sticks, 1½ inches each

4 teaspoons sliced ginger

1 tablespoon cardamom pods

1½ teaspoons fennel seeds

¼ teaspoon cloves

⅛ teaspoon black peppercorns

1 vanilla bean, split

¼ cup honey, or as needed

3 cups milk

1. Bring the water to a boil in a medium saucepan. Add the tea bags, cinnamon, ginger, cardamom, fennel, cloves, peppercorns, and vanilla bean. Reduce the heat and simmer the mixture for 10 minutes, stirring occasionally, until aromatic and the mixture is a medium brown. Add the honey and milk and stir to dissolve the honey. Bring to a boil and remove from the heat.

2. Strain the liquid through a sieve, pressing on the tea bags and spices to extract as much liquid and flavor as possible. Taste the liquid for sweetness and add more honey if desired.

3. Serve the chai immediately as a hot drink or chill and serve over ice.

Bubble Tea

MAKES 8 SERVINGS

1 F YOU don't have a cocktail shaker, you can shake up the drink in a covered jar instead. It is important to use double-strength tea for this recipe because the flavor of the tea is diluted when you shake it up with the milk and ice. You can replace the brown sugar with honey for a slightly different flavor.

3 quarts plus 2 cups water, divided use

¾ cup granulated sugar

⅓ cup packed light brown sugar

1 cup small tapioca pearls

12 bags black tea

1 quart whole milk

1. Combine 1 cup water with the sugars and bring to a boil, stirring constantly to dissolve the sugar. Reduce the heat to medium and simmer 2 or 3 minutes to make a syrup. Set aside.

2. To prepare the tapioca, bring 7 cups of water to a boil in a large saucepot and add the tapioca pearls. Simmer uncovered, stirring frequently, until they are mostly transparent and slightly gummy, about 30 minutes. Remove the tapioca from the heat and cover the pan. Cool for 30 minutes, then drain through a wire-mesh sieve and rinse with cool water.

3. Add the cooked tapioca pearls to the sugar syrup and stir to coat the pearls with the syrup. Store in the refrigerator until ready to make the bubble tea. *(recipe continues on next page)*

Making Bubble Tea

Bubble tea got its start in Taiwan and has become popular throughout the world. It is known by several names: boba drink, pearl tea drink, boba ice tea, boba, boba nai cha, zhen zhou nai cha, pearl milk tea, pearl ice tea, black pearl tea, tapioca ball drink, BBT, PT, pearl shake, QQ (which means chewy in Chinese).

MAKE A SUGAR SYRUP

Simmering sugar and water together makes a simple syrup. This syrup is blended with the softened tapioca pearls to give them some flavor, as well as to sweeten the tea and milk mixture. Sugar dissolves more readily in hot water to help avoid having the sugar drop to the bottom of the glass.

SOFTEN THE TAPIOCA PEARLS

There are large and small tapioca pearls, as well as white and black tapioca pearls. We've used small pearls since they fit more easily through a straw. If you can find black pearls, they give the drink an interesting appearance. Large pearls call for very fat straws. You may even find that one of the straw/spoon combinations that you get with a root beer float at your favorite soft-serve ice cream store makes it easier to drink the bubble tea, as well as scoop up the pearls.

As the tapioca simmers, it will become translucent. The texture changes too, becoming gummy and slippery. When the softened and sweetened tapioca pearls are combined with the tea, they give the drink the appearance of big bubbles (hence the name).

BREW AND FLAVOR THE TEA

We've used a black tea for this drink, but some bubble teas call for adding herbs and spices to the tea as it brews. Cardamom, clove, or cinnamon are all good choices. Be sure to strain them out of the tea before serving. Let the tea steep a little longer than you would if you were drinking it plain so that the finished drink has a definite taste of tea.

Shake the tea and milk together with ice until it is frothy, so that you get a layer of bubbles on top of the bubble tea, as well as the tapioca "bubbles" at the bottom of the glass.

4. Place the tea bags in a teapot or a pitcher. Bring the remaining 6 cups of water to a full boil and pour over the tea bags. Brew until you have a double-strength tea, 5–6 minutes. Discard the tea bags and allow the tea to cool to room temperature.

5. For each serving of bubble tea, put ⅓ cup cooked tapioca pearls into a large glass. Combine ¾ cup tea, ½ cup milk, 3 tablespoons sugar syrup, and a few cubes of ice in a cocktail shaker. Shake thoroughly and pour over the tapioca pearls. Serve immediately with a wide straw.

LEFT TO RIGHT *Add the tapioca pearls to plenty of water. As the tapioca cooks, it will be necessary to stir more often so that the tapioca doesn't stick to the bottom of the pan. The tapioca has swelled considerably after cooking and is slightly translucent. It should be slightly gummy and a little slippery. Before mixing the tea in the shaker, have the glasses set up with the tapioca mixture in the bottom.*

Agua de Jamaica *(Hibiscus Cooler)*

AGUA DE jamaica is a delicious herbal tea from Mexico with a refreshing taste and a beautiful ruby-red color that comes from hibiscus flowers, known as *jamaica* in Spanish (pronounced ha-MIKE-ah). Although it does take some looking to find hibiscus flowers, you may be able to find them in natural foods stores that sell bulk herbs and spices. The flowers can leave stains, so use stainless steel or glass containers instead of plastic, aluminum, or ceramic.

2 quarts water, or as needed

2 cups jamaica flowers (hibiscus)

1¼ cups sugar, plus as needed

3 medium oranges, cut in half

1. Bring the water to a boil. Add the hibiscus and sugar; stir while the mixture boils for 1 minute.

2. Squeeze the juice from the oranges into a noncorrosive bowl and place the orange halves in the bowl as well. Pour the hibiscus mixture into the bowl and steep for 1 hour.

3. Strain through a sieve, pressing on the hibiscus and oranges to extract as much liquid as possible. Taste the liquid for strength and sweetness. If it is too pungent, add water. If it is too tart, add sugar. Cover and refrigerate in a pitcher until you are ready to serve.

Carrot-Ginger Cocktail

IF YOU don't have a juicer, you can still make this delicious vegetable cocktail. Replace the whole carrots called for here with 1½ cups carrot juice, which can be found in larger markets or at natural foods stores. Puree the carrot juice with the celery, apples, and ginger in a blender, and serve.

4 medium carrots, trimmed and sliced

2 stalks celery, trimmed

2 apples, cored and chopped

1 slice peeled fresh ginger, about ¼ inch thick

1. Put all of the ingredients through a juice machine following the manufacturer's instructions.

2. Stir the cocktail well to even out the flavor before serving. Serve at once in tall glasses.

Raspberry-Lime Rickey

MAKES 8 SERVINGS

*R*ICKEYS ARE sparkling drinks. You can add some vodka, gin, or rum if you like.

⅔ cup raspberry puree

⅔ cup fresh lime juice, about 5 limes

2 liters club soda or sparkling water

8 lime wedges for garnish

1. Combine the raspberry puree and lime juice in a pitcher. Add the carbonated water and stir gently to combine.

2. Serve in tall glasses over ice, garnished with lime wedges.

Mediterranean Cooler

MAKES 8 SERVINGS

*L*OOK FOR bottled pomegranate juice in the produce section of some stores. You can substitute other juices for those we recommend here. Grapefruit and cranberry juice make a Sea Breeze. Orange and cranberry make a Madras. A modest amount of club soda gives the drink a little spritz without getting too bubbly. You can also add some vodka, gin, or rum to give the drink a more potent kick.

4 cups tangerine juice, about 16 tangerines

2 cups pomegranate juice

2 cups club soda

1. If using fresh tangerines juice them and strain the juice to remove any seeds or unwanted pulp. Combine the tangerine juice with the pomegranate juice in a pitcher; chill.

2. When ready to serve, add the club soda and stir to combine. Serve over ice, if desired.

Tropical Fruit Smoothie

MAKES 2 SERVINGS

*T*HE AVERAGE blender can usually hold enough to make two servings of a smoothie at once, so if you are planning to make more, dice as much fruit as you need, then purée the smoothies in several batches.

1 cup diced pineapple

¼ cup diced mango

¼ cup diced papaya

¼ cup peeled and diced kiwi

½ cup fresh orange juice, divided use

¼ cup coconut milk

¼ cup plain nonfat yogurt, optional

⅓ cup ice

1 tablespoon sugar, or as needed

¼ teaspoon vanilla extract

2 pineapple slices for garnish

Toasted shredded unsweetened coconut for garnish, optional

1. In a blender, combine pineapple, mango, papaya, kiwi, and ¼ cup orange juice; puree until smooth. With the machine running, add the remaining orange juice, coconut milk, yogurt (if using), ice, sugar, and vanilla extract. Blend the fruit mixture until smooth and thick.

2. Serve the smoothies at once in chilled tall glasses garnished with a pineapple slice and a sprinkle of toasted coconut.

Peach Smoothie

MAKES 2 SERVINGS

*T*RY OTHER fruit juices instead of peach juice or nectar. Cranberry, mango, apple, or pineapple juices are all good choices.

2 ripe peaches, peeled and pit removed

1 banana, sliced

1 cup peach juice or nectar

½ cup plain yogurt

3 tablespoons honey, or to taste

2 peach slices for garnish

1. In a blender, combine peaches, banana, peach juice or nectar, yogurt, and honey. Puree until smooth and thick.

2. Serve the smoothies at once in chilled tall glasses garnished with a peach slice.

Cappuccino Smoothie

MAKES 2 SERVINGS

*I*F YOU don't have an espresso maker, use triple the amount of coffee you normally use to brew coffee.

1 cup espresso, cold

½ cup coffee ice cream

¼ cup crushed or cracked ice

⅓ cup milk

¼ cup heavy cream, whipped

¼ teaspoon ground cinnamon, or as needed

Blend the espresso, ice cream, ice, and milk in a blender until smooth. Serve at once in chilled tall glasses garnished with a dollop of whipped cream and a sprinkle of cinnamon.

Mango Lassi

MAKES 8 SERVINGS

THIS TRADITIONAL Indian drink was originally made from yogurt, water, toasted cumin, salt, and chiles. Sweet lassis, such as this one, have become very popular in recent years. They are quite similar to smoothies. To make a mango puree, cut a very ripe mango and push the flesh through a wire-mesh sieve or a food mill. If you have any leftover puree, you can store it in the refrigerator or freezer.

4 cups mango puree

4 cups whole-milk yogurt

½ cup whole milk

½ cup water

4 teaspoons lime juice, about 1 lime

4 teaspoons honey, plus more if needed

¾ teaspoon ground cardamom

1. In a large mixing bowl, whisk together the mango puree, yogurt, milk, water, lime juice, honey, and cardamom thoroughly. Taste the mixture and add more honey if necessary.

2. Serve the lassi at once in chilled glasses.

Lemonade

MAKES 8 SERVINGS

WHEN YOU buy lemons, select fruit that is heavy for its size with relatively thin skin. They will have the most juice. Let the lemons warm to room temperature and roll them under your palm before juicing them to get even more juice from the lemons.

6⅔ cups cold water, divided use

½ cup sugar

1 cup lemon juice

8 lemon slices for garnish

1. Combine ⅔ cup water with the sugar in a small saucepan and bring to a boil. Stir to dissolve the sugar.

2. Combine the sugar-water with the lemon juice and add the 6 cups cold water. Stir to combine.

3. Serve immediately over ice garnished with a lemon slice or store in the refrigerator until ready to use.

Raspberry Lemonade

MAKES 8 SERVINGS

TO MAKE the raspberry puree for this lemonade, push fresh or thawed frozen raspberries through a wire-mesh sieve into a small bowl. You'll need about 1 cup berries to make ⅓ cup puree.

6⅔ cups cold water, divided use

½ cup sugar

1 cup lemon juice

⅓ cup raspberry puree

24 raspberries for garnish

1. Combine ⅔ cup water with the sugar in a small saucepan and bring to a boil. Stir to dissolve the sugar.

2. Combine the sugar-water with the lemon juice and add the 6 cups cold water and the raspberry puree. Stir to combine.

3. Serve immediately over ice garnished with 3 raspberries or store in the refrigerator until ready to use.

Ginger Lemonade

MAKES 8 SERVINGS

SIMMERING THE ginger along with the sugar and water infuses its flavor throughout the lemonade. Try adding the stems of fresh herbs such as mint, lavender, or lemon balm, or pieces of orange or lime zest for even more flavor.

6⅔ cups cold water, divided use

½ cup sugar

¾ inch piece ginger, sliced

1 cup lemon juice

8 thin slices ginger for garnish

1. Combine ⅔ cup water with the sugar and ginger in a small saucepan and bring to a boil. Stir to dissolve the sugar. Remove the pan from the heat and allow the ginger to steep in the sugar-water for 10 minutes. Strain the mixture, pressing the ginger to extract all its juices.

2. Combine the ginger sugar-water with the lemon juice and add the 6 cups cold water. Stir to combine.

3. Serve immediately over ice garnished with a ginger slice or store refrigerated until ready to use.

OPPOSITE *In the pitchers, from left to right, Ginger Lemonade, Raspberry Lemonade, and Lemonade*

Greyhound

MAKES 8 SERVINGS

SQUEEZE YOUR own grapefruit for this bracing brunch cocktail. To make a Salty Dog, rub the rim of each glass with a piece of grapefruit and dip in coarse salt, as you would to prepare a margarita glass.

4 cups grapefruit juice

1¼ cups vodka

Ice as needed

Combine the grapefruit juice and vodka in a pitcher and stir to blend well. Serve over ice in tall glasses.

Mojito

MAKES 8 SERVINGS

MOJITOS ARE a delicious blend of rum, lime, and mint for an interesting change from mimosas and Bloody Marys at brunch. They get their fizz from a splash of club soda. Bartenders use a special tool known as a muddler to crush the limes and mint. A muddler looks like a miniature baseball bat. A wooden spoon works, too. Sugarcane swizzle sticks are a great touch if you can find them. You may be able to find them shelved along with cocktail mixes in large supermarkets.

6½ limes

⅔ cup sugar, or to taste

½ cup coarsely chopped peppermint

2 cups white rum

4 cups club soda

8 sugarcane swizzle sticks for garnish, optional

1. Cut the limes into quarters and add them to a pitcher along with the sugar. Mash the limes and sugar together using the back of a wooden spoon until the juices from the limes have been released and the sugar has mostly dissolved into the lime juice.

2. Add the mint to the pitcher and mash it together with the lime-sugar mixture. Pour the rum and the club soda into the pitcher and stir together.

3. Put two pieces of the quartered limes in each tall glass and add ice cubes. Pour the mojito over the ice and garnish with a sugarcane swizzle stick, if desired, and serve immediately.

Mimosa

MAKES 7 SERVINGS

MIMOSAS ARE enduringly popular champagne cocktails that have become a brunch classic. Use freshly squeezed orange juice and good-quality champagne. If blood oranges are in season and available, try them for a dramatic twist on the standard mimosa.

One 750-ml bottle champagne or sparkling wine

2¼ cups fresh orange juice

Fill your glasses one-quarter of the way with champagne, allow the bubbles to settle, then fill glasses half full. After the bubbles have settled, add 2½ ounces of orange juice to each glass of champagne, or until glasses are three-quarters full.

Pouring Champagne and Other Sparkling Beverages

Champagne is sold in a number of different-sized bottles from the diminutive quarter-bottle or "split" (6.3 fluid ounces) to half-bottles (12.7 fluid ounces) to 750-milliliter bottles (the standard size, which supplies 25.4 fluid ounces) to the magnum (50.8 fluid ounces and equal to 2 standard bottles). Even bigger bottles are sold, though they are difficult to find and unwieldy to pour from: the Jeroboam (equal to 4 bottles), Rehoboam (equal to 6 bottles), Methuselah (equal to 8 bottles), Salmanazar (equal to 12 bottles), the Balthazar (equal to 16 bottles), and the Nebuchadnezzar (equal to 20 bottles). When you buy champagne, get the right sized bottle for your party. Unpoured champagne doesn't hold all that well, though you can carefully stopper it and keep it refrigerated for up to 12 hours. There will be some loss of carbonation, however.

A standard 750-milliliter bottle yields five 5-ounce glasses, assuming you are using a standard champagne flute. Of course, your glass may be larger or smaller. There are some tricks for pouring champagne whether you plan to serve it on its own or in a cocktail such as a mimosa or kir.

OPEN CHAMPAGNE BOTTLES CAREFULLY

Loosen and remove the foil wrapper around the cork. Then, untwist the wire "cage" that holds the cork in place. Keep your finger on top of the cork so that it doesn't fly out when you aren't ready.

Wrap a clean napkin around the bottle and the cork to get a secure grip. Be sure you aren't aiming the bottle in anyone's direction and keep the bottle at a 45° angle as you open it. Then, twist the cork in one direction and the bottle in the other and gently ease the cork out. If you've done this properly, there may be a small pop, but there shouldn't be a big bang or an eruption of champagne. The point, after all, is to keep the bubbles in the champagne and to get the champagne into your glass.

PRIME THE GLASS

Champagne and other sparkling beverages won't run over the top of your glass if you use a two-stage approach to pouring. The first pour, sometimes referred to as "priming" the glass, doesn't fill the glass. Carefully pour in enough champagne to fill the glass only one-half to one-quarter full.

THE SECOND POUR

When you prime the glass with a little champagne, the bubbles may rise almost to the top of the glass. When they settle down, you can finish filling the glass without overflows. If you are filling a lot of glasses, prime them all first, then make a second pass to fill them all.

Kir Royale

KIR ROYALE is made by combining champagne with crème de cassis, a deep-red liqueur made from black currants that was first made by French monks in the 16th century as a cure for snakebites and jaundice. Try other fruit-flavored liqueurs (peach, orange, or raspberry) instead of cassis if you like.

5 ounces (10 tablespoons) crème de cassis

One 750-ml bottle champagne or sparkling wine

10 blackberries

Add 2 tablespoons of crème de cassis to each glass. Pour in enough champagne to fill the glasses one-quarter of the way with champagne; allow the bubbles to settle. Add more champagne to fill the glasses three-quarters full. Garnish each glass with two blackberries. Serve at once.

1. Add the crème de cassis to the glass after measuring it or add it directly from the bottle after you have practiced making the drink a few times. 2. Prime the glass with champagne by filling the glass one-quarter full. Finish by adding champagne until the glasses are three-quarters full.

Sangria

*T*RY A white sangria, made from a fresh, fruity white wine mixed with a combination of stone fruits: plums, peaches, apricots, nectarines, and cherries. Instead of Grand Marnier, try a nut-flavored liqueur like Amaretto.

3 tablespoons water

3 tablespoons sugar

4 strawberries, quartered

½ cup raspberries

½ cup blueberries

½ cup blackberries

8 slices peeled orange

2½ cups dry red wine

¾ cup orange juice

⅓ cup Grand Marnier

¾ cup sparkling water

1. Combine the water and sugar in a small saucepan and bring to a boil, stirring to dissolve the sugar. Remove from heat and let cool.

2. Combine the fruit in a bowl. In a large pitcher, combine the sugar-water, wine, orange juice, and Grand Marnier. Add the fruit and stir gently to combine. (The sangria can be prepared ahead to this point and held in the refrigerator for up to 12 hours before serving.)

3. Just before serving, add the sparkling water to the pitcher. Serve the sangria in wineglasses.

Chapter Three

MUFFINS, QUICK BREADS
& COFFEE CAKES

FRESHLY BAKED MUFFINS, quick breads, and coffee cakes are perfect additions to a brunch menu. Choose from sweet favorites like Banana Nut Loaf (page 47) or Morning Glory Muffins (page 44) or try something savory instead: Cheddar Thyme Muffins (page 43) or Jalapeño Jack and Cheddar Cornbread (page 65).

Choosing Ingredients

All-purpose flour works beautifully in the recipes in this chapter. It has enough protein to maintain a quick bread's shape and volume as the batter bakes, but not so much that it becomes tough or rubbery. There are recipes in this chapter that call for whole wheat, cornmeal, and even oat flour in addition to all-purpose flour.

Most quick breads include at least a little sweetener for flavor and color, as well as an appealing texture. White granulated and brown sugars are the most common sweeteners, but molasses and honey are sometimes used, too. These syrups are well suited for recipes made using the well mixing method (see opposite) because they are already liquid.

The garnishes you choose for a quick bread can change its character from a sweet treat to something savory or spicy. Streusels, coarse sugar, or even a bit of flour or oatmeal are simply scattered on the top or swirled into the batter. Some garnishes or add-ins are blended or folded into the batter just before you put it in the pan to bake.

A common problem for bakers is finding that the add-in has dropped to the bottom of the muffin or bread. To keep that from happening, take the time to prepare the add-ins according to the recipe directions. Some should be dusted with a bit of flour, and others need to be cut or grated to the right size.

Sifting

Sifting dry ingredients like flour, confectioners' sugar, cocoa, ground spices, baking powder, and baking soda serves two important purposes. It breaks apart any tightly packed pockets and it distributes ingredients like spices and leaveners evenly. This means you can mix the batter easily without overmixing.

The recipes in this book call for the flour and other dry ingredients to be measured out first and then sifted. To sift more than one ingredient together, add the properly measured ingredients to a sieve or sifter. Shake or tap the sieve to encourage the dry ingredients to fall through the sieve into a bowl or directly onto a piece of parchment or waxed paper. If you use paper, you can simply lift the paper, fold it to create a cone, and pour the dry ingredients directly into the mixing bowl.

Preparing and Filling Pans

When baking pans are prepared and filled correctly, baked goods rise properly for a wonderful texture and a nicely browned crust.

Quick bread and cake batters contain a great deal of flour, which makes them tend to stick to untreated surfaces. Greasing and flouring your baking pans or using liners makes it easier to get breads, cakes, or muffins out of the pans.

GREASING

The fastest way to apply a light, even coating of oil to a baking pan, whether the sides are straight, fluted, or scalloped, is with a cooking spray. Sprays made from canola oil have a neutral flavor. Some sprays include flour; while these are fine for coating pans and tins, be sure not to use them on griddles, skillets, sauté pans, or waffle irons where the flour might burn. You can also brush or rub the pan with oil, softened butter, or shortening. Be sure to brush it evenly into corners and edges.

LINING WITH PARCHMENT PAPER

Lining a baking pan with parchment paper helps you remove even the most delicate quick breads and cakes. If you are using a round baking pan, trace the pan on your parchment and cut it to fit your pan.

Biscuits and scones may also be baked on parchment paper–lined baking sheets. The paper keeps egg wash from sticking and burning on the pan. Muffin liners are pleated so that they can expand when filled with batter. They are sold in sizes to fit miniature, regular, and large muffin tins.

FILLING BAKING PANS AND MUFFIN TINS

Batters leavened with baking powder or baking soda continue to rise during the first stage of baking. When you fill pans about two-thirds to three-quarters full, the batter expands to fill the pan and rises slightly over the top for a dome-shaped crust.

If pans are filled too high, the batter could run over the edges before rising is complete. If they are not filled enough, the batter may rise too rapidly and too high in the center during the initial stages of baking. Eventually, the center, which is not supported by the sides of the pan, may fall from its own weight and the entire item turn out dense or chewy rather than light and airy.

If your recipe makes enough batter for two or more loaves, divide the batter evenly between the pans so both loaves bake in the same amount of time.

Storing and Reheating

For many home bakers, one of the best things about quick breads is their simplicity. You can easily double the recipes in this book, making some to enjoy right away and some to store for later. Most muffins and quick breads can be stored in resealable plastic bags or rigid plastic containers and will last in the freezer for up to 2 months.

To defrost them, simply take them out of the freezer and let them rest at room temperature for an hour or so; a frozen muffin tucked into a bagged lunch in the morning will be perfect by the time you're ready to eat.

The Well Mixing Method

The well mixing method boils down to three basic steps. First, the dry ingredients are measured and sifted together to blend. Second, the wet ingredients, such as milk, cream, or juice, are measured and blended separately from the dry ingredients. Third, the wet ingredients are added to the dry ingredients and stirred just until combined.

COMBINE THE DRY INGREDIENTS AND MAKE A WELL

Measure your ingredients carefully before starting to combine them. Dry ingredients, such as flour, sugar, salt, and baking powder or soda, are blended before they are mixed into a batter by either sifting them together or combining them in a bowl and using a whisk to blend them evenly. Read through the ingredient list and method before you combine the dry ingredients. You may be asked to reserve a quantity of the flour or sugar to add with a garnish or use as a topping. Some recipes may call for garnish ingredients (dried fruits, grated cheese, minced herbs, and so forth) to be tossed together with the dry ingredients. Make a well by pushing the dry ingredients from the center of the bowl to the sides.

BLEND THE WET INGREDIENTS

Wet ingredients commonly used in quick bread batters include milk, buttermilk, cream, water, fruit juices, oil, and melted butter. Eggs are also considered a liquid. All of these ingredients should be properly measured and, when necessary, warmed enough to blend easily with the rest of the wet ingredients. Batters blend most evenly when the liquid ingredients are all close to room temperature. Use a whisk or a table fork to blend the wet ingredients together until they are smooth.

COMBINE THE WET AND DRY INGREDIENTS

Most quick bread batters made with the well mixing method are best mixed by hand. They are normally not heavy enough to make stirring difficult, and a short mixing time produces the most tender baked goods. Pour the wet ingredients into the well in the dry ingredients. Use a wooden spoon or a rubber spatula to stir and fold together the batter until the dry ingredients are evenly moistened.

Raspberry Muffins *with Pecan Streusel*

R ASPBERRIES MAKE a great change from the ever popular blueberry muffin. Since this recipe works with either fresh or frozen berries, you can make it year-round.

1½ cups all-purpose flour

½ cup sugar

2 teaspoons baking powder

½ teaspoon salt

½ cup milk

½ cup butter, melted and cooled

1 large egg, beaten

1 cup raspberries, fresh or frozen, divided use

¾ cup Pecan Streusel (recipe follows)

1. Preheat the oven to 375°F. Prepare the muffin tins by spraying them lightly with cooking spray or lining with muffin liners.

2. Sift the flour, sugar, baking powder, and salt together into a mixing bowl. Make a well in the center of the flour mixture.

3. In a separate bowl, blend the milk, butter, and egg. Add the milk mixture to the flour mixture and stir by hand just until the batter is evenly moistened. Fold in ½ cup of the raspberries.

3. Fill the prepared muffin tins about three-quarters full. Gently tap the filled tins to release any air bubbles. Divide the remaining raspberries among the muffins and sprinkle the tops with the streusel. Bake until a skewer inserted into the center of a muffin comes out clean, 25–30 minutes.

4. Cool the muffins in the pan for about 10 minutes before removing them from the pan. *(recipe continues on page 40)*

LEFT TO RIGHT *Make a well in the center of the dry ingredients and add the wet ingredients; fold the wet ingredients into the dry ingredients and mix until thoroughly combined. Gently fold the raspberries into the batter by lifting and folding the batter over the raspberries; if you simply stir the raspberries into the thick batter, the raspberries will break and color the batter. Use scoops or measuring cups to divide the batter evenly among the prepared muffin cups.*

The muffins can be served warm, or transfer them to a cooling rack to finish cooling before storing in an airtight container. Muffins can be frozen for up to 6 weeks.

Pecan Streusel

MAKES 2 CUPS

SUBSTITUTE OTHER nuts for the pecans, such as walnuts or hazelnuts. Try this streusel instead of the oatmeal streusel on the Honey Almond Crumb Cake (page 52).

⅔ cup chopped toasted pecans
   (see the sidebar *Toasting and Chopping Nuts*, **opposite**)
⅔ cup packed brown sugar
⅔ cup all-purpose flour
5 tablespoons butter, melted

Combine the pecans, brown sugar, and flour in a small bowl. Stir in the melted butter with a table fork until the mixture resembles moist crumbs. Use as directed in the recipe.

Raisin Bran Muffins

MAKES 12 MUFFINS

YOUR FAVORITE bran cereal takes on a whole new life in these wonderful muffins. Try other dried fruits such as diced apricots or prunes instead of the golden raisins.

1½ cups bread flour
1 cup plus 2 tablespoons sugar
4½ teaspoons baking powder
1 teaspoon baking soda
¾ teaspoon salt
2½ cups bran flakes
1½ cups buttermilk
2 large eggs
1 tablespoon canola oil
1 teaspoon vanilla extract
¾ cup golden raisins

1. Preheat the oven to 375°F. Prepare the muffin tins by spraying lightly with cooking spray or lining with muffin liners.

2. Sift the flour, sugar, baking powder, baking soda, and salt together into a mixing bowl. Make a well in the center of the flour mixture.

3. In a separate bowl, blend the bran flakes, buttermilk, eggs, oil, and vanilla. Add the buttermilk mixture to the flour mixture and stir by hand just until the batter is evenly moistened. Fold in the raisins.

4. Fill the prepared muffin tins about three-quarters full. Gently tap the filled tins to release any air bubbles. Bake until a skewer inserted into the center of a muffin comes out clean, 20–25 minutes.

5. Cool the muffins in the pan for about 10 minutes before removing them from the pan. The muffins can be served warm, or transfer them to a cooling rack to finish cooling before storing in an airtight container. Muffins can be frozen for up to 6 weeks.

Bran Muffins

MAKES 12 MUFFINS

To make moister muffins, gently fold ½ cup chopped, plumped-up dried fruit such as prunes, dates, apricots, or raisins into the batter just before baking.

1½ cups all-purpose flour

1 cup wheat or oat bran

1½ teaspoons baking powder

½ teaspoon salt

¼ teaspoon ground cinnamon

¼ cup butter, room temperature

⅓ cup sugar

½ cup milk

1 large egg

2 tablespoons dark molasses or barley malt

1. Preheat the oven to 400°F. Prepare the muffin tins by spraying lightly with cooking spray or lining with muffin liners.

2. Sift the flour, bran, baking powder, salt, and cinnamon together. Set aside.

3. Cream the butter and sugar together until very smooth and light by hand with a wooden spoon or with an electric mixer using the paddle attachment, about 3 minutes.

4. Whisk together the milk, egg, and molasses. Gradually add the egg mixture to the butter mixture while mixing on medium speed and continue mixing until smooth. Scrape down the bowl to blend evenly.

5. Stir the flour mixture into the creamed butter mixture until the batter is evenly blended. Do not overmix.

6. Fill the prepared muffin tins about three-quarters full. Gently tap the filled tins to release any air bubbles. Bake until a skewer inserted into the center of a muffin comes out clean and the tops are golden brown, 16–18 minutes.

7. Cool the muffins in the pan for about 10 minutes before removing them from the pan. The muffins can be served warm or room temperature, or transfer them to a cooling rack to finish cooling before storing in an airtight container. Muffins can be frozen for up to 6 weeks.

Toasting and Chopping Nuts

Nuts hold better if they are purchased raw. Once they are roasted, their oils are drawn to the surface, making it easier for them to turn rancid. Toasting nuts right before you want to use them heightens their flavor and improves their texture. You can toast small amounts of nuts in a dry skillet as follows:

Heat a small dry skillet over high heat (cast iron is ideal). Add the nuts and swirl the pan over the heat to keep them from scorching. Continue until the nuts begin to give off a rich, toasted aroma and are just starting to brown, usually about 2 minutes. Immediately transfer them to a bowl to keep them from burning.

Once the nuts are cool, chop them by hand using a chef's knife, or place them in a mini–food processor and pulse it on and off just until the nuts are coarsely chopped.

Cheddar & Thyme Muffins

MAKES 12 MUFFINS

ADD THESE muffins to your repertoire as a savory alternative. They are perfect to enjoy at dinner, too.

2 cups all-purpose flour

2 tablespoons Coleman's dry mustard

1 tablespoon baking powder

1 teaspoon salt

¼ teaspoon freshly ground black pepper

Pinch cayenne pepper

1 cup grated sharp cheddar cheese

1 tablespoon chopped thyme

1½ cups milk

1 large egg

¼ cup butter, melted

¼ teaspoon hot sauce such as Tabasco,
   or to taste

1. Preheat the oven to 350°F. Prepare the muffin tins by spraying them lightly with cooking spray or lining them with muffin liners.

2. Sift the flour, mustard, baking powder, salt, and peppers together into a mixing bowl. Add the grated cheddar and thyme; toss together until evenly distributed. Make a well in the center of the flour mixture.

3. In a separate bowl, blend the milk, egg, butter, and hot sauce. Add the milk mixture to the flour mixture and stir by hand just until the batter is evenly moistened.

4. Fill the prepared muffin tins about three-quarters full. Gently tap the filled tins to release any air bubbles. Bake until a skewer inserted into the center of a muffin comes out clean, 20–25 minutes.

5. Cool the muffins in the pan for about 10 minutes before removing them from the pan. The muffins can be served warm, or transfer them to a cooling rack to finish cooling before storing in an airtight container. Muffins can be frozen for up to 6 weeks.

OPPOSITE *Cheddar and Thyme Muffins are pictured here with Morning Glory Muffins (with the oatmeal on top; page 44) and Cranberry Orange Muffins (page 45).*

Morning Glory Muffins

MAKES 12 MUFFINS

*T*HESE SWEET, rich muffins really stick with you, making them a perfect choice to tuck into a lunch box or briefcase for breakfast on the road or at your desk.

⅔ cup pastry flour

⅔ cup all-purpose flour

⅔ cup sugar

¾ teaspoon baking soda

½ teaspoon cinnamon

½ teaspoon salt

⅔ cup grated carrots

½ cup shredded coconut

½ cup dark raisins

½ cup peeled and shredded apple

⅓ cup crushed and drained pineapple

⅓ cup chopped toasted walnuts

2 large eggs

½ cup canola oil

½ teaspoon vanilla

¼ cup rolled oats for topping

1. Preheat oven to 375°F. Prepare the muffin tins by spraying them lightly with cooking spray or lining with muffin liners.

2. Sift the flours, sugar, baking soda, cinnamon, and salt together into a mixing bowl. Add the carrots, coconut, raisins, apple, pineapple, and walnuts, tossing together until evenly distributed. Make a well in the center of the flour mixture.

3. In a separate bowl, blend the eggs, oil, and vanilla. Add the egg mixture to the flour mixture and stir by hand just until the batter is evenly moistened.

4. Fill the prepared muffin tins about three-quarters full. Gently tap the filled tins to release any air bubbles. Scatter a little of the rolled oats over each muffin. Bake until a skewer inserted into the center of a muffin comes out clean, 20–25 minutes.

5. Cool the muffins in the pan for about 10 minutes before removing them from the pan. The muffins can be served warm, or transfer them to a cooling rack to finish cooling before storing in an airtight container. Muffins can be frozen for up to 6 weeks. *See photo on page 42.*

The Creaming Mixing Method

Creamed batters, often used to make cakes as well as quick breads, result in rich baked goods with an exceptionally smooth, light, and even texture. Warm the butter to room temperature so you can beat it easily to a smooth consistency together with the sugar, usually white granulated or brown sugar. As the butter and sugar are beaten, or "creamed," small pockets of air are trapped in the butter and distributed evenly throughout the batter. Eventually, these tiny air pockets expand in the oven's heat. This action, along with any other leavener you use, produces a very fine texture and a soft, moist crumb. Adding eggs to the creamed butter and sugar adds moisture; this moisture eventually turns to steam, further leavening the cake.

CREAMING BUTTER AND SUGAR

Take the butter from the refrigerator 15–20 minutes (slightly longer in colder kitchens, less time on warm days) before you begin to let it soften slightly so it is easier to whip. Cream the butter on its own to soften it enough to make it easier to blend in the sugar. To do this, beat it with the paddle attachment of a stand mixer on low speed for about 2 minutes. You can also soften the butter by hand; use a wooden spoon and stir vigorously. When the butter is light in texture, add the sugar

Cranberry Orange Muffins

MAKES 12 MUFFINS

CRANBERRIES ADD moisture and tartness to these muffins. Making orange zest is easy with a microplane. If you don't have one yet, we highly recommend getting one. You'll wonder how you got along without one before.

3 cups all-purpose flour

1 tablespoon baking powder

1½ teaspoons salt

⅓ cup butter, softened

1½ cups sugar

3 large eggs

⅔ cup buttermilk

1 tablespoon vanilla extract

⅓ cup canola oil

2¾ cups cranberries, fresh or frozen

2 tablespoons grated orange zest

3 tablespoons coarse sugar for topping

1. Preheat the oven to 350°F. Prepare the muffin tins by spraying them lightly with cooking spray or lining with muffin liners.

2. Sift the flour, baking powder, and salt together. Set aside.

3. Cream the butter and sugar together until very smooth and light by hand with a wooden spoon or with an electric mixer using the paddle attachment, about 3 minutes.

4. Whisk the eggs, buttermilk, vanilla, and oil together. Gradually add the egg mixture to the butter mixture while mixing on medium speed and continue mixing until smooth. Scrape down the bowl to blend evenly.

5. Stir the flour mixture into the creamed butter mixture until the batter is evenly blended. Do not overmix. Fold in the cranberries and orange zest.

6. Fill the prepared muffin tins about three-quarters full. Gently tap the filled tins to release any air bubbles. Sprinkle the tops of the muffins with the coarse sugar. Bake until a skewer inserted into center of a muffin comes out clean and the tops are golden brown, 30–35 minutes.

7. Cool the muffins in the pan for about 10 minutes before removing them from the pan. The muffins can be served warm or room temperature, or transfer them to a cooling rack to finish cooling before storing in an airtight container. Muffins can be frozen for up to 6 weeks. *See photo on page 42.*

and mix until blended. The sharp edges of the sugar crystals trap some air and create small pockets in the batter that give the finished baked good a light texture.

ADDING THE EGGS

Any eggs and other wet ingredients you add to the creamed butter-and-sugar mixture should be at room temperature. If they are very cold, they may cause the butter to harden into little flecks; if this happens, keep mixing until the flecks disappear before adding more ingredients. Eggs are usually added to the creamed butter-and-sugar mixture before any other liquid ingredients so that they can mix evenly into the butter.

ADDING THE DRY INGREDIENTS

Add the sifted dry ingredients as directed in your recipe. Some call for the dry ingredients to be added all at once, while others indicate to add them in two or three additions, alternating with the liquid ingredients.

ADDING OTHER INGREDIENTS

Hot ingredients like melted chocolate should be cooled to room temperature before they are added to the batter and will combine with it most readily if they are blended with a small amount of the batter first.

Banana Nut Loaf

MAKES 2 LOAVES

IF YOUR bananas are ready to make into banana bread before you are ready to use them, freeze them (in their peels) until your next baking day. They'll keep for up to 2 months. After they thaw, they will practically puree themselves.

6 bananas, very ripe

1 teaspoon lemon juice

3¼ cups all-purpose flour

½ teaspoon baking powder

1¼ teaspoons baking soda

½ teaspoon salt

2 cups sugar

2 large eggs

½ cup vegetable oil

¾ cup chopped toasted pecans

1. Preheat the oven to 350°F. Prepare two 8-inch loaf pans by spraying lightly with cooking spray or rubbing with softened butter.

2. Puree the bananas and lemon juice together using a blender or by hand. You should have about 2 cups mashed bananas.

3. Sift together the flour, baking powder, baking soda, and salt. Set aside.

4. Combine the banana puree, sugar, eggs, and oil and mix on medium speed with a paddle attachment until blended, about 3 minutes. Scrape the bowl as needed. Add the sifted dry ingredients and mix until just combined. Mix in the pecans.

5. Divide the batter evenly between the loaf pans. Gently tap the filled pans to burst any air bubbles. Bake until the bread springs back when pressed and a tester inserted near the center comes out clean, about 55 minutes.

6. Cool the loaves in the pans for a few minutes, then remove the bread from the pans, transfer to cooling racks, and cool completely before slicing and serving or wrapping. They can be held at room temperature for up to 3 days or frozen for up to 6 weeks.

Pumpkin Loaf

MAKES 2 LOAVES

CHOCOLATE CHIPS are a great addition to pumpkin bread. Use regular or miniature chips.

3⅓ cups all-purpose or cake flour

2 tablespoons plus 1½ teaspoons baking powder

1 tablespoon plus 1 teaspoon pumpkin pie spice

¾ teaspoon salt

1¼ cups pumpkin puree

1 cup water

1 cup butter

2 cups plus 2 tablespoons sugar

3 large eggs

1½ cups chocolate chips

1. Preheat the oven to 350°F. Prepare two 9-inch loaf pans by spraying them lightly with cooking spray or rubbing with softened butter. Dust them lightly with flour, shaking out any excess.

2. Sift the flour, baking powder, pumpkin pie spice, and salt together. Set aside.

3. Blend the pumpkin puree and water in a small bowl. Set aside.

4. Cream the butter and sugar together until very smooth and light by hand with a wooden spoon or with an electric mixer using the paddle attachment, about 3 minutes.

5. Add the eggs one at a time, mixing until smooth and scraping down the bowl between each addition. Scrape down the bowl to blend evenly.

6. Stir the flour mixture into the creamed butter mixture in four additions, alternating with the pumpkin mixture, beginning and ending with the flour. Mix the batter until it is evenly blended after each addition, scraping down the bowl as needed. After the final addition, continue to mix the batter until smooth, 2–3 minutes. Fold in the chocolate chips.

7. Divide the batter evenly between the prepared loaf pans, filling them about three-quarters full. Gently tap the filled pans to release any air bubbles. Bake until a skewer inserted into center of the loaf comes out clean and the tops are golden brown, 50–60 minutes.

8. Cool the pumpkin bread in the pans for about 10 minutes before removing from the pan. Transfer them to a cooling rack to finish cooling before slicing and serving or wrapping to store. They can be held at room temperature for up to 3 days or frozen for up to 6 weeks.

Date Nut Bread

MAKES 2 LOAVES

*T*RY TOASTING slices of this rich, moist bread and spreading them with cream cheese or peanut butter. This bread holds well.

4 cups all-purpose or cake flour

1 tablespoon baking powder

1 teaspoon baking soda

1 teaspoon salt

½ cup butter, room temperature

1 cup packed light brown sugar

2 large eggs

2 cups chopped pitted dates

1 cup chopped toasted pecans

1¾ cups water, divided use

1. Preheat the oven to 350° F. Prepare two 9-inch loaf pans by spraying lightly with cooking spray or rubbing with softened butter. Dust them lightly with flour, shaking out any excess.

2. Sift together the flour, baking powder, baking soda, and salt. Set aside.

3. Cream the butter and sugar together until very smooth and light by hand with a wooden spoon or with an electric mixer using the paddle attachment, about 3 minutes.

4. Add the eggs one at a time, mixing until smooth and scraping down the bowl between each addition. Scrape down the bowl to blend evenly.

5. Stir the flour mixture into the creamed butter mixture until it is evenly blended, scraping down the bowl as needed. Add the dates, pecans, and half the water and stir until smooth. Add the remaining water and stir until smooth.

6. Divide the batter evenly between the prepared loaf pans, filling them about three-quarters full. Gently tap the filled pans to release any air bubbles. Bake until a skewer inserted into center of the loaf comes out clean and the tops are golden brown, 50–60 minutes.

7. Cool the date bread in the pans for about 10 minutes before removing from the pan. Transfer them to a cooling rack to finish cooling before slicing and serving or wrapping to store. They can be held at room temperature for up to 3 days or frozen for up to 6 weeks.

Marbleized Pound Cake

MAKES 2 LOAVES

MARBLING TWO batters by gently folding them together results in a beautiful baked cake. Cutting a slit in the top layer of the cake once a crust has started to form is an extra step you can take to be sure your cake looks as beautiful on the outside as it does on the inside.

¾ cup chopped bittersweet chocolate

3½ cups all-purpose flour

1 teaspoon baking powder

1 teaspoon salt

2 cups butter

2¼ cups sugar

9 large eggs, beaten

1 teaspoon vanilla extract

1. Preheat the oven to 375°F. Prepare two 9-inch loaf pans by spraying lightly with cooking spray or rubbing with softened butter. Dust them lightly with flour, shaking out any excess.

2. Melt the chocolate over very low heat or in the microwave. Transfer to a mixing bowl and let the chocolate cool to room temperature.

3. Sift together the flour, baking powder, and salt. Set aside.

4. Cream the butter and sugar together until very smooth and light by hand with a wooden spoon or with an electric mixer using the paddle attachment, about 3 minutes.

5. Add the eggs in three to four additions, mixing until smooth and scraping down the bowl between each addition. Scrape down the bowl to blend evenly. Blend in the vanilla.

6. Stir the flour mixture into the creamed butter mixture until it is evenly blended, scraping down the bowl as needed.

7. Add half of the batter to the melted chocolate and mix thoroughly. Gently fold the chocolate mixture into the remaining batter just until the chocolate batter is swirled throughout.

8. Divide the batter evenly between the prepared loaf pans, filling them about three-quarters full. Gently tap the filled pans to release any air bubbles. Bake the cakes until a skin has formed on the cakes, about 15 minutes. Use a sharp paring knife to cut a slit down the center of each loaf. Continue to bake until a skewer inserted into center of the loaf comes out clean and the tops are golden brown, another 40–45 minutes.

9. Cool the cakes in the pans for about 10 minutes before removing from the pan. Transfer them to a cooling rack to finish cooling before slicing and serving or wrapping to store. They can be held at room temperature for up to 3 days or frozen for up to 6 weeks.

Honey Almond Crumb Cake

MAKES 12–14 SERVINGS

*T*OP THIS sweet fragrant cake with 2 cups of berries (strawberries, blueberries, blackberries, raspberries, or a combination) instead of the streusel, if you prefer.

3⅓ cups all-purpose or cake flour

1 teaspoon salt

½ teaspoon baking powder

¾ cup sour cream

½ cup canola oil

3 tablespoons honey

1 tablespoon vanilla extract

½ cup almond paste

6 large eggs, beaten, divided use

1¼ cups butter, softened

1¼ cups sugar

2 cups Oatmeal Streusel (recipe follows)

1. Preheat the oven to 350°F. Prepare an 11 × 17-inch jelly roll pan by spraying it lightly with cooking spray. Dust the pan lightly with flour, shaking out any excess.

2. Sift the flour, salt, and baking powder together. Set aside.

3. Blend the sour cream, oil, honey, and vanilla in a small bowl. Set aside.

4. Cream the almond paste with 2 tablespoons of the beaten eggs in an electric mixer using the paddle attachment on medium speed until smooth and light, about 2–3 minutes. Scrape down the bowl to blend evenly. Add the butter and sugar and continue to beat until very smooth and light.

5. Add the remaining beaten eggs in three additions, mixing until smooth and scraping down the bowl between each addition.

6. Stir the flour mixture into the creamed butter mixture. Mix the batter until it is evenly blended, scraping down the bowl as needed. Fold in the sour cream mixture until just combined.

7. Spread the batter in an even layer in the prepared jelly roll pan. Sprinkle the streusel evenly over the top of the cake. Bake until a skewer inserted into center of the cake comes out clean and the edges are golden brown, about 30 minutes.

8. Cool the cake in the pan on a cooling rack before slicing and serving or wrapping to store. Hold the cake at room temperature for up to 3 days or freeze it for up to 6 weeks.

Oatmeal Streusel

MAKES 2 CUPS

*U*SE THIS delicious streusel to add more flavor and texture to virtually any muffin or quick bread. It is easy to double or triple and can be held in the refrigerator for up to 2 weeks. It can also be frozen for up to 3 months.

¾ cup all-purpose or cake flour

⅔ cup rolled oats

6 tablespoons sugar

1 teaspoon ground cinnamon

¼ teaspoon salt

3 tablespoons butter, room temperature

Combine the flour, oats, sugar, cinnamon, and salt in a mixing bowl and stir until evenly blended. Add the butter and mix by hand or in a mixer with the paddle attachment until crumbly, about 5 minutes.

Sour Cream Streusel Coffee Cake

MAKES 1 BUNDT CAKE

W E'VE SUGGESTED a Bundt pan for this cake, but you can also use a loaf pan or even bake the batter and streusel in muffin tins. This cake keeps extremely well, as long as it is carefully wrapped. Freeze it for up to 2 months.

STREUSEL MIXTURE

¼ cup plus 2 tablespoons packed light brown sugar

⅓ cup finely chopped toasted walnuts

¼ cup chocolate chips

½ teaspoon ground cinnamon

½ teaspoon cocoa powder

SOUR CREAM BATTER

2¼ cups all-purpose or cake flour

1 teaspoon baking powder

½ teaspoon baking soda

½ teaspoon salt

3 large eggs

¾ cup sour cream

1 teaspoon vanilla extract

¾ cup unsalted butter, room temperature

¾ cup sugar

1. Preheat the oven to 350° F. Prepare a Bundt pan by spraying it lightly with cooking spray or rubbing with softened butter.

2. To prepare the streusel, toss together the brown sugar, walnuts, chocolate chips, cinnamon, and cocoa until evenly blended. Set aside.

3. Sift the flour, baking powder, baking soda, and salt together. Set aside.

4. In a separate bowl, blend the eggs, sour cream, and vanilla. Set aside.

5. Cream the butter and sugar together until very smooth and light by hand with a wooden spoon or with an electric mixer using the paddle attachment, about 3 minutes.

6. Add the egg mixture in three additions, alternating with the flour mixture. Mix the batter until it is evenly blended after each addition, scraping down the bowl as needed. After the final addition, continue to mix the batter until smooth, 2–3 minutes.

7. Spoon half of the batter into the Bundt pan. Scatter the streusel mixture evenly over the batter and swirl with a skewer to blend the streusel in slightly. Add the remaining batter over the streusel.

8. Gently tap the filled pan to release any air bubbles. Bake until a skewer inserted into center of the cake comes out clean and the top is golden brown, about 1 hour and 15 minutes.

9. Cool the cake in the pan for about 10 minutes before removing from the pan. Transfer to a cooling rack to finish cooling before slicing and serving or wrapping to store. This cake can be held at room temperature for up to 3 days or frozen for up to 2 months.

Carrot and Pear Cake

MAKES 2 LOAVES

CARROTS AND pears give this cake a wonderful sweet flavor and a beautiful color. If you are making the cakes in advance, wrap them tightly and store at room temperature for up to 3 days or freeze for up to 6 weeks.

2 ⅔ cups all-purpose flour

1½ teaspoons ground cinnamon

¾ teaspoon salt

¾ teaspoon baking powder

¼ teaspoon baking soda

1⅓ cups chopped toasted walnuts

1⅓ cups shredded coconut

2½ cups shredded carrot

2 cups shredded pear

1½ cups sugar

1⅓ cups vegetable oil

5 large eggs

1. Preheat the oven to 350° F. Prepare two 9-inch loaf pans by spraying lightly with cooking spray or rubbing with softened butter.

2. Sift the flour, cinnamon, salt, baking powder, and baking soda together into a mixing bowl. Add the walnuts and coconut to the flour mixture and stir until evenly distributed. Make a well in the center of the flour mixture.

3. In a separate bowl, blend the carrot, pear, sugar, oil, and eggs. Add the carrot mixture to the flour mixture and stir by hand just until the batter is evenly moistened.

4. Divide the batter evenly between the prepared loaf pans, filling them about three-quarters full. Gently tap the filled pans to release any air bubbles. Bake until a skewer inserted into center of the loaf comes out clean and the tops are golden brown, about 1 hour and 15 minutes.

5. Cool the carrot and pear cakes in the pans for about 10 minutes before removing from the pan. Transfer them to a cooling rack to finish cooling. The cakes are ready to slice and serve now.

Scottish Bannocks

MAKES 12 BANNOCKS

BANNOCKS ARE traditionally served with breakfast or afternoon tea in Scotland. They are wonderful hot from the oven, but they don't hold well.

1 cup quick-cooking oats

¼ cup all-purpose flour

2 tablespoons sugar

1 tablespoon baking powder

Pinch salt

¼ cup butter, diced and chilled

⅓ cup cold milk, plus as needed

1. Preheat the oven to 450°F.

2. Combine the oats, flour, sugar, baking powder, and salt in a large bowl. Add the butter, cutting it into the dry ingredients until the mixture resembles coarse meal.

3. Add the milk to the oat mixture, stirring until barely combined. The dough will look coarse and shaggy at this point. If the dough is too dry, add a few teaspoons more milk.

4. Turn the mixture out onto a lightly floured surface and knead just until dough holds together. Press or roll out to a thickness of ½ inch. Cut out the bannocks using a 2½-inch cutter. Gather scraps together, reroll, and cut additional bannocks. Place the bannocks on an ungreased baking sheet about 1 inch apart.

5. Bake until light brown, 10–12 minutes. Serve very hot, directly from the oven.

Jalapeño Biscuits

MAKES 12 BISCUITS

YOU CAN use the layering and folding technique described here to add a wide variety of garnishes to your biscuits. Instead of jalapeños, try finely diced ham, grated cheese, or diced roasted peppers.

2 cups all-purpose flour

1 tablespoon baking powder

¾ teaspoon salt

⅓ cup butter, diced

¾ cup buttermilk

2 teaspoons minced jalapeño pepper

Pinch freshly ground black pepper

1. Preheat the oven to 425°F. Prepare a baking sheet by spraying it lightly with cooking spray or lining with parchment paper.

2. Sift the flour, baking powder, and salt into a large bowl.

Add the butter, cutting it into the dry ingredients until the mixture resembles coarse meal. You should still be able to see small pieces of butter.

3. Add the buttermilk to the flour mixture, stirring until barely combined. The dough will look coarse and shaggy at this point.

4. Transfer the dough to a lightly floured work surface, press into a ball, and knead once or twice. Press or roll the dough out to a thickness of ½ inch. Sprinkle the jalapeños and black pepper over two-thirds of the dough. Fold the dough in thirds, like a letter, then reroll it out to a thickness of ½ inch. Cut out the biscuits using a 2½-inch cutter. Gather scraps together, reroll, and cut additional biscuits. Place the biscuits on the prepared pan about 1 inch apart. Refrigerate uncovered for 15 minutes.

5. Bake the biscuits until they have risen and the tops are golden brown, 18–20 minutes. Serve very hot, directly from the oven.

Making Biscuits

The technique used to make biscuits, as well as scones and soda bread, is known as a rubbed dough method. Instead of soft batters that drop easily from a spoon, biscuits, scones, and soda bread are made from a stiff dough that can be rolled and cut.

KEEP INGREDIENTS COOL

Any liquids or fats that you add to these doughs should be kept very cold. Cold ingredients are important if you want a light flaky texture.

CUT THE FAT INTO THE FLOUR

Instead of blending the ingredients to make a smooth batter, as you do for muffins and cakes made with the straight or creaming mixing meth-

ods, you should cut the butter into the flour with a pastry knife or two table knifes, just long enough to produce a mealy texture. You should still be able to see small pieces of butter.

ADD THE LIQUID INGREDIENTS AND BLEND BRIEFLY

Although the mixing method for biscuits and soda bread is similar to that for pie dough (page 158) and blitz puff pastry (page 96), these doughs contain enough liquid to make a soft dough. Chill the liquid (and eggs, if called for) and add them to the fat and flour mixture. Work quickly and instead of stirring, use a fork to pull the flour into the liquid. The dough is properly blended when it looks very rough, a condition bakers sometimes refer to as a "shaggy mass."

Angel Biscuits

MAKES 12 BISCUITS

A TOUCH OF yeast gives these biscuits their light, ethereal texture. If you are new to yeast baking, they make a perfect introduction.

¾ teaspoon dry yeast

3 tablespoons warm water, about 110°F

¾ cup buttermilk

6 tablespoons shortening, melted and cooled

1¾ cups all-purpose flour

1½ tablespoons sugar

1¼ teaspoons baking powder

¼ teaspoon baking soda

½ teaspoon salt

Egg wash of 2 egg whites blended with 1 tablespoon cold water

1. Preheat the oven to 425°F. Prepare a baking sheet by spraying it lightly with cooking spray or lining with parchment paper.

2. Stir together the yeast and warm water in a small bowl and let stand for 5 minutes, or until the yeast foams. Add the buttermilk and melted shortening. Set aside.

3. Sift the flour, sugar, baking powder, baking soda, and salt together into a mixing bowl. Make a well in the center of the flour mixture.

4. Add the yeast-buttermilk mixture to the flour mixture and stir by hand just until the batter is moistened. The dough will look coarse and shaggy at this point.

5. Transfer the dough to a lightly floured work surface, press into a ball, and knead once or twice. Press or roll the dough out to a thickness of ½ inch. Cut out the biscuits using a 2-inch cutter. Gather scraps together, reroll, and cut additional biscuits. Place the biscuits on the prepared pan about 1 inch apart and lightly brush the tops with egg wash. Let the biscuits rise until they are nearly doubled, about 20 minutes.

6. Bake the biscuits until the tops are golden brown, 12–14 minutes. Serve very hot, directly from the oven.

KNEAD THE DOUGH BRIEFLY

The purpose of kneading these doughs is simply to gather them together into a smooth ball. Turn the dough out onto a lightly floured surface and press it together. Knead the dough two or three times. It is ready to shape by either rolling and cutting or molding into a loaf.

PAT OR ROLL THE DOUGH INTO AN EVEN LAYER
AND CUT THE BISCUITS

Keep the dough very lightly dusted, just enough so that it doesn't stick. Your biscuit cutter should have sharp, clean edges. Press the cutter into the dough and twist it slightly to lift the biscuit up. Make your cuts as close together as possible. Once you've cut out all you can, gather the scraps together, pressing them enough so that you can roll out the dough. Then cut additional biscuits.

COOL THE DOUGH ONCE MORE BEFORE
BAKING THE BISCUITS

This final cooling lets the dough relax and counteracts the potential toughness that might result from blending flour and liquid. It also gives the oven time to come up to the right temperature. You'll notice that the suggested baking temperature for biscuits and soda bread is usually 400° to 425° F. They need to bake quickly in a hot oven for a good rise and a great color. If your recipe recommends it, apply a thin layer of egg wash or cold milk for a rich color and a slight sheen.

Buttermilk Biscuits *with Sausage Gravy*

*B*UTTERMILK BISCUITS are a great bread to serve at breakfast or brunch, but you can make them into the main course by adding a substantial gravy.

1¼ cups cold buttermilk

1 large egg

2 cups bread flour

1¾ cups all-purpose flour

3 tablespoons sugar

2 tablespoons baking powder

1¼ teaspoons salt

¾ cup cold butter, diced

Egg wash of 1 egg yolk whisked with 2 tablespoons heavy cream

Sausage Gravy (recipe follows), optional

1. Preheat oven to 425°F. Prepare a baking sheet by spraying it lightly with cooking spray or lining with parchment paper.

2. Combine the buttermilk and egg in a small bowl and blend until evenly mixed. Set aside.

3. Sift the flours, sugar, baking powder, and salt into a large bowl. Add the butter, cutting it into the dry ingredients until the mixture resembles coarse meal. You should still be able to see small pieces of butter.

4. Add the buttermilk mixture to the flour mixture, stirring until barely combined. The dough will look coarse and shaggy at this point.

5. Transfer the dough to a lightly floured work surface, press into a ball, and knead once or twice. Press or roll the dough out to a thickness of ½ inch. Cut out the biscuits using a 2½-inch cutter. Gather scraps together, reroll, and cut additional biscuits. Place the biscuits on the prepared pan about 1 inch apart and lightly brush the tops with egg wash. Refrigerate uncovered for 15 minutes.

6. Bake the biscuits until they have risen and the tops are golden brown, 18–20 minutes. Serve the biscuits very hot, directly from the oven, accompanied by the sausage gravy.

Sausage Gravy

*S*ERVE THIS simple and satisfying gravy over biscuits or use it as a topping for a plain omelet.

8 ounces Breakfast Sausage (page 211)

1 tablespoon vegetable oil

2 tablespoons flour

2 cups milk, plus as needed

1 teaspoon salt

½ teaspoon ground black pepper

1. Heat a large skillet over medium heat. Crumble the sausage into the pan and sauté, stirring frequently with a wooden spoon and breaking up the sausage as it cooks, until it is golden brown and thoroughly cooked, about 5 minutes. Transfer the sausage from the pan to a colander set in a bowl and let it drain.

2. Add the vegetable oil and the flour to the same pan used to cook the sausage. Stir to blend and cook over medium heat, stirring well to scrape up any brown bits on the bottom of the pan. Continue to cook, stirring constantly, until the mixture is a pale golden brown, about 3 minutes.

3. Add the milk, whisking constantly to remove any lumps. Simmer over low heat, stirring frequently, until the gravy is thickened, about 20 minutes. Taste the gravy and add salt and pepper to taste. If the gravy is too thick, thin it with a little additional milk; use only enough to get a pourable consistency.

4. Return the cooked sausage to the gravy. Adjust the seasoning with additional salt and pepper, if necessary.

Soda Bread

MAKES 2 LOAVES OR 16 ROLLS

*T*RADITIONAL RECIPES for soda bread suggest wrapping the freshly baked loaves in a clean tea towel. This keeps the soda bread moist and preserves its unique texture.

4 cups cake flour

2 tablespoons baking soda

½ cup sugar

¼ teaspoon salt

¼ cup vegetable shortening

1 cup dark raisins

1 tablespoon caraway seeds

1 cup cold milk

1. Preheat the oven to 400°F. Prepare a baking sheet by spraying it lightly with cooking spray or lining it with parchment paper.

2. Sift the flour, baking soda, sugar, and salt together into a large bowl. Using a pastry cutter or 2 knives, cut the shortening into the dry ingredients until it resembles coarse meal.

3. Add the raisins, caraway seeds, and milk. Mix the dough just until it forms a shaggy mass.

4. Turn the dough out onto a lightly floured surface. Press the dough into a ball. Form the dough into 2 equal loaves, or cut into 16 equal pieces to make rolls. Dust with flour and lightly score a cross into the top of each roll or loaf with a sharp knife.

5. Bake the soda bread until it is lightly browned and sounds hollow when tapped on the bottom, about 8–10 minutes for rolls and 25 minutes for loaves. Wrap the bread in a tea towel directly out of the oven.

6. Cool the soda bread in the tea towel on a wire rack before serving. It can be held at room temperature for up to 2 days or frozen for up to 4 weeks.

Cornbread

*T*O GET a crisp crust on the bottom and sides of your cornbread, use a cast-iron skillet. (A 10-inch pan is perfect for this recipe.) Alternately, this batter can be used to make corn sticks, using a cast-iron corn stick pan as shown here; most of these pans bake 7 corn sticks at a time. Put the skillet or corn stick pan into the oven while you mix the batter so that it gets very hot. Brush the hot pan liberally with oil just before pouring in the batter.

1¼ cups all-purpose flour

½ cup yellow cornmeal

½ cup sugar

⅓ cup powdered milk

2 tablespoons baking powder

½ teaspoon salt

2 large eggs

½ cup water

⅓ cup corn oil

¼ teaspoon vanilla extract

1. Preheat the oven to 350°F. Spray an 8-inch square baking pan with cooking spray, or prepare a cast-iron skillet or corn stick pan as directed above.

2. Combine the flour, cornmeal, sugar, powdered milk, baking powder, and salt in a bowl and mix thoroughly. Make a well in the center of the flour mixture.

3. Combine the eggs, water, oil, and vanilla in a separate bowl and mix thoroughly. Add the egg mixture to the flour mixture and stir by hand just until the batter is moistened.

4. Pour the batter into the pan and bake until a knife inserted in the center comes out clean and the top of the cornbread springs back lightly to the touch, 25–30 minutes.

5. Allow the cornbread to cool slightly before cutting. Serve the cornbread warm or at room temperature.

Jalapeño Jack & Cheddar Cornbread

*T*HE ADDITION of the two cheeses makes this cornbread extremely moist. Look for a good aged cheddar, which will have a sharp bite and pronounced flavor.

1½ cups yellow cornmeal

1½ cups all-purpose flour

¼ cup sugar

1 teaspoon baking powder

½ teaspoon baking soda

¼ teaspoon salt

1 cup buttermilk

3 large eggs

¼ cup butter, melted

⅓ cup shredded sharp cheddar cheese

⅓ cup shredded jalapeño Jack cheese

1 tablespoon minced jalapeños

1. Preheat the oven to 375°F. Lightly grease a 9 × 12-inch baking pan.

2. Sift the cornmeal, flour, sugar, baking powder, baking soda, and salt together into a mixing bowl. Make a well in the center of the cornmeal mixture.

3. In a separate bowl, blend the buttermilk, eggs, and butter. Add the buttermilk mixture to the cornmeal mixture and stir by hand just until the batter is evenly moistened. Add the cheeses and jalapeños and blend just until evenly distributed throughout the batter.

4. Spread the batter evenly in the prepared pan. Bake until a skewer inserted into center of the cornbread comes out clean and the top is golden brown, 30 minutes.

5. Cool the cornbread in the pan before cutting into individual servings. Serve warm or at room temperature.

Ham & Cheddar Scones

MAKES 10 SCONES

THE CHEESE gets nice and brown and bubbly on the outside, and the ham adds a lot of flavor. The green onions provide a nice counterpoint to the ham and cheese and give the scones a fantastic fresh flavor. These scones are so moist that they almost fall apart.

3 cups all-purpose flour

½ cup sugar

2 tablespoons baking powder

½ teaspoon salt

1 cup medium-diced ham

½ cup medium-diced cheddar cheese

½ cup sliced scallions

2 cups heavy cream

1. Cut two 10-inch circles of parchment paper. Use one to line a 10-inch round cake pan. Reserve the second piece.

2. Sift the flour, sugar, baking powder, and salt together into a mixing bowl. Add the ham, cheese, and scallions and toss together with the dry ingredients until evenly distributed. Make a well in the center of the flour mixture.

3. Add the cream to the flour mixture and stir by hand just until the batter is evenly moistened.

4. Place the dough in the lined cake pan and press into an even layer. Cover the dough with the second parchment paper circle. Freeze the dough until very firm, at least 2 hours.

5. Preheat the oven to 350° F. Prepare a baking sheet by spraying it lightly with cooking spray or lining with parchment paper.

6. Thaw the dough for 5 minutes at room temperature; turn it out of the cake pan onto a cutting board. Cut the dough into 10 equal wedges and place the individual wedges on the baking sheet about 2 inches apart.

7. Bake the scones until golden brown, 30–40 minutes. Cool the scones on the baking sheet for a few minutes, then transfer to cooling racks. Serve scones warm or at room temperature. Serve baked scones the same day they are made or freeze for up to 4 weeks.

LEFT TO RIGHT *Mix the cream with the dry ingredients until it is just combined. This is known as the shaggy mass stage. Cut the dough evenly into 10 pieces so that each scone will bake evenly. Opposite, the finished Ham and Cheddar Scones are shown with Cream Scones (page 68) and Dried Cherry Scones (page 69).*

Cream Scones

MAKES 10 SCONES

BE SURE your cream is very cold for the best texture. Look for coarse sugar along with other baking items in your grocery store, but if it isn't available, you can use regular granulated sugar instead.

3 cups all-purpose flour

½ cup sugar

2 tablespoons baking powder

½ teaspoon salt

2 cups heavy cream, cold

2 tablespoons milk

3 tablespoons coarse sugar for topping

1. Cut two 10-inch circles of parchment paper. Use one to line a 10-inch round cake pan. Reserve the second piece.

2. Sift the flour, sugar, baking powder, and salt together into a mixing bowl. Make a well in the center of the flour mixture.

3. Add the cream to the flour mixture and stir by hand just until the batter is evenly moistened.

4. Place the dough in the lined cake pan and press into an even layer. Cover the dough with the second parchment paper circle. Freeze the dough until very firm, at least 2 hours.

5. Preheat the oven to 350°F. Prepare a baking sheet by spraying it lightly with cooking spray or lining it with parchment paper.

6. Thaw the dough for 5 minutes at room temperature; turn it out of the cake pan onto a cutting board. Cut the dough into 10 equal wedges and place the individual wedges on the baking sheet about 2 inches apart. Brush the scones with milk and sprinkle with the sugar.

7. Bake the scones until golden brown, 30–40 minutes. Cool the scones on the baking sheet for a few minutes, then transfer to cooling racks. Serve scones warm or at room temperature. Serve baked scones the same day they are made or freeze for up to 4 weeks. *See photo on page 67.*

Dried Cherry Scones

MAKES 10 SCONES

*D*RIED FRUITS give scones a magnificent flavor. A touch of salt in the dough is the perfect counterpoint to their sweetness. As the scones bake, dried cherries plump up and take on a great jammy texture. Try dried currants or apricots instead of cherries.

3 cups all-purpose flour

½ cup sugar

2 tablespoons baking powder

1½ teaspoons salt

1 cup dried cherries

2 cups heavy cream

SUGAR GLAZE (optional)

2 tablespoons milk

1 cup confectioners' sugar, sifted

1. Cut two 10-inch circles of parchment paper. Use one to line a 10-inch round cake pan. Reserve the second piece.

2. Sift the flour, sugar, baking powder, and salt together into a mixing bowl. Add the dried cherries and toss them together with the dry ingredients until evenly distributed. Make a well in the center of the flour mixture.

3. Add the cream to the flour mixture and stir by hand just until the batter is evenly moistened.

4. Place the dough in the lined cake pan and press into an even layer. Cover the dough with the second parchment paper circle. Freeze the dough until very firm, at least 2 hours.

5. Preheat the oven to 350° F. Prepare a baking sheet by spraying it lightly with cooking spray or lining it with parchment paper.

6. Thaw the dough for 5 minutes at room temperature; turn it out of the cake pan onto a cutting board. Cut the dough into 10 equal wedges and place the individual wedges on the baking sheet about 2 inches apart.

7. Bake the scones until golden brown, 30–40 minutes. Cool the scones on the baking sheet for a few minutes, then transfer to cooling racks.

8. Mix the milk and confectioners' sugar together to make a glaze, if desired, and spoon over the scones while they are still warm. Serve scones warm or at room temperature. Serve baked scones the same day they are made or freeze for up to 4 weeks. *See photo on page 67.*

Lemon Curd

MAKES 2 CUPS

*Y*OU CAN use a double boiler for this recipe, but it is actually easier to whisk the lemon curd as it cooks if you make a double boiler setup from a stainless-steel bowl set into a saucepan with an inch or two of simmering water. The bottom of the bowl should not sit directly in the water and the water should be kept below a rolling boil for the best results. You can strain the curd to remove the zest for a silky smooth texture, or leave it unstrained for a more textured curd.

9 large egg yolks

⅔ cup lemon juice

¾ cups sugar

4 teaspoons lemon zest

14 tablespoons butter, cubed, room temperature

1. Bring an inch or two of water to a simmer in a saucepan or the bottom of a double boiler.

2. Combine the egg yolks, lemon juice, sugar, and zest in a stainless mixing bowl or the top of a double boiler and whisk until the sugar is completely dissolved. Set the mixture over the simmering water and continue to whisk until the eggs are thickened and warm, about 12 minutes.

3. Add the butter a few pieces at a time, stirring until each addition is blended into the eggs before adding more. Continue stirring until all of the butter is blended into the curd.

4. Transfer the curd (straining if desired) to a bowl set in an ice bath and cool, stirring from time to time. Once the curd has reached room temperature, it is ready to serve or store in a covered container in the refrigerator for up to 3 days.

BELOW, LEFT TO RIGHT *Whisk the egg mixture over a hot water bath until it is thick enough to hold a line drawn through it on the back of a wooden spoon; this is called the nappé stage. Stir the butter into the curd a little bit at a time. The curd should pile up on itself slightly after it is strained; this is the proper consistency of the finished curd. Serve the cooled lemon curd as an accompaniment to scones, as shown opposite, or use it to make individual tartlets or a pie.*

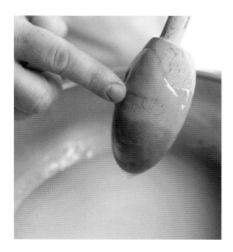

Funnel Cakes

MAKES 20 CAKES

A WRAPPER MADE of folded parchment or waxed paper is the perfect "plate" for these delicious fried cakes.

3⅓ cups all-purpose flour

¼ cup sugar

1¼ teaspoons baking powder

½ teaspoon baking soda

¼ teaspoon salt

2½ cups cold milk

3 large eggs, beaten

½ teaspoon vanilla extract

1 quart canola oil, for deep frying

¾ cup confectioners' sugar

1. Sift the flour, sugar, baking powder, baking soda, and salt together into a mixing bowl. Make a well in the center of the flour mixture.

2. Whisk together the milk, eggs, and vanilla in a separate bowl. Add the milk mixture to the flour mixture and stir by hand just until the batter is evenly moistened.

3. Heat the oil to 350°F in a deep pan or deep fryer. Using a 2-ounce ladle, drizzle the batter into the oil in a spiral pattern to form a loose cake approximately 4 inches in diameter.

4. Fry until golden brown on the first side, about 30 seconds. Turn the cake over and fry until golden brown on the second side, about 30 seconds. Remove the cake from the oil and drain on paper toweling. Repeat with the remaining batter.

5. Dust the hot funnel cakes with confectioners' sugar. For a quick, clean way to get an even layer of sugar on the cakes, tie the confectioners' sugar in a cheesecloth pouch with some kitchen twine and use it to dust the funnel cakes. Serve immediately.

SWEET AND SAVORY BREADS & PASTRIES

ASKETS OR TRAYS filled with freshly baked pastries, luscious sticky rolls, or buttery brioche are the perfect way to add some elegance and extravagance to breakfast or brunch. We've collected several recipes that give you the option of making your own pastries that feature fresh and dried fruits, nuts, cheeses, and even chocolate.

Classic breakfast breads, including English Muffins (page 81), Sticky Buns (page 84), Raisin Cinnamon Swirl Bread (page 79), and Cinnamon Rolls (page 82), give you the opportunity to try your hand at some sweet breads, while Cottage Cheese Dill Rolls (page 92) and Cheddar Onion Rye Rolls (page 93) have a decidedly savory taste. Try them on the weekend when you have a bit more time to keep track of the dough as it rises.

Most yeast doughs can be left to rise overnight in the refrigerator. Simply take them from the refrigerator and let them warm to room temperature while you brew the coffee or tea, make juice, or set the table. Brioche (page 88) and Challah (page 89) are a bit more complex so you may prefer to bake them the day before. (Both of these rich, butter-and-egg enriched breads are perfect for sandwiches, toast, in bread puddings, or for French toast.)

Unlike lunch and dinner when we usually save sweets for a dessert that follows the meal, breakfast and brunch give us full permission to savor a sweet pastry, cake, or cookie right along with the "main" course. Try substituting the filling for the Mushroom, Leek, and Brie Turnovers (page 104) where a fruit filling is called for, to create a savory pastry that can be a meal on its own.

The Best Ingredients

Although any of the recipes in this chapter can be made successfully with all-purpose flour, you'll get the best results if you use the type of flour suggested in the recipe.

FLOURS AND MEALS

Bread flour has a slightly higher protein content than all-purpose flour. That means yeast-raised doughs can rise a little better and will have a satisfyingly chewy texture after they bake.

Cake flour is a soft wheat flour that produces delicate and tender cakes. Because it is softer, it has a tendency to clump. Be sure to sift cake flour to lighten it and break it apart.

Rye flour can be either medium or light. Medium rye has a more noticeable flavor and deeper color than light rye. Compared to white wheat flours, rye flours contain more of the whole grain's germ and bran. You can keep it fresh longer by storing it in a zip-close bag in the freezer.

YEAST

All of the recipes for breads and rolls in this chapter call for active dry yeast, the kind you can find readily in envelopes or jars in your supermarket. If you want to use fresh yeast, then you will need to double the amount of yeast we call for. Instant dry yeast, typically sold in vacuum-sealed pouches, is becoming more widely available. If you want to substitute it for active dry yeast, make your first batch with the same amount as indicated for active dry yeast. Then, if you find it necessary, you can adjust the amount slightly up or down for future batches.

SUGAR

White sugar, brown sugar, and molasses are used in recipes in this chapter to add sweetness and moisture to baked goods.

DAIRY AND EGGS

Butter is at the base of many of the pastries and cakes in this chapter. It is a major component of our basic pastry dough, Blitz Puff Pastry (page 96). If European-style butters are available in your area, try them to see what a difference they can make.

We've featured cream cheese fillings for a few of our pastries; you can substitute reduced-fat versions of cream cheese or Neufchâtel if you prefer. Cottage cheese is an important component of one of our simplest savory breads, the Cottage Cheese Dill Rolls. Our recipes call for full-fat sour cream; you may substitute reduced-fat, but avoid nonfat sour cream.

NUTS AND FRUITS

Cherries, apples, and raisins are some of the fruits we've used to create sweet fillings for pastries. Feel free to experiment with other fruits when they are in season. Pears, peaches, and plums can usually stand in for apples or cherries. Try dried apricots, cranberries, cherries, or blueberries for the raisins we've called for in some recipes.

Almonds and pecans add a rich taste to coffee cakes and pastries. Try substituting other nuts you like—hazelnuts, walnuts, or pistachios, for instance. Toasting whole, slivered, or sliced nuts before adding them to a batter boosts their flavor. Almond paste can be purchased in cans or tubes.

Equipment

The right equipment can make all the difference. A good selection of baking sheets and pans, a sturdy mixer, and assorted hand tools are all you really need.

BAKING SHEETS AND PANS

Baking sheets and cake pans are made in many different sizes and materials. We've used standard sizes, but you may need to make some adjustments to our recipes if you have special bakeware that you like to use.

Dark pans tend to absorb heat. They are great for creating rich, golden crusts. Lighter pans reflect heat and are often suggested for more delicate pastries that should be golden but not brown. If you use glass or ceramic baking dishes, you may need to lower the temperature by 10 or 15 degrees.

Use cooking spray, vegetable shortening, or butter to lightly grease baking pans. If you have parchment paper or a silicone baking mat, they are excellent to use when baking turnovers, elephant ears, and biscotti.

PASTRY BRUSH

A good pastry brush is essential for applying egg wash before baking and a thin coating of apricot glaze after baked goods come out of the oven. Clean the brush in soapy water after you use it and let it dry completely before you put it away.

MIXER

We prepared these recipes using a stand mixer. A dough hook makes quick work of yeast doughs and blitz puff pastry. However, you can also mix batters and doughs with a handheld mixer or by hand. You will need to increase mixing times slightly.

THE OVEN

Preheating the oven properly means that your baked goods come out of the oven with a good texture and color. Most ovens require at least 15 minutes to come fully up to temperature. Position the racks in the middle third of the oven, if possible, to obtain the most even color in your baked goods. Turn pans part way through baking or move them from higher to lower shelves (or vice versa) if your baked goods are starting to develop an uneven color.

Making Yeast Doughs

Use the guidelines given here to make any of the yeast dough recipes included in this chapter.

REHYDRATE THE YEAST

Dried yeast needs to soften in some liquid. To be sure that your yeast is still active, our bread recipes call for blending the yeast with some or all of the liquid before adding the remaining ingredients. This step is sometimes referred to as "proofing" the yeast. If a foam develops on the top of the liquid after the yeast has rested for a few minutes, then it is still alive.

ADD THE DRY INGREDIENTS AND MIX

If you are mixing a yeast dough in a stand mixer, use the dough hook to blend in most of the flour. Reserve about 1 cup to add at the end. If your mixer is struggling with a heavy dough, turn it out onto a lightly floured surface and knead the rest of the flour into the dough, adding it just a bit at a time and using the least amount possible to keep the dough from sticking to your hands or the work surface.

KNEADING

Kneading dough stretches the gluten in the flour, making it strong, flexible, and elastic. To knead by machine, simply increase the speed of the machine. (The mixing times in our recipes are for machine kneading.) To knead by hand, turn the dough out of the bowl onto a floured work surface. Press the heels of your hands into the dough and use them to push the dough away from you.

Give the ball of dough a quarter turn with your fingertips to fold the far edge back over onto the dough. As you continue to push and pull the dough, stretching all sides evenly, dust the dough, the work surface, and your hands with flour to keep the dough from sticking. Kneading a dough by hand can take anywhere from 10 to 15 minutes or more. The dough should feel smooth, satiny, and springy when it is fully kneaded.

THE FIRST RISE

Bakers call this stage of bread-making "bulk fermentation." Put the kneaded dough into a lightly greased bowl, cover it with a cloth or plastic wrap, and let it rise in a warm place, away from any drafts. As the dough rises, it will double in volume. Some doughs rise enough in 20 or 30 minutes, others require longer rising times. Consult the recipe for guidance.

FOLDING OVER THE DOUGH

You may have heard or read the instruction to "punch down" yeast doughs after the first rise. Actually, you should treat the dough with a gentle touch. Press down on the dough in three or four places to deflate the dough.

Some doughs call for a second rise; replace the cover and let it rise once more. The second rise usually takes less time than the first. After completing the appropriate number of rises, fold the dough over on itself and turn it out onto a lightly floured work surface. It is ready now to shape into rolls or loaves as directed in the recipe.

Raisin Cinnamon Swirl Bread

MAKES 2 LOAVES

*T*HIS WONDERFUL bread develops a deep brown and very shiny crust as it bakes, giving it an almost lacquered look. If you have any leftover bread, it is great for toasting to enjoy the next morning. Or, you can use it in place of brioche or challah to make delicious French toast.

1½ teaspoons active dry yeast

1½ cups whole milk, warmed to 110°F

4½ cups bread flour

¼ cup butter, softened

¼ cup sugar

1 large egg, lightly beaten

2 teaspoons salt

⅔ cup packed raisins

4 teaspoons ground cinnamon, divided use

Egg wash of 1 egg whisked with 2 tablespoons cold milk or water

¼ cup brown sugar, packed

1. Place the yeast and warm milk in the bowl of a mixer and stir to completely dissolve. Let the yeast proof until foamy, about 5 minutes. Add the flour, butter, sugar, egg, and salt. Mix the ingredients together on low speed using the dough hook just until the dough begins to come together (it will look rather rough), about 2 minutes.

2. Increase the speed to medium-high and mix until the dough is smooth, an additional 4 minutes. Transfer the dough to a lightly floured work surface; add the raisins and 2 teaspoons of the cinnamon. Knead just long enough to swirl them through the dough, about five or six times.

3. Shape the dough into a ball and place it in a lightly greased bowl. Cover with plastic wrap and let the dough rise in a warm place until doubled in size, about 2 hours.

4. Fold the dough gently over on itself in three or four places, turn the dough out onto a lightly floured work surface, and cut it into 2 equal pieces. Cover the dough and let it rest until relaxed, about 15 minutes.

5. Lightly grease two 9-inch loaf pans.

6. Working with one piece of dough at a time, roll the dough into a rectangle 8 × 12 inches and ½ inch thick. Dust the dough and rolling pin lightly with flour if necessary to prevent the dough from sticking. Brush lightly with egg wash. Mix the brown sugar with the remaining 2 teaspoons cinnamon and sprinkle half of this mixture evenly over the dough. Roll the dough into a cylinder, starting with the long side of the dough. Pinch the dough together to seal the seams and tuck the ends under. Place the loaf seam side down in a loaf pan. Brush lightly with egg wash. Repeat with the second piece of dough to make the second loaf.

7. Cover the loaves and let them rise in a warm place until they nearly fill the pans and spring back slowly to the touch without collapsing, about 1½–2 hours.

8. Preheat the oven to 375°F.

9. Gently brush the bread again with egg wash. Bake the loaves until the crust is brown and the sides spring back when pressed, about 25–30 minutes. Remove the bread from the pans and cool completely on a rack before slicing and serving.

English Muffins

ENGLISH MUFFINS are a traditional British breakfast bread, though they are not known as English muffins in England. Instead of being baked, they are cooked on a griddle. English muffins are split apart with a fork to take advantage of their "spongy" texture, which traps butter or jam.

1½ teaspoons active dry yeast

1 cup water, warmed to 110°F

2 cups all-purpose flour

1 tablespoon unsalted butter, softened

1 teaspoon sugar

1 teaspoon salt

¼ cup cornmeal, or as needed

Oil or solid vegetable shortening, as needed

1. Place the yeast and warm water in the bowl of a mixer and stir to completely dissolve. Let the yeast proof until foamy, about 5 minutes. Add the flour, butter, sugar, and salt to the yeast mixture. Mix the ingredients together on low speed using the dough hook until well blended, about 2 minutes.

2. Increase the speed to medium-high and mix until the dough is smooth, another 5 minutes.

3. Shape the dough into a ball and place it into a lightly greased bowl. Cover with plastic wrap and let the dough rise in a warm place until doubled in size, about 2 hours.

4. Fold the dough gently over on itself in three or four places and turn the dough out onto a lightly floured work surface.

5. Divide dough into 12 equal pieces. Shape into rounds and place on sheet pans that have been heavily dusted with cornmeal. Turn each muffin over to coat both sides with cornmeal. Cover and let rise until slightly risen, about 30 minutes.

6. Preheat a griddle over medium heat and brush lightly with oil or shortening. Cook the English muffins until lightly brown on the bottom, about 5 minutes. Turn the muffins over and cook until golden brown, another 5 minutes.

7. Split the English muffins by pulling them apart with a table fork. Toast them just before serving. Serve very hot.

Raspberry Compote

RASPBERRIES HAVE a rich, garnet color and a heady aroma. We've blended them with pomegranate juice here. You could substitute other fruit juices, including cranberry, cherry, or raspberry. Offer this compote as a spread for English muffins or other breakfast breads.

2 cups raspberries

¼ cup pomegranate juice

¼ cup Triple Sec

¼ cup sugar, plus as needed

2 teaspoons orange zest

1 cup orange segments

1. Combine the raspberries, pomegranate juice, Triple Sec, sugar, and orange zest in a saucepan and bring to a slow simmer over medium heat, stirring to dissolve the sugar. Reduce the heat, cover the pan, and let simmer, stirring occasionally, until all the berries have softened and the liquid starts to thicken, 15–20 minutes.

2. Remove from the heat and stir in the orange segments. Taste the compote and add more sugar, if desired.

3. The compote is ready to serve now, or it can be cooled and stored in a container in the refrigerator for up to 10 days. Reheat over low heat or in the microwave.

Cinnamon Rolls *with Apricot Glaze*

SPRINKLE SOME raisins or currants over the cinnamon sugar before rolling and slicing the dough, if you like.

½ cup sugar, divided use

1½ teaspoons ground cinnamon

2¼ teaspoons active dry yeast

¾ cup milk, warmed to 110°F

2½ cups bread flour

¼ cup butter, softened

2 large eggs, lightly beaten

1 teaspoon salt

Egg wash of 1 egg whisked with 1 tablespoon milk

2 tablespoons butter, melted

½ cup Apricot Glaze (recipe follows)

1. To make cinnamon sugar, combine ¼ cup sugar with the cinnamon and set aside.

2. Combine the yeast and milk in the bowl of a mixer and stir until completely dissolved. Let the yeast proof until foamy, about 5 minutes. Add the flour, the remaining ¼ cup sugar, ¼ cup butter, eggs, and salt to the yeast mixture.

3. Mix the ingredients together on low speed using the dough hook just until the dough begins to come together (it will look rather rough), about 2 minutes. Increase the speed to medium-high and mix until the dough is smooth, an additional 5 minutes.

4. Turn the dough out onto a lightly floured surface, knead once or twice, and gather it into a smooth ball. Place in a lightly greased bowl, cover with plastic wrap, and let the dough rise in a warm place until doubled in size, about 2 hours.

5. Fold the dough gently over on itself in three or four places. Cover once more and let the dough rise a second time until doubled in size, about 1 hour

6. Preheat the oven to 400°F. Line 2 baking sheets with parchment or spray them lightly with cooking spray.

7. Dust the work surface and rolling pin lightly with flour to prevent the dough from sticking. Roll the dough into a rectangle 10 × 20 inches and about ¼-inch thick. Lightly brush a 1-inch wide strip of egg wash along one long side of the dough. Brush the rest of the rectangle with the melted butter and sprinkle the cinnamon sugar evenly over the butter. Roll the dough up to form a log, starting with the edge opposite the

Making Sweet Rolls

After the dough is risen and folded over, roll it into an even layer with regular dimensions. Brush one of the long edges with a little egg wash. The egg wash will help hold the seams together and keep the buns from unrolling as they bake.

A light coating of melted butter holds the cinnamon sugar for these Cinnamon Rolls in place and gives it a richer flavor. The cinnamon smear for the Sticky Buns (page 86) has some butter in it. Be sure it is at room temperature as you spread it so you won't tear the dough.

Starting with the edge that was not brushed with egg wash, begin to roll the dough up into a cylinder. Try to keep the tightness of the roll even from one end to the other for a smooth, regularly shaped roll. Continue to roll up, and press gently to seal the seam. Slice the roll into pieces to make buns of the desired size and set them in a baking pan that has been coated with Pan Smear (page 86).

egg-washed strip. Pinch the dough together to seal the seam. Slice into 12 equal pieces. Arrange the rolls in even rows on the prepared baking sheets. Brush them with some of the remaining egg wash.

8. Cover the rolls and let them rise in a warm place until they nearly double in size and spring back slowly to the touch without collapsing, about 1 hour.

9. Bake until golden brown, about 25–30 minutes. Warm the apricot glaze in a saucepan. While the rolls are still warm, brush each roll lightly with the glaze. Allow to cool before serving.

Apricot Glaze

MAKES 2 CUPS

*T*HIS GLAZE adds sheen and flavor to baked goods like the pastries on pages 97–102, as well as our cinnamon rolls. It holds well, so you can make a double batch and keep it on hand. Try apple jelly instead of apricot jam for a glaze with a subtle flavor. If you use apple jelly, there is no need to strain the glaze. Brush a thin, even coating of warm glaze on cooled baked goods with a pastry brush, wiping away any pools that develop on the surface.

¾ cup apricot jam

¾ cup water

¾ cup corn syrup

⅓ cup brandy

1. Combine the jam, water, corn syrup, and brandy in a saucepan; bring to a boil over high heat, stirring until the jam is completely melted. Strain the glaze through a wire-mesh sieve into a bowl.

2. The glaze is ready to use once it has cooled to room temperature or store it in a covered container in the refrigerator for up to 3 weeks. Warm the glaze over low heat or in the microwave until it is thin enough to brush easily.

Sticky Buns with Pecans

MAKES 12 STICKY BUNS

*I*F YOU and your family love sticky buns, you can double or even triple the recipes for the cinnamon smear and pan smear and store them for later use. Keep them in airtight containers in the refrigerator for up to 2 weeks. Our recipe produces oversized buns with plenty of sticky caramel, but you can make smaller versions if you prefer. You will need to reduce the overall baking time somewhat.

2¼ teaspoons active dry yeast

¾ cup milk, warmed to 110°F

2½ cups bread flour

¼ cup sugar

¼ cup butter, softened

2 large eggs, lightly beaten

1 teaspoon salt

Egg wash of 1 egg whisked with 2 tablespoons cream or milk

2 cups Pan Smear (recipe follows)

1 cup Cinnamon Smear (recipe follows)

1. Place the yeast and warm milk in the bowl of a mixer and stir to completely dissolve. Let the yeast proof until foamy, about 5 minutes. Add the flour, sugar, butter, eggs, and salt. Mix the ingredients together on low speed using the dough hook just until the dough begins to come together (it will look rather rough), about 2 minutes.

2. Increase the speed to medium-high and mix until the dough is smooth, an additional 5 minutes.

3. Shape the dough into a ball and place it in a lightly greased bowl. Cover with plastic wrap and let the dough rise in a warm place until doubled in size, about 2 hours. Fold the dough gently over on itself in three or four places. Cover again and let rise until doubled a second time, about 1 hour.

4. Preheat the oven to 400°F. Prepare two 9-inch square baking pans by pouring 1 cup of the pan smear into each of them. *(recipe continues on page 86)*

LEFT TO RIGHT *Roll up the sticky bun dough with your fingertips, using light, even pressure to make sure that the log is of an even thickness. Place the sticky buns in the pan on top of the smear; they should be evenly spaced and just touch each other slightly. Notice the size of the sticky buns now that they have proofed properly; they should nearly fill the pan.*

5. Roll the dough into a rectangle that is 8 × 14 inches and about ¼ inch thick. Dust the dough and rolling pin lightly with flour if necessary to prevent the dough from sticking. Lightly brush a 1-inch wide strip of egg-wash along the long side of the dough closest to you. Spread the cinnamon smear evenly over the remaining dough. Roll the dough up to form a log, starting with the edge opposite the egg washed strip. Pinch the dough together to seal the seam. Slice into 12 equal pieces. Place 6 rolls in each of the prepared pans. Cover the rolls and let them rise until they have nearly doubled, about 30 minutes. Brush lightly with egg wash.

6. Bake the rolls until they are baked through and the crust is golden brown, about 25–30 minutes. As soon as you remove the pans from the oven, turn each pan over onto a plate. Lift the pan away and let the rolls cool before serving them. If the sticky buns cool down and are hard to get out of the pan, you can warm the bottom of the pan to loosen them.

Pan Smear

MAKES 2 CUPS

*I*F YOU prepare the pan smear in advance, be sure to re-combine it by stirring it with a wooden spoon before adding it to your baking pan.

1 cup light brown sugar

¾ cup dark corn syrup

1 cup heavy cream

Combine all of the ingredients together in a saucepan and heat to thread stage (220°F), stirring frequently to prevent scorching. Cool to room temperature before using.

Cinnamon Smear

MAKES 1 CUP

½ cup bread flour

⅓ cup sugar

2 teaspoons ground cinnamon

3 tablespoons butter

3 large egg whites

½ cup pecans, toasted and chopped

1. Mix together the flour, sugar, and cinnamon in the bowl of a mixer. Add the butter to the flour mixture. Using the paddle attachment, mix on medium speed for 1 minute, or until it looks like coarse meal and there are no visible chunks of butter.

2. With the mixer on medium speed, add the egg whites one at a time. Continue to mix until fully combined, scraping down the bowl as necessary. Stir in the nuts and mix just until combined.

Brioche à Tête

THESE CLASSIC French rolls are baked in a fluted mold. You can find individual sized molds or large molds to make a single large brioche. If you don't have brioche molds, use muffin tins instead. Brioche dough holds well in the refrigerator and, in fact, needs a long, slow rise overnight for the best texture, so plan accordingly. If the dough becomes too warm as you shape the brioche, return it to the refrigerator until it firms up.

2¼ teaspoons active dry yeast

¼ cup whole milk, warmed to 110°F

2 cups bread flour

2 large eggs, lightly beaten

1 tablespoon salt

¾ cup butter, diced and at room temperature

Egg wash of 2 egg yolks whisked with 2 tablespoons heavy cream

1. Place the yeast and milk in the bowl of a mixer and stir to completely dissolve. Let the yeast proof until foamy, about 5 minutes. Add the flour, eggs, and salt. Mix the ingredients together on low speed using the dough hook just until the dough begins to come together (it will look rather rough and crumbly), about 4 minutes. Increase the speed to medium-high and add the butter gradually until it has all been added and the dough is extremely smooth and satiny, an additional 15 minutes. Scrape the bowl down from time to time to blend the dough evenly. Transfer the dough to a clean bowl, cover tightly, and refrigerate the dough overnight.

2. Fold the dough gently over on itself in three or four places, turn the dough out onto a lightly floured work surface, and cut it into 12 equal pieces. Loosely roll each piece of dough into a ball. Place the pieces on a baking sheet and let them rest in the refrigerator until relaxed, about 15 minutes.

3. Place the dough ball on a work surface dusted with flour, pinch down ⅓ of the dough ball with the side of your hand and roll it back and forth, making a depression in the dough but not detaching it. Gently twist the head, make a deep depression in the center of the larger ball with your fingertips, and gently press the head into the depression. Place each tête into a lightly greased brioche-a-tête mold. Lightly brush the brioches with egg wash. Cover the brioches and allow to rise until doubled in size, 1–2 hours.

4. Preheat the oven to 400°F.

5. Lightly brush the brioches with egg wash and bake until golden brown, about 20 minutes. Cool slightly in the pan and then unmold and cool completely on a wire rack before serving.

Brioche Loaf

MAKES 1 LOAF

BRIOCHE BAKED into a loaf is perfect for making into a rich, almost decadent toast. Or slice it very thin and use it to make the tea sandwiches found in Chapter 9.

2¼ teaspoons active dry yeast

¼ cup whole milk, warmed to 110°F

2 cups bread flour

2 large eggs, lightly beaten

1 tablespoon salt

¾ cup butter, diced and at room temperature

Egg wash of 2 egg yolks whisked with 2 tablespoons heavy cream

1. Place the yeast and milk in the bowl of a mixer and stir to completely dissolve. Let the yeast proof until foamy, about 5 minutes. Add the flour, eggs, and salt. Mix the ingredients together on low speed using the dough hook just until the dough begins to come together (it will look rather rough and crumbly), about 4 minutes. Increase the speed to medium-high and add the butter gradually until it has all been added and the dough is extremely smooth and satiny, an additional 15 minutes. Scrape the bowl down from time to time to blend the dough evenly. Transfer the dough to a clean bowl, cover tightly, and refrigerate the dough overnight.

2. Fold the dough gently over on itself in three or four places, turn the dough out onto a lightly floured work surface, and cut it into 8 equal pieces. Shape each piece into a ball and place in a lightly greased loaf pan in two rows of four. Brush the dough lightly with egg wash, cover with plastic wrap, and let it rise in a warm place until doubled in size, about 2 hours.

3. Preheat the oven to 400°F.

4. Lightly brush the brioche with egg wash and bake until the bread has a golden crust, about 30 minutes. Cool the bread slightly in the pan then remove from pan and cool completely on a wire rack before slicing and serving.

Challah

MAKES 1 LARGE LOAF OR 2 SMALL LOAVES

*T*HIS RICH bread gets its color and flavor from egg yolks. If you are lucky enough to have any left over, cut thick slices to make the French Toast with Orange Sauce (page 134).

1½ teaspoons active dry yeast

1 cup water, warmed to 110°F

3 cups bread flour

3 large egg yolks

¼ cup canola oil

1 tablespoon sugar

1 teaspoon salt

Egg wash of 2 egg yolks whisked with 2 tablespoons heavy cream

1. Place the yeast and water in the bowl of a mixer and stir to completely dissolve. Let the yeast proof until foamy, about 5 minutes. Add the flour, egg yolks, canola oil, sugar, and salt. Mix the ingredients together on low speed using the dough hook just until the dough begins to come together (it will look rather rough), about 2 minutes. Increase the speed to medium and mix until the dough is smooth and soft but not sticky, an additional 5 minutes.

2. Turn the dough out onto a lightly floured surface, knead once or twice, and gather it into a smooth ball. Place the dough in a lightly greased bowl, cover with plastic wrap, and let rise in a warm place until doubled in size, about 2 hours.

3. Fold the dough gently over on itself in three or four places, turn the dough out onto a lightly floured work surface, and cut it into 3 equal pieces. (For 2 small loaves, divide into 6 equal pieces.) Cover the pieces and let them rest until relaxed, about 15 minutes.

4. Form each piece into 12-inch long strands that are evenly tapered at each end. Pinch 3 strands of dough together at one end and braid them together. To finish, pinch the loose ends together and tuck them under the loaf. (If you are making 2 loaves, repeat the process to braid the loaf.)

5. Place the loaf (or loaves) on a parchment-lined baking sheet, brush dough lightly with egg wash, cover lightly, and let rise until the dough springs back slowly to the touch without collapsing, about 20 minutes.

6. Preheat the oven to 375°F.

7. Lightly brush the dough with egg wash and bake until the loaf is golden brown and makes a hollow thump when tapped on the bottom, about 45 minutes for a large loaf or 30 minutes for smaller loaves.

8. Transfer the challah to a cooling rack and cool completely before slicing and serving.

Knot Rolls with Poppy Seeds

MAKES 24 ROLLS

*T*HESE BUTTERY rolls are best served warm. Enjoy them with big cups of frothy cappuccino or hot chocolate for breakfast. You can let the dough rise very slowly in a cool spot or overnight in the refrigerator. Let the dough return to room temperature before final shaping and baking.

¾ cup milk

½ cup water, warmed to 110°F

2 teaspoons active dry yeast

2 tablespoons sugar

3 tablespoons butter, room temperature

2 large eggs, lightly beaten

2½–3 cups bread flour, divided use, plus extra as needed

1 teaspoon salt

Egg wash of 1 large egg whisked with 2 tablespoons milk

2 tablespoons poppy seeds

1. Scald the milk by bringing it just to a boil over medium heat, then allow to cool to room temperature.

2. Combine the water, yeast, and sugar in a large bowl and stir well. Let sit for 2–3 minutes or until it is quite frothy.

3. Add the cooled milk, butter, eggs, 1½ cups of the flour, and the salt. Stir well for several minutes until the dough begins to form long elastic strands. Gradually add more flour until the dough is too heavy to stir.

4. Turn the dough onto a lightly floured work surface and knead for about 10 minutes, adding only enough flour to prevent the dough from sticking. The dough should be moist, smooth, and springy when it is properly kneaded.

5. Transfer the dough to a lightly oiled bowl, turn to coat, cover with a clean cloth, and place in a warm, draft-free spot to rise until doubled in volume, 1–2 hours.

6. Fold the dough over and let it rest for 10 minutes. While the dough is resting, spray two 9 × 11-inch baking pans with cooking spray.

7. Turn the dough out onto a lightly floured surface. With your fingertips, press the dough down and flatten to about ¼-inch thickness. Cut rectangles of dough about 1 inch long by 2 inches wide. Roll each piece into a long cylinder, about 6 inches long. Wrap the cylinder around the index and middle fingers of one hand to make a circle of dough. Bring one end up and through the circle to make the knot and pinch the two ends together. Place the rolls in the prepared pans, leaving at least 3 inches between the rolls. Cover the rolls and let them rise until nearly doubled in size.

8. Preheat the oven to 350°F.

9. Brush the rolls lightly with egg wash and sprinkle with poppy seeds. Bake until golden brown and baked through, 15–20 minutes. Let the rolls cool slightly before serving.

The Knot Rolls with Poppy Seeds are shown here with the Cottage Cheese Dill Rolls (page 92) and the Cheddar Onion Rye Rolls (page 93).

Cottage Cheese Dill Rolls

MAKES 24 ROLLS

COTTAGE CHEESE gives these rolls a slightly tart flavor and a tender texture. Dill is a perfect counterpoint flavor. You can also add a bit of dill seed or even substitute other fresh herbs for the dill—chives, scallions, or oregano would all be good choices.

4½ teaspoons active dry yeast

⅓ cup water, warmed to 110°F

4¼ cups bread flour

1½ cups small-curd cottage cheese

¼ cup minced yellow onions

2 large eggs

1 tablespoon butter, softened

3 tablespoons chopped fresh dill

2 teaspoons prepared horseradish

2 tablespoons sugar

1½ teaspoons salt

2¼ teaspoons baking soda

⅓ cup butter, melted, divided use

3 tablespoons coarse salt for sprinkling

1. Place the yeast and warm water in the bowl of the mixer and stir to completely dissolve. Let the yeast proof until foamy, about 5 minutes. Add the flour, cottage cheese, onions, eggs, 1 tablespoon softened butter, dill, horseradish, sugar, salt, and baking soda to the yeast mixture. Mix the ingredients together on low speed using the dough hook just until the dough begins to come together (it will look rather rough), about 2 minutes. Increase the speed to medium-high and mix until the dough is smooth, an additional 5 minutes.

2. Turn the dough out onto a lightly floured surface, knead once or twice, and gather it into a smooth ball. Place in a lightly greased bowl, cover with plastic wrap, and let the dough rise in a warm place until doubled in size, about 2 hours.

3. Fold the dough gently over on itself in three or four places. Cover once more and let the dough rise a second time until doubled in size, about 1 hour.

4. Preheat the oven to 400°F. Line 2 baking sheets with parchment paper or grease lightly.

5. Fold the dough gently over on itself in three or four places, turn the dough out onto a lightly floured work surface and cut it into 16 equal pieces (about 2 ounces each). Cover the pieces and let them rest until relaxed, about 15 minutes. Round each piece into a smooth ball and place in even rows on the prepared baking sheets. Cover and let rise until the dough springs back when lightly touched but does not collapse, 20–30 minutes.

6. Brush the top of each roll with a little of the melted butter. Bake until golden brown, about 20–30 minutes. As soon as the rolls are removed from the oven, brush lightly with the remaining melted butter and sprinkle lightly with salt.

7. Transfer to wire racks to cool completely before serving. *See photo on page 90.*

Cheddar & Onion Rye Rolls

MAKES 20 ROLLS

SERVE THESE rolls slightly warmed to bring out the great taste of cheese and onions. Make a double batch of rolls so that you can tuck some away in the freezer. Then you can just grab one or two on your way out the door to enjoy on your drive or at your desk.

1½ teaspoons active dry yeast

2 cups water, warmed to 110°F

4 cups bread flour

1 cup medium rye flour, plus more for dusting

1 tablespoon sugar

1 tablespoon molasses

1 tablespoon canola oil

1½ teaspoons salt

2 cups cheddar cheese, large dice

½ cup yellow onions, large dice

1. Place the yeast and water in the bowl of a mixer and stir to completely dissolve. Let the yeast proof until foamy, about 5 minutes. Add the bread and rye flours, sugar, molasses, oil, and salt. Mix the ingredients together on low speed using the dough hook just until the dough begins to come together (it will look rather rough), about 4 minutes. Increase the speed to medium-high and mix until the dough is smooth, an additional 2 minutes. Add the cheese and onions and continue to mix on medium speed until the cheese and onions are evenly distributed throughout the dough, about 1 minute.

2. Turn the dough out onto a lightly floured surface. Knead by hand until the cheese and onions are completely worked into the dough. (The dough will feel rather tight.) Gather it into a smooth ball. Place in a lightly greased bowl, cover with plastic wrap, and let the dough rise in a warm place until doubled in size, about 1 hour.

3. Fold the dough gently over on itself in three or four places, turn the dough out onto a lightly floured work surface, and cut it into 20 equal pieces. Cover the pieces and let them rest until relaxed, about 15 minutes.

4. Preheat the oven to 425°F. Line 2 baking sheets with parchment paper or grease lightly.

5. Round each piece of dough into a smooth ball and place in even rows on the prepared baking sheets. Cover and let rise until the dough springs back when lightly touched but does not collapse, 30 minutes.

6. Make a small slit down the center of each roll with a very sharp paring knife or a razor blade. Dust the tops of the rolls lightly with rye flour, if desired.

7. Bake until the rolls have a golden brown crust and sound hollow when thumped on the bottom, 15–18 minutes. Cool completely on racks before serving. *See photo on page 90.*

Gugelhopf

MAKES 2 CAKES

*T*HERE ARE five traditional ways to spell the name of this cake, including kouglof, gugelhupf, kugelhopf, and gouglehopf. Gugelhopf is typically thought of as a Viennese specialty. Some say that its shape is meant to resemble a turban.

3 cups bread flour, divided use

1 cup milk

4½ teaspoons active dry yeast

Seeds from 1 vanilla bean

½ cup butter

½ cup sugar

2 teaspoons salt

3 large eggs

⅔ cup golden raisins or dried cranberries

1 cup whole blanched almonds

1. To make a sponge, mix 1 cup of the bread flour, the milk, yeast, and seeds from the vanilla bean in a mixing bowl. Stir with a wooden spoon or mix on low speed with the dough hook attachment until evenly blended. Cover the bowl and let the sponge rest at room temperature until it has risen slightly and just begun to fall, about 20 minutes.

2. Cream the butter, sugar, and salt in a separate mixing bowl with the paddle attachment on medium speed until light and fluffy, about 5 minutes. Add the eggs and continue to mix, scraping down the bowl as necessary, until evenly blended and very smooth.

3. Switch to the dough hook. Add the sponge mixture and the remaining flour to the butter-and-sugar mixture. Mix on low speed for 5 minutes. Increase the speed to medium and mix the dough until it is smooth and elastic, another 5 minutes.

4. Add the raisins or cranberries to the dough and continue to mix or knead the dough until it pulls cleanly away from the sides of the bowl, about 15 minutes.

5. Shape the dough into a ball and place it in a lightly greased bowl. Cover with plastic wrap and let the dough rise in a warm place until doubled in size, about 20 minutes. Fold the dough gently over on itself in three or four places and turn the dough out onto a lightly floured work surface. Divide the dough into two equal pieces and shape them into rounds. Let them rest on a lightly floured surface, covered loosely, until the dough relaxes, 15 minutes.

6. Spray 2 gugelhopf molds or Bundt pans with cooking spray or brush them lightly with softened butter. Arrange the almonds in a row in the bottom of the pans.

7. Poke a hole in the center of each ball of dough using the handle of a rolling pin (dust the handle lightly with flour so it doesn't stick to the dough or tear it). Gently expand the openings with your fingers until the openings can fit over the tube in the center of the gugelhopf molds or Bundt pans. Place the dough in the pan, smooth side facing up, cover loosely, and let rise until the dough rises nearly to the top of the pan, 1½–2 hours.

8. Preheat the oven to 375°F. Bake the gugelhopf until the crust is golden brown and it springs back when lightly pressed, about 30 minutes.

9. Remove the gugelhopf from the oven, turn it out of the pan onto a cooling rack. Cool completely before slicing and serving the gugelhopf.

Blitz Puff Pastry

MAKES 2½ POUNDS OF DOUGH

BLITZ PUFF pastry lives up to its name. It is as flaky and buttery as the classic puff pastry, but you can put it together quickly. The rolling and folding process may appear lengthy, but most of that time is taken up by letting the dough chill enough to handle easily. Double or even triple the recipe if you like. For larger batches, you can use a stand mixer with a dough hook to blend the dough. Divide the dough into smaller pieces before wrapping and freezing to have your own pastry on hand to make sweet and savory pastries.

2 cups butter

3½ cups all-purpose flour

1¾ teaspoons salt

1 cup cold water

1. Cut the butter into ¼-inch cubes. Refrigerate until the cubes are chilled and firm.

2. Combine the flour and salt in a large mixing bowl. Add the butter and toss with your fingertips until the butter is coated with flour. Add all but about 2 tablespoons of the cold water. Mix with a pastry blender or a table fork until an evenly moist but still rough dough forms. Add additional water if necessary as you mix the dough if it is not moist enough to hold together when pressed into a ball.

3. Cover the dough tightly with plastic wrap. Cool in the refrigerator until the butter is firm but not brittle, about 20 minutes.

4. Turn the dough out onto a lightly floured work surface. Roll it into a rectangle approximately 12 × 30 inches; the dough should be about ½ inch thick.

5. Fold the dough in thirds like a letter (this is the first of four 3-folds). Turn the dough 90 degrees. Roll the dough out again to a rectangle as described above and fold once more (this is the second of four 3-folds). Wrap the dough tightly in plastic wrap and chill for 30 minutes in the refrigerator. Remove the dough from the refrigerator, and working quickly, continue rolling and folding the dough for the third and fourth 3-folds as described above, chilling the dough in between each of these folds for 30 minutes at a time.

Shaping Breakfast Pastries

We've replaced Danish dough in our breakfast pastries with our Blitz Puff Pastry. You can substitute frozen prepared puff pastry sheets if you prefer.

KEEP BLITZ OR PREPARED PUFF PASTRY DOUGH VERY COOL

Keeping the pastry dough chilled preserves the layers of fat. These layers are responsible for the flaky texture and dramatic rise of breakfast pastries like turnovers, cheese pockets, Bear Claws (page 100) and Elephant Ears (page 105).

USE THE LEAST POSSIBLE AMOUNT OF FLOUR WHEN ROLLING THE DOUGH

Dust the work surface and the rolling pin lightly with flour as you work.

Use enough pressure to roll the dough to the appropriate thickness, but don't press down too hard in any one place. Stop rolling just short of the edges of the dough. If the pin runs over the edge of the dough, the layers there will be pressed together and your pastries may not have the best possible texture or height. If the dough starts to soften too much as you work, put it back in the refrigerator for 10 or 12 minutes to firm up before you go on to cut out the shapes for your pastries. (The dough should feel cool to the touch.)

CUT SHAPES WITH A SHARP KNIFE

If the dough is cool, it won't stretch out as you cut it into squares or rectangles. Use a very sharp knife to cut the dough so that the dough is not torn or pulled out of shape as you work.

6. After completing the final 3-fold, wrap the dough in plastic wrap and allow it to firm under refrigeration for at least 1 hour before using. The dough will last up to 1 week in the refrigerator or it may be frozen for up to 2 months.

Cherry Cheese Baskets

MAKES 12 BASKETS

*B*AKE THESE flaky pastries with the cheese filling, then add the cherry filling after they bake for a wonderful, fresh look and flavor.

1½ pounds Blitz Puff Pastry (page 96)

¾ cup Cheese Filling (recipe follows)

¾ cup Apricot Glaze (page 83), warmed

¾ cup Cherry Filling (recipe follows), warmed

1. Line a baking sheet with parchment paper.

2. Roll the puff dough into a rectangle 12 × 16 inches. Dust the dough and rolling pin lightly with flour if necessary to prevent the dough from sticking. Cut the dough into twelve 4-inch squares. Place the squares on a baking sheet and let them chill in the refrigerator until firm, about 10 minutes.

3. To make a basket, fold squares of dough in half to make a triangle. Position the triangle so the closed point of the triangle is away from you. Use a sharp knife to make a cut parallel to the two shorter sides of the triangle. These cuts should come to within ¼ inch of the point but should not cut entirely through the point. These two cuts make the rim for the basket.

4. Open out the triangle and brush very lightly with egg wash. Fold one basket rim over to line up with the opposite side. Repeat with the second rim. Add 1 tablespoon of the cheese filling to each basket. Transfer to the baking sheet and chill for several minutes while you preheat the oven.

5. Preheat the oven to 425°F.

6. Bake the baskets until golden brown, about 20 minutes. Transfer to cooling racks and brush with apricot glaze while they are still hot. Spoon 1 tablespoon of the cherry filling into each basket. Cool completely before serving. *(recipe continues on page 99)*

LEFT TO RIGHT *Fold the squares in half on the diagonal to form a triangle; make the two parallel cuts, as shown, but be sure not to cut through the point. Fold one of the cut pieces of dough over to the opposite corner, as shown; repeat with the other piece of cut dough to finish shaping the pastry. Fill the pastries with the desired filling before baking; be sure that the filling doesn't go over the edges of the dough.*

Cheese Filling

MAKES 2 CUPS

THE CORNSTARCH in this filling helps it hold together as it bakes. You can store the filling in a zip-close plastic bag. When you are ready to fill your pastries, simply cut away one corner and use the bag as a disposable pastry bag.

12 ounces cream cheese

6 tablespoons granulated sugar

⅓ cup sifted cornstarch

¾ teaspoon lemon zest

¾ teaspoon orange zest

1 teaspoon vanilla extract

2 eggs

1. Cream the cheese, sugar, cornstarch, lemon zest, orange zest, and vanilla extract together until very smooth and light by hand with a wooden spoon or with an electric mixer using the paddle attachment. Add the eggs one at a time, mixing until smooth and scraping down the bowl between each addition. Scrape down the bowl to blend evenly.

2. The filling is ready to use now or store in a covered container in the refrigerator for up to 2 days.

Cherries

Cherries fall into two major categories: sour (also called "tart" or "pie" cherries) and sweet.

SOUR CHERRIES

Sour cherries have a short season and don't keep well once picked. Two of the more familiar varieties of sour cherries are Montmorency and Morello. Sour cherries are smaller and rounder than sweet ones and have a brighter red color.

When sour cherries are at the peak of ripeness, most of them are picked and pitted, then immediately frozen, jarred, or dried. Sometimes, processed sour cherries have already been sweetened, so be sure to check the label. If you use jarred cherries for the filling, drain the cherries and reserve the liquid to use as part of the cherry juice called for in the filling recipe.

SWEET CHERRIES

Sweet cherry varieties like Bing (deep red to almost black skin and flesh), Lambert, and Rainier (golden cherries with a reddish blush) are usually larger than sour cherries. They are usually eaten fresh, but can be used to replace some or all of the sour cherries you require as long as you cut back a little on the amount of sugar.

Cherry Filling

MAKES 2 CUPS

YOU CAN find bottled cherry juice in the produce section and in some specialty shops. If you are using frozen cherries, let them thaw in a colander set in a bowl. Use the juices the cherries release to replace some of the cherry juice.

2 tablespoons cornstarch

½ cup cherry juice or water, divided use

½ cup sugar, plus as needed

¾ teaspoon lemon juice

¼ teaspoon ground cinnamon

⅛ teaspoon ground nutmeg

⅛ teaspoon salt

3 cups pitted sour cherries, fresh, frozen, or jarred

1 tablespoon butter

1. Combine the cornstarch with ¼ cup of the cherry juice or water in a small bowl and stir until the cornstarch is completely dissolved.

2. Combine the remaining cherry juice or water, the sugar, the lemon juice, cinnamon, nutmeg, and salt in a saucepan; bring to a boil over high heat, stirring until the sugar is dissolved. Add the dissolved cornstarch and return the mixture to a boil, stirring constantly, until thickened and smooth, about 3 minutes. Add the cherries to the mixture and simmer until the cherries are very tender and the liquid is very flavorful, 5–6 minutes. Taste the filling as it simmers and add more sugar, if desired.

3. Remove the filling from the heat and stir in the butter until it melts and is evenly blended. Transfer to a bowl set in an ice bath and cool, stirring from time to time. Once the filling has reached room temperature, it is ready to use or store in a covered container in the refrigerator for up to 10 days.

Cheese Pockets

MAKES 12 PASTRIES

*T*HESE POCKETS are simple to shape, once you've rolled out the blitz puff pastry.

1½ pounds Blitz Puff Pastry (page 96)
1½ cups Cheese Filling (page 99)
¼ cup sliced almonds, as needed
¾ cup Apricot Glaze (page 83), warmed

1. Line a baking sheet with parchment paper.

2. Roll the puff dough into a rectangle 12 × 16 inches. Dust the dough and rolling pin lightly with flour if necessary to prevent the dough from sticking. Cut the dough into twelve, 4-inch squares. Place the squares on a baking sheet and let them chill in the refrigerator until firm, about 10 minutes.

3. Spoon or pipe 2 tablespoons of the cheese filling into the center of each pastry square. Fold each corner into the center, overlapping them. Press the overlapped corners gently to seal them, and pierce each one with some almond slices to keep the pocket closed as it bakes. Transfer to the prepared baking sheet and chill for several minutes while you preheat the oven.

4. Preheat the oven to 425°F.

5. Bake the pockets until golden brown, about 20 minutes. Transfer to cooling racks and brush with apricot glaze while they are still hot. Cool completely before serving.

Bear Claws

MAKES 12 PASTRIES

*S*HAPING THESE pastries is a little tricky the first time you try it, but they taste delicious, even if the almond filling oozes out a little.

2 pounds Blitz Puff Pastry (page 96)
2 cups Almond Filling (recipe follows)
Egg wash of 1 egg whisked with 2 tablespoons cream or milk
2 cups sliced almonds
1 cup Apricot Glaze (page 83)

1. Line a baking sheet with parchment paper.

2. Cut the dough in half. Work with one piece of dough at a time, placing the second piece in the refrigerator to keep it firm. Roll the dough into a rectangle 6½ × 24 inches × ⅛ inch thick. Turn the dough so that the longest edge runs widthwise.

2. Pipe half of the almond filling widthwise in a line just below the center of the dough. Lightly brush the puff pastry below the filling with egg wash.

3. Fold the top edge of the dough over the filling and line it up with the bottom edge of the dough. Press this excess dough together firmly to form a seal around the filling. If the dough has become soft, refrigerate until it becomes firm again.

4. Using a knife, cut vertically through the strip of excess dough in ½-inch increments, making sure not to cut past the seal into the filling; this strip will form the toes of the bear claws. Brush the dough lightly with egg wash and sprinkle with sliced almonds. Cut the dough into 3½-inch segments and space these evenly on the prepared baking sheet, cut strip up. Gently pull the lower two corners (opposite the cut strip) of each bear claw down and tuck back under the filling slightly, pressing firmly, causing the toes to separate. *(recipe continues on page 102)*

(recipe continues on page 102)

OPPOSITE *Clockwise from bottom left: Bear Claws, Cheese Pockets (with almonds), Apple-Filled Turnovers (page 102), and Cherry Cheese Baskets (page 97).*

5. Repeat with the remaining dough, filling, and almonds. Refrigerate the shaped bear claws for 15–20 minutes.

6. Preheat the oven to 425°F.

7. Bake until golden brown, about 20 minutes. Brush the pastries with the Apricot Glaze while they are still hot.

Almond Filling

MAKES 2 CUPS

PROFESSIONAL BAKESHOPS often have cake crumbs on hand. Use ladyfingers to make your own: Remove the ladyfingers from the package and let them air dry for a few hours. Break them into pieces and put them in the bowl of a food processor. Pulse the processor off and on until the ladyfingers are ground into even crumbs. One 4-ounce package of ladyfingers makes 1½ cups cake crumbs.

½ cup almond paste

2 tablespoons dark rum

2½ cups cake crumbs or ground ladyfingers

6–7 large egg whites, or as needed

1. Mix the almond paste and rum on medium speed using the paddle attachment until thoroughly combined and the almond paste has formed a smooth paste, about 1–2 minutes. Add the cake crumbs and mix until just combined, about 1 minute.

2. Add 6 of the egg whites slowly and mix until the filling reaches piping consistency, about 1 minute. Add the remaining egg white if necessary.

3. The filling is ready to use now or store in a covered container in the refrigerator for up to 2 days. To make the filling easier to pipe, let the filling warm at room temperature for about 15 minutes before using and stir well by hand or in a mixer until spreadable.

Apple-Filled Turnovers

MAKES 12 PASTRIES

THIS RECIPE provides the basic instructions for filling and folding turnovers. Once assembled, you can keep the pastries in the freezer for up to 3 months. These turnovers are full-sized pastries, but you may want to make miniature versions instead. Resist the temptation to overfill the pastry though, or the filling can ooze out as the pastries bake. To dress these turnovers up, make a thin icing of confectioners' sugar and milk (see the glaze used for the Dried Cherry Scones, page 69).

1½ pounds Blitz Puff Pastry (page 96)

Egg wash of 1 egg whisked with 2 tablespoons cream or milk

1½ cups Apple Filling (recipe follows)

1 cup Apricot Glaze, warm (page 83)

1. Line a baking sheet with parchment paper.

2. Roll the puff dough into a rectangle 12 × 16 inches. Dust the dough and rolling pin lightly with flour if necessary to prevent the dough from sticking. Cut the dough into twelve 4-inch squares. Place the squares on the prepared baking sheet and let them chill in the refrigerator until firm, about 10 minutes.

3. To assemble the turnovers, take the puff pastry from the refrigerator. Brush the squares lightly with egg wash. Place 2 tablespoons of the filling in the center of each square. Fold one corner of the dough over the filling and line it up with the opposite corner of the dough to make a triangle. Press the edges firmly together to seal in the filling. Chill the turnovers for 10 minutes before baking.

4. Preheat the oven to 425°F.

5. Brush the turnovers lightly with egg wash. Cut a small opening in the center of each turnover with a sharp knife to allow steam to vent.

5. Bake the turnovers until golden brown, about 20 minutes. Transfer to cooling racks and brush with apricot glaze while they are still hot. Cool the turnovers completely before serving. *See photo on page 101.*

Apple Filling

MAKES 2 CUPS

*Y*OU CAN use this filling for the Apple-Filled Crêpes on page 127, or try substituting it for other fruit fillings called for in your favorite breakfast pastry recipe.

¼ cup applejack or apple-flavored brandy

¼ cup apple juice

3 tablespoons canola oil, divided use

4 cups Granny Smith apples, peeled, cored, and sliced

6 tablespoons granulated sugar

3 tablespoons currants

¾ teaspoons orange zest

½ teaspoon vanilla extract

¼ teaspoon ground cinnamon

⅛ teaspoon ground nutmeg

1. Combine the applejack or brandy and the apple juice in a small bowl and set aside.

2. Heat a sauté pan over medium-high heat and add 1 tablespoon of the oil. Toss the sliced apples with the sugar.

3. Add about one-third of the sugared apples (they should be in a single layer) and sauté the apples until golden on both sides, about 4 minutes. Transfer the apples to a bowl. Add one-third of the apple juice mixture to the pan, stirring to release the sugar from the pan, and simmer until slightly reduced and thickened, 30 seconds. Pour the apple juice mixture over the sautéed apples.

4. Sauté the remaining apples in two more batches as directed above. When you add the final third of the applejack mixture to the pan, stir in the currants, orange zest, vanilla, cinnamon, and nutmeg. Add the mixture to the bowl and stir the filling gently until the currants are evenly distributed throughout.

5. Place the filling in a bowl set in an ice bath and cool, stirring from time to time. Once the filling has cooled, it is ready to use or store in a covered container in the refrigerator for up to 5 days. Warm the filling over low heat or in the microwave if necessary.

Mushroom, Leek & Brie Turnovers

MAKES 12 TURNOVERS

*T*HIS SAVORY turnover recipe capitalizes on the rich, almost smoky flavor of sautéed mushrooms and creamy, pungent Brie. As you cook the mushrooms and leeks to a light caramel, they develop a slightly smoky taste. Look for a ripe, runny Brie for the most flavor.

1 tablespoon extra virgin olive oil

¾ cup coarsely chopped mushrooms

1 cup sliced leeks

1 teaspoon minced garlic

2 tablespoons Madeira

½ teaspoon salt

¼ teaspoon freshly ground black pepper

1½ pounds Blitz Puff Pastry (page 96)

Egg wash of 1 egg whisked with 2 tablespoons cream or milk

3 ounces Brie cheese

1. Preheat the oven to 425° F. Line a baking sheet with parchment paper.

2. Heat the olive oil in a sauté pan over medium-high heat until it shimmers. Add the mushrooms to the pan and sauté until lightly caramelized, about 2–3 minutes. Add the leeks to the pan and reduce the heat to medium. Sauté the leeks until they are light golden brown, about 3–4 minutes. Add the garlic and cook for 1 minute.

3. Deglaze the pan with the Madeira and reduce until nearly dry, about 1 minute. Season the mixture with salt and pepper. Cool the mixture to room temperature.

4. Roll the dough into a rectangle 12 × 16 inches. Cut the dough into twelve 4-inch squares. Place the squares on the prepared baking sheet and let them chill in the refrigerator until firm, about 10 minutes.

5. Brush each square lightly with egg wash. Place 1 tablespoon of the mushroom filling in the center of each square. Top the filling with 1½ teaspoons Brie. Fold one corner of the dough over the filling and line it up with the opposite corner of the dough. Press the edges firmly together to seal the filling inside the puff pastry dough. Chill the turnovers for about 10 minutes before baking. Brush the turnovers lightly with egg wash. Cut a small opening in the center of each turnover to allow steam to vent.

6. Bake the turnovers until golden brown, about 20–25 minutes. Serve immediately.

Elephant Ears *(Palmiers)*

MAKES 2 DOZEN

Ｅ LEPHANT EARS are a delicate cookie made of puff pastry sprinkled with granulated sugar. The name reflects the palm-leaf shape of the pastry.

1⅔ cups sugar, divided use, plus more as needed

1¼ pounds Blitz Puff Pastry (see page 96)

1. Sprinkle ½ cup sugar in an even layer on the work surface and place the dough on top of the sugar. Sprinkle ½ cup sugar in an even layer on top of the dough. Roll the dough into a rectangle 16 × 20 inches × ⅛ inch thick. Sprinkle additional sugar on the work surface and the dough as needed to keep it from sticking. Sprinkle ⅓ cup sugar on top of the dough after it has been rolled out. Turn the dough so that the longest edge faces toward you.

2. Roll the 2 longest edges of the dough toward each other to meet in the middle, leaving a ½-inch gap. Sprinkle the remaining sugar on top of the length of the dough. Fold one piece of dough on top of the other piece of dough as if you were closing a book.

3. Cover the dough and refrigerate until firm, about 1 hour.

4. Preheat the oven to 400°F. Line 2 baking sheets with parchment paper or spray lightly with cooking spray.

5. Slice the dough crosswise into ½-inch-thick pieces and arrange the cookies in even rows on the prepared baking sheets, spacing them about 1 inch apart.

6. Bake until the bottom side of the cookies are golden brown, about 10 minutes. Remove the baking sheets from the oven and turn each cookie over. Return the pan to the oven and continue to bake the cookies until the other side is golden brown, 5–7 minutes. Allow the cookies to cool slightly before removing from the baking sheets. If the cookies cool too much before they are removed from the sheet tray, the caramel may harden and stick to the surface, making the cookies difficult to remove. Store in an airtight container.

Palmiers with Prosciutto

MAKES ABOUT 3 DOZEN

*T*HIS IS a savory variation of the classic pastry. Here prosciutto and a dusting of Parmesan cheese replace the sugar. The palmiers can be made in batches and frozen. They can then be baked from the frozen state as needed and served warm.

½ pound Blitz Puff Pastry (page 96)

6 tablespoons tomato paste

12 thin slices prosciutto, about 5 ounces

¼ cup finely grated Parmesan cheese, divided use

1. Preheat the oven to 400°F. Line 2 baking sheets with parchment paper.

2. Roll the puff pastry into a 10-inch square. Brush one side of the pastry with the tomato paste. Lay the prosciutto over the tomato paste, then dust with the cheese.

3. Roll the top and bottom edges of the dough toward each other to meet in the middle, leaving a ½-inch gap. Sprinkle the remaining cheese on top of the length of the dough. Fold one piece of dough on top of the other piece of dough as if you were closing a book. Cover the dough and refrigerate until firm, about 1 hour.

4. Slice the dough crosswise into ¼-inch-thick pieces and bake on the prepared baking sheets until golden brown, about 10 minutes. A sheet of parchment paper placed on top of the palmiers during baking will help them to stay flat; it can be removed for the last few minutes of baking to allow for browning.

Paillettes

MAKES ABOUT 3 DOZEN

*T*HESE CHEESE sticks are a quick and simple way to add a signature look to your table. The sticks may be twisted, curled, or shaped as desired before baking. The fanciful shapes reaching from tall glasses or jars serve as eye-catching edible decorations. Cajun spice blend, cayenne, poppy seeds, and sesame seeds may also be used to flavor the sticks.

½ pound Blitz Puff Pastry (page 96)

Egg wash of 1 egg yolk whisked with 1 tablespoon cream or milk

½ cup grated Parmesan cheese

Sweet paprika to taste

1. Preheat the oven to 400°F. Line 2 baking sheets with parchment paper.

2. Roll the puff pastry into a 10-inch square. Brush one side of the puff pastry sheet with the egg wash. Sprinkle the cheese and paprika evenly over the puff pastry. Cut the pastry lengthwise into ¼-inch strips.

3. Transfer the pastry strips to the prepared baking sheets, leaving 1 inch between each strip to allow for expansion. Bake until golden brown, about 10 minutes.

OPPOSITE *Palmiers with Prosciutto (right) are shown with Paillettes and Gougères (page 240).*

Chocolate Biscotti

MAKES 4 DOZEN

*T*RY ADDING macadamia nuts, almonds, or hazelnuts to the batter for a delicious variation.

1¾ cups cake flour

¼ cup cocoa powder

1 teaspoon baking powder

3 large eggs

¾ cup sugar

1 tablespoon instant coffee powder

1 teaspoon vanilla extract

¼ teaspoon almond extract

¼ teaspoon salt

1 cup bittersweet chocolate chunks

1. Preheat the oven to 300°F. Line 2 cookie sheets with parchment paper or a silicone baking mat.

2. Sift together the flour, cocoa powder, and baking powder and set aside.

3. Whip the eggs, sugar, instant coffee, vanilla and almond extracts, and salt in a mixer with the whisk attachment on high speed until thick and pale yellow, about 5 minutes. Add the flour mixture and blend on low speed until the dough is just blended. Scrape down the bowl as needed.

4. Fold the chocolate chunks into the dough by hand with a rubber spatula. The dough will be slightly sticky.

5. Divide the dough evenly between the prepared cookie sheets, mounding the dough to make logs that are 3 inches wide, 12 inches long, and about 1 inch thick.

6. Bake until a skewer inserted in the center of the logs comes out clean, about 30–35 minutes. Remove from the oven and cool on the pans for 10 minutes.

7. Reduce the oven temperature to 275°F. Cut each log crosswise into ½-inch slices with a serrated knife. Return the slices to the cookie sheets, cut side down, and bake for 10 minutes. Turn the biscotti over and continue baking on the other side until they are completely dry and crisp, another 10–12 minutes. Transfer to wire racks and cool completely before serving or storing in airtight containers.

Orange Biscotti

MAKES 4 DOZEN

*A*LMONDS ARE a great addition to these orange-flavored biscotti, but they are equally good with pistachios.

2 cups cake flour

1 teaspoon baking powder

3 large eggs

1 cup sugar

1 tablespoon orange zest, about 1 orange

1 teaspoon vanilla extract

¼ teaspoon almond extract

¼ teaspoon salt

1 cup slivered almonds

1 cup minced candied orange peel

1. Preheat the oven to 300°F. Line 2 cookie sheets with parchment paper or a silicone baking mat.

2. Sift together the flour and baking powder and set aside.

3. Whip the eggs, sugar, orange zest, vanilla and almond extracts, and salt in a mixer with the whisk attachment on high speed until thick and pale yellow, about 5 minutes. Add the flour mixture and blend on low speed until the dough is just blended. Scrape down the bowl as needed.

4. Fold the slivered almonds and candied orange peel into the dough by hand with a rubber spatula. The dough will be slightly sticky.

5. Divide the dough evenly between the prepared cookie sheets, mounding the dough to make logs that are 3 inches wide, 12 inches long, and about 1 inch thick.

6. Bake until a skewer inserted in the center of the logs comes out clean, about 30–35 minutes. Remove from the oven and cool on the pans for 10 minutes.

7. Reduce the oven temperature to 275°F. Cut each log crosswise into ½-inch slices with a serrated knife. Return the slices to the cookie sheets and bake for 10 minutes. Turn the biscotti over and continue baking on the other side until they are completely dry and crisp, another 10–12 minutes. Transfer to wire racks and cool completely before serving or storing in airtight containers.

Chapter Five

PANCAKES, WAFFLES
& CRÊPES

THIS CHAPTER INTRODUCES a wide range of griddle cakes, from hearty, nubbly buckwheat blinis to tender blintzes to moist and luscious French toast. Many other countries have some sort of griddle cake they love, but they don't always serve them for breakfast, the meal at which most Americans have grown to enjoy them.

One of the best things about griddle cakes of all sorts is that you have virtually limitless options when it comes to toppings and garnishes. Hot spiced apples or a honeyed compound butter spiked with citrus zest are just some of the suggestions you'll find in these recipes. Another great thing about griddle cakes and waffles is they can be cooked ahead of time, cooled, and frozen in zip-close bags for a quick alternative to a hot, homemade breakfast. Just pop them in the toaster or toaster oven straight from the freezer. This is a great way to use any leftovers that might linger after breakfast.

Griddle cakes are made from relatively simple batters that blend quickly and can actually be held for a few days in some cases. In fact, crêpes are more tender and delicate when the batter rests overnight. We've included tips and tricks to accompany the recipes throughout this chapter for everything from streamlining your work in the morning to changing a familiar dish from sweet to savory.

The Best Ingredients

Pancake, crêpe, and waffle recipes boil down to just four or five basic ingredients: flour, eggs, milk or buttermilk, and butter, shortening, or oil. With so much riding on each individual ingredient, it pays to choose the best raw materials you can find.

FLOURS AND MEALS

The best pancakes and waffles are tender, moist, and delicate. To get that texture you can use all-purpose flour; most brands of all-purpose flour have a moderate protein content. For even more delicate batters, you may wish to try cake or pastry flour. These flours have even less protein.

Many recipes in this chapter include some measure of flours or meals made from other grains, including buckwheat, corn, and oats. When cornmeal is included in a recipe, we have used stone-ground yellow cornmeal. The coarser the cornmeal, the more textured your pancakes and waffles will be.

When a recipe calls for oatmeal, you can use either quick-cooking or rolled oats. (Rolled oats are sometimes labeled "old-fashioned.") Look for oat flour in natural foods shops, or make your own by processing rolled oats in a food processor until a fine meal or powder forms.

Some specialty flours and meals, including buckwheat, oat or wheat bran, or cornmeal, stay fresher and more flavorful if you store them in the freezer. Be sure to use containers or bags that seal tightly and label and date the package.

EGGS AND MILK

Eggs hold pancakes together, give the batter a wonderful golden color, and add flavor and nutritional value. In some recipes the eggs are separated so that the whites can be beaten into a foam. When the beaten whites are folded into the batter, they produce a light, delicate texture.

Buttermilk gives many recipes in this chapter a pleasant tang. In addition, buttermilk reacts with baking soda for exceptionally light pancakes. If you like buttermilk pancakes and waffles but find it hard to keep buttermilk on hand in the refrigerator, look for powdered buttermilk in the baking goods section of most supermarkets.

BUTTER, OIL, AND SWEETENERS

Butter and oil give batters additional tenderness and flavor. Apart from adding butter or oil as an ingredient, you also need oil to keep griddles lubricated. Oil won't burn as readily as butter. If you like to use cooking spray, be sure to take the pan off the heat before you spray it to prevent flare-ups and smoke.

Sugar and other sweeteners are added to batters to provide extra moisture and flavor. In addition, they help pancakes and waffles develop richly colored exteriors. You can usually substitute sweeteners such as honey, molasses, corn syrup, or maple syrup in recipes. Since these ingredients are normally added in relatively small amounts, you can usually substitute using equal amounts.

A gentle touch for mixing pancake batters is one important factor in success. The other is selecting and preparing your pan properly.

Moderate or heavy-gauge pans can hold heat evenly and tend to develop few hot spots. If one part of the pan is significantly hotter than other parts, your pancakes will not cook evenly.

The pan or griddle must have a very flat, smooth surface as well. To keep your pans from becoming warped or buckled, use the following guidelines:

- *Preheat pans and griddles completely before adding oil or butter.*
- *Adjust the heat whenever your sense of smell or touch or sight tells you that the pan is getting too hot or too cold.*
- *Use a thin layer of oil or butter to lubricate the pan.*
- *If your pan or griddle has a nonstick surface, use tools designed to prevent scratches when you turn the cakes.*

If you like to use cast-iron griddles or skillets, condition them before using them the first time: Get the pan hot, add a liberal amount of oil, and let the oil heat up. Pour out the oil and rub the pan or griddle with paper toweling. (This is the same method you should use to condition unlined crêpe pans.)

Once cast-iron pans are conditioned, maintain their surfaces by wiping out the pan with paper toweling. You can use a little salt as an abrasive if necessary. Do not wash cast-iron pans with soap and water if you can avoid it. Be sure cast-iron pans, skillets, and griddles are completely dry before you put them away, otherwise they can rust.

Soapstone griddles are another classic choice for making griddle cakes. Like cast iron, soapstone has the advantage of being heavy enough to hold and release heat very evenly. Also like cast iron, soapstone griddles require some special maintenance to keep them properly seasoned: Oil the griddle before using it and whenever the surface starts to stick; clean the griddle with a sponge and hot water; avoid abrasives and detergents. (Both cast iron and soapstone can be scrubbed and washed when necessary; you simply need to repeat the seasoning process.)

Waffle irons are a must to make any kind of waffle. To read more about waffle irons and their proper use, see page 135.

The well method is the most common way to blend a batter, whether you are making pancakes, waffles, or crêpes. The method gets its name from the fact that you literally make a "well" in the center of the dry ingredients. The well lets you blend the dry ingredients into the wet ingredients quickly. Consult your recipe to see if the batter should rest or if it is ready to use directly after mixing.

A few recipes in this chapter (Buckwheat Blinis on page 122 and Raised Waffles on page 139) include a small amount of yeast. The yeast needs some time to do its work, so these batters are generally mixed using the same well method as that for a buttermilk pancake. Once blended, the batter is left to "ferment" for several hours or even overnight. If your kitchen is warm, put the batter in the refrigerator to ferment. Let it rest at room temperature while you preheat your griddle or waffle iron.

Buttermilk Pancakes
with Grand Marnier-Infused Strawberries

MAKES 8 SERVINGS

*I*F YOU have a 1-quart measuring cup or a bowl with a spout, use that to mix the batter. You can simply pour the batter out onto a preheated griddle or skillet. If you don't use up all of the batter, you can save it for a day or two. Cover it tightly and stir the batter to blend it again the next morning. The batter may be slightly thinner, but the pancakes will still be tender and delicious. Choose your favorite toppings: butter, syrup, honey, fruit purees, or other toppings as desired.

2 cups all-purpose flour

¼ cup sugar

4 teaspoons baking powder

½ teaspoon baking soda

½ teaspoon salt

2¼ cups buttermilk

4 large eggs

¼ cup butter, melted and cooled

Cooking spray or vegetable oil to coat pan, as needed

4 cups Grand Marnier–Infused Strawberries (recipe follows)

1. Sift the flour, sugar, baking powder, baking soda, and salt together into a mixing bowl. Make a well in the center of the flour mixture.

2. In a separate bowl, blend the buttermilk, eggs, and butter. Add the buttermilk mixture to the flour mixture and stir by hand just until the batter is evenly moistened. The batter is ready to use or may be stored covered and refrigerated for up to 12 hours.

3. Heat a large skillet or griddle over medium-high heat. Oil it lightly by brushing or spraying with cooking oil. Drop the pancake batter into the hot pan by large spoonfuls, about ¼ cup. Leave about 2 inches between the pancakes to allow them to spread and to make turning easier.

4. Cook on the first side until small bubbles appear on the upper surface of the pancake and the edges are set, about 2 minutes. Use an offset spatula or a palette knife to turn the pancakes and finish cooking on the second side, another 2–3 minutes. Adjust the temperature beneath the skillet or griddle to produce a good brown color.

5. Serve the pancakes at once topped with the strawberries.

Grand Marnier-Infused Strawberries

MAKES 4 CUPS

*T*HIS POTENT strawberry dish is perfect as a topping for ultra-adult pancakes or waffles at Sunday brunch. If you have any left, serve it over ice cream or on its own, topped with whipped cream, for a great dessert dish at night.

2 cups sugar

1¾ cups Grand Marnier, divided use

6 cups hulled and quartered strawberries

1. Mix together the sugar and 1¼ cups Grand Marnier, then add the strawberries and stir together. Cover the strawberries and marinate refrigerated overnight. The strawberries will be submerged in liquid when they are properly marinated.

2. Using a slotted spoon, transfer the strawberries from the liquid to a separate bowl and set aside. Pour the liquid into a saucepan and bring to a boil. *(recipe continues on page 116)*

Reduce the heat and simmer slowly until reduced to a syrupy consistency, about 30 minutes. It may be necessary to reduce the heat while the liquid is reducing.

3. Cool the syrup to room temperature and add the remain-ing ½ cup Grand Marnier. Pour this syrup over the reserved strawberries.

4. The strawberries are ready to serve now, or they can be stored in a covered container in the refrigerator for up to 5 days.

Making Pancakes

Whether you enjoy "silver dollar" size pancakes or great big cakes that fill up your plate, a few simple steps can ensure that your griddlecakes are light and tender with a rich color and flavor.

SIFTING AND BLENDING THE DRY INGREDIENTS

The way you handle the dry ingredients has a direct effect on a grid-dlecake's texture. The more evenly the dry ingredients are blended, the fewer strokes it takes to blend the batter. Keeping stirring time to a min-imum means that your batter won't be overmixed. The less you have to mix the batter, the more tender your pancakes and waffles will be.

We recommend sifting all of the dry ingredients—flour, salt, sugar, baking powder or baking soda—together into a mixing bowl large enough to hold the finished batter.

COMBINING THE WET INGREDIENTS

Blend together the wet ingredients, such as buttermilk or milk, eggs, and oil or melted butter, until they are smooth. This is another way you can be sure your batter is handled gently and mixed quickly.

BLENDING THE BATTER

Use a wooden spoon to blend these batters. Before you actually add the wet ingredients to the dry ones, use your spoon to create a well in the center by pushing the dry ingredients from the center to the sides of the bowl but don't pack them down too much.

Add the wet ingredients all at once and stir the dry ingredients from the edge into the center, mixing just long enough to moisten all of the dry ingredients. You may leave lumps in some batters; others, like crêpes, are strained. See specific recipes for instructions.

CHECKING THE GRIDDLE OR PAN

Set your pan over medium to medium-high heat and let it get very hot while you either blend the batter or gather together the syrup, but-ter, or other toppings. If you use nonstick pans, use slightly lower heat. The pan is hot enough when a few drops of water skitter over the sur-face and evaporate in a few seconds. (For more about waffle irons, see page 135.)

Brush or rub a coating of oil on the pan once it is hot with a piece of folded paper toweling. Keep the towel and the oil handy to wipe out the pan and re-lubricate it between batches.

ADDING THE BATTER TO THE PAN

More than one pancake can be cooked on the griddle at once. Pancake batter will spread: the thinner the batter, the more it spreads. Be sure to leave enough room between the pancakes to allow them to spread without touching. Leaving some room means that you'll have an easier time of turning the pancakes.

TURNING PANCAKES

You can tell when pancakes are ready to turn by looking for bubbles that break on the surface. Lift the pancake with a spatula or palette knife and check the color. The color should be an even golden brown. Turn the cake and finish on the second side.

Blueberry Pancakes

MAKES 8 SERVINGS

*I*F FRESH blueberries aren't in season, you can use frozen berries. There is no need to thaw the berries before folding them into the batter. Substitute other berries, including raspberries, strawberries, or blackberries, for the blueberries.

2 cups all-purpose flour

¼ cup sugar

4 teaspoons baking powder

½ teaspoon baking soda

½ teaspoon salt

2¼ cups buttermilk

4 large eggs

¼ cup butter, melted and cooled

1 cup blueberries, fresh or frozen

Cooking spray or vegetable oil to coat pan, as needed

1. Sift the flour, sugar, baking powder, baking soda, and salt together into a mixing bowl. Reserve 3 tablespoons of the flour mixture in a zip-close bag. Make a well in the center of the flour mixture.

2. In a separate bowl, blend the buttermilk, eggs, and butter. Pour the buttermilk mixture into the well in the flour mixture and stir by hand just until the batter is evenly moistened. The batter is ready to use or may be stored covered and refrigerated for up to 12 hours.

3. Heat a large skillet or griddle over medium-high heat. Oil it lightly by brushing or spraying with cooking oil. Just before making the pancakes, add the blueberries to the reserved flour mixture; shake gently until the berries are evenly coated. Fold the berries into the batter. Drop the pancake batter into the hot pan by large spoonfuls (about ¼ cup). Leave about 2 inches between the pancakes to allow them to spread and to make turning easier.

4. Cook on the first side until small bubbles appear on the upper surface of the pancake and the edges are set, about 2 minutes. Use an offset spatula or a palette knife to turn the pancakes and finish cooking on the second side, another 2–3 minutes. Adjust the temperature beneath the skillet or griddle to produce a good brown color.

5. Serve the pancakes at once.

Banana Pancakes *with Blueberry Maple Syrup*

A FINE PUREE of sweet ripe bananas gives these pancakes a fine texture, but feel free to leave them a little coarser so that you get nuggets of tender banana in your pancakes.

2 cups all-purpose flour

¼ cup sugar

4 teaspoons baking powder

½ teaspoon baking soda

½ teaspoon salt

1¾ cups buttermilk

4 large eggs

¼ cup butter, melted and cooled

Cooking spray or vegetable oil to coat pan, as needed

¾ cup mashed ripe bananas

Powdered sugar for garnish

Blueberries for garnish

2 cups Blueberry Maple Syrup (recipe follows)

1. Sift the flour, sugar, baking powder, baking soda, and salt together into a mixing bowl. Make a well in the center of the flour mixture.

2. In a separate bowl, blend the buttermilk, eggs, and butter. Add the buttermilk mixture to the flour mixture and stir by hand just until the batter is evenly moistened. The batter is ready to use or may be stored covered and refrigerated for up to 12 hours.

3. Heat a large skillet or griddle over medium-high heat. Oil it lightly by brushing or spraying with cooking oil. Just before making the pancakes, fold the bananas into the batter. Drop the pancake batter into the hot pan by large spoonfuls, about ¼ cup. Leave about 2 inches between the pancakes to allow them to spread and to make turning easier.

4. Cook on the first side until small bubbles appear on the upper surface of the pancake and the edges are set, about 2 min-utes. Use an offset spatula or a palette knife to turn the pan-cakes and finish cooking on the second side, another 2–3 min-utes. Adjust the temperature beneath the skillet or griddle to produce a good brown color.

5. Serve at once, dusted with powdered sugar and garnished with blueberries, accompanied by the blueberry maple syrup.

Blueberry Maple Syrup

WE'VE STRAINED the syrup for a smooth, pourable con-sistency. You may prefer to skip the straining step for a more rustic texture, similar to that of a fruit topping. In that case, simply add the maple syrup once the blueberries and their liquid have a soft, jamlike texture.

4 cups blueberries, fresh or frozen

1 teaspoon lemon zest

1 cup maple syrup

1. Combine the blueberries and lemon zest in a medium-sized saucepan. Bring to a simmer over medium heat and sim-mer, stirring occasionally, until most of the juice has been re-leased and the mixture develops a saucelike consistency, about 10 minutes.

2. Strain the mixture through a fine-mesh sieve into a clean saucepan, making sure to press all of the juice out of the blue-berry mixture. Return the juice to a simmer and add the maple syrup. Simmer over low heat until the syrup is slightly reduced and thickened, about 10 minutes.

3. The syrup is ready to serve now, or it can be cooled and stored in a container in the refrigerator for up to 10 days. Re-heat over low heat or in the microwave.

Chocolate Chip Pancakes

MAKES 8 SERVINGS

CHOCOLATE LOVERS got good news from the health community recently. A small amount of dark chocolate is actually good for you, and these delicious pancakes are a great way to get a big chocolate flavor. They are so moist you may not even want to put butter on them. If you have some leftover pancakes, freeze them and reheat in your toaster on your next busy morning.

2 cups all-purpose flour

¼ cup sugar

4 teaspoons baking powder

½ teaspoon baking soda

½ teaspoon salt

2¼ cups buttermilk

4 large eggs

¼ cup butter, melted and cooled

Cooking spray or vegetable oil to coat pan, as needed

¾ cup chocolate chips

⅓ cup chopped pecans, toasted

1. Sift together the flour, sugar, baking powder, baking soda, and salt into a large bowl and make a well in the center of the dry ingredients.

2. In a separate bowl, blend the buttermilk, eggs, and butter. Add the buttermilk mixture to the flour mixture and stir by hand just until the batter is evenly moistened. The batter is ready to use or may be stored covered and refrigerated for up to 12 hours.

3. Heat a large skillet or griddle over medium-high heat. Oil it lightly by brushing or spraying with cooking oil. Just before making the pancakes, fold the chocolate chips and pecans into the batter. Drop the pancake batter into the hot pan by large spoonfuls (about ¼ cup). Leave about 2 inches between the pancakes to allow them to spread and to make turning easier.

4. Cook on the first side until small bubbles appear on the upper surface of the pancake and the edges are set, about 2 minutes. Use an offset spatula or a palette knife to turn the pancakes and finish cooking on the second side, another 2–3 minutes. Adjust the temperature beneath the skillet or griddle to produce a good brown color.

5. Serve at once.

Corn & Scallion Pancakes

MAKES 8 SERVINGS

*T*HESE ARE a wonderful savory take on a basic breakfast pancake. If sweet corn is in season, cut the kernels away from the cob and then scrape the cob with a table knife to remove some of the milk. Add the corn milk with the buttermilk mixture for a great fresh flavor.

1½ cups all-purpose flour

½ cup cornmeal

1 tablespoon baking powder

½ teaspoon baking soda

½ teaspoon salt

1 tablespoon sugar

2¼ cups buttermilk

3 large eggs

¼ cup butter, melted

Cooking spray or vegetable oil to coat pan, as needed

½ cup corn kernels, fresh or frozen

2 scallions, thinly sliced

1. Sift together the flour, cornmeal, baking powder, baking soda, salt, and sugar into a large bowl and make a well in the center of the dry ingredients.

2. In a separate bowl, blend the buttermilk, eggs, and butter. Add the buttermilk mixture to the flour mixture and stir by hand just until the batter is evenly moistened. The batter is ready to use or may be stored covered and refrigerated for up to 12 hours.

3. Heat a large skillet or griddle over medium-high heat. Oil it lightly by brushing or spraying with cooking oil. Just before making the pancakes, fold the corn and scallions into the batter. Drop the pancake batter into the hot pan by large spoonfuls (about ¼ cup). Leave about 2 inches between the pancakes to allow them to spread and to make turning easier.

4. Cook on the first side until small bubbles appear on the upper surface of the pancake and the edges are set, about 2 minutes. Use an offset spatula or a palette knife to turn the pancakes and finish cooking on the second side, another 2–3 minutes. Adjust the temperature beneath the skillet or griddle to produce a good brown color.

5. Serve immediately.

Buckwheat Blinis *with Apple Butter*

MAKES 8 SERVINGS

*T*HIS BLINI recipe makes breakfast-sized pancakes. Serve them with the apple butter for a hearty breakfast on a cold winter morning. Or you can make smaller blini to top with sour cream and caviar for a classic Russian hors d'oeuvre.

1 tablespoon plus 2 teaspoons dry active yeast

5 cups milk, warmed to 110°F

3⅓ cups all-purpose flour

¾ cup buckwheat flour

1 tablespoon sugar

1½ teaspoons salt

3 large egg yolks, beaten

5 large egg whites

¼ cup butter or oil

2 cups Apple Butter (recipe follows)

1. Dissolve the yeast in the warmed milk and set aside for 5–10 minutes or until yeast blooms.

2. Sift the flours, sugar, and salt together into a large bowl and make a well in the center of the dry ingredients.

3. Add the egg yolks and yeast mixture to the flour and stir until smooth. Cover with plastic and let rise until doubled, 2–3 hours.

4. To make the blini, beat egg whites to soft peaks and fold into batter. Preheat a griddle on medium heat and lightly grease with butter or oil. Ladle ⅓ cup batter for each blini onto the griddle. Turn once, when bubbles break on the upper surface and the bottom is golden brown, about 2 minutes. Finish cooking on the second side, about 1 minute. Repeat until the batter is finished.

5. Serve immediately with the Apple Butter.

Apple Butter

MAKES 2 CUPS

*T*ART, JUICY apples make a flavorful apple butter that doesn't get too sweet. You can choose a single variety, such as MacIntosh, or mix several varieties. Use a saucepan with a heavy-gauge bottom to prevent the apple butter from scorching as you cook it. A flame diffuser, if you have one, also keeps the heat even and gentle as the apple butter simmers.

12 cups peeled and sliced apples

1½ cups apple cider

1¼ cups sugar

½ cinnamon stick

½ teaspoon ground cardamom

½ teaspoon grated lemon zest

¼ teaspoon salt

1. Combine the apples and apple cider in a saucepan and bring to a slow simmer over medium heat. Reduce the heat, cover the pan, and let simmer, stirring occasionally, until all the apples are soft and pulpy, about 30 minutes.

2. Remove from the heat and puree the apples with a food mill or a sieve into a clean saucepan. Add the sugar, cinnamon, cardamom, zest, and salt to the apple puree and simmer over low heat, stirring frequently, until very thick and deep brown, about 2 hours.

3. Transfer the apple butter to a bowl set in an ice bath and cool, stirring from time to time. Once the apple butter has cooled, it is ready to serve or store in a covered container in the refrigerator for up to 3 weeks.

Strawberry Honey Butter

MAKES 1 CUP

*F*LAVORED BUTTERS are a perfect accompaniment to pancakes and waffles. You can also serve them with hot biscuits, muffins, or toast. Shape the butter by piping, as shown here, or roll it into a log to chill and slice. A simple and attractive option is to simply pack it into a pretty cup or crock.

¾ cup butter, softened

½ cup minced, hulled strawberries

2 tablespoons honey

1 tablespoon lemon juice, about ½ lemon

¼ teaspoon orange zest

Combine butter, strawberries, honey, lemon juice, and orange zest and beat together until very smooth but not soft or oily. The butter is ready to transfer to a pastry bag to pipe into rosettes and serve as a topping or spread now, or cover and store in the refrigerator for up to 2 days. Let the butter soften to room temperature before serving.

ABOVE *Pipe the strawberry butter into shapes either directly onto a plate or onto a baking sheet lined with parchment paper. The butter can be frozen after it is piped into the shapes.*

Crêpes *with Spicy Mushroom & Queso Fresco Filling*

MAKES 8 SERVINGS

YOU MAY want to make a double batch of this master crêpe recipe so you can freeze some to have on hand for a quick meal. Here we accompany the basic crêpes with a savory filling to create a delicious brunch dish.

2 cups all-purpose flour

¼ cup sugar

½ teaspoon salt

2 cups milk

2 large eggs

1 tablespoon butter, melted

½ teaspoon vanilla extract

Melted butter or vegetable oil to coat pan, as needed

2 cups Spicy Mushroom and Queso Fresco Filling (recipe follows), optional

1. Sift the flour, sugar, and salt together into a mixing bowl. Make a well in the center of the flour mixture.

2. In a separate bowl, blend the milk, eggs, butter, and vanilla. Add the milk mixture to the flour mixture and stir by hand just until the batter is smooth. Let the batter rest in the refrigerator at least 1 and up to 12 hours before preparing the crêpes. Strain the batter if necessary to remove lumps before preparing the crêpes.

3. Heat a crêpe pan or small skillet over medium-high heat. Brush with melted butter. Pour about ¼ cup batter into the crêpe pan, swirling and tilting the pan to coat the bottom with batter. Cook until the first side is set and has a little color, about 2 minutes. Adjust the temperature under the pan if necessary. Use a thin metal or heatproof rubber spatula to lift the crêpe and turn it over. Cook on the other side until the crêpe is cooked through, 1 minute more.

Making Crêpes

The thinner the crêpe the better, but don't be discouraged if the first crêpe or two is a little uneven. With each crêpe you make, you'll get better at gauging the right amount of batter and level of heat for your pan.

MIX THE BATTER

Crêpe batters have a more liquid consistency than other pancake batters. Whisk well to remove any lumps, and then let the batter rest for at least 1 hour to ensure tender crêpes.

PREPARE THE PAN

Crêpes are typically prepared in a small, flat, round pan with short, sloped sides. Small nonstick skillets also work well. Heat the pan over medium heat and grease lightly with butter or oil to prevent sticking or, in the case of nonstick pans, to add flavor.

COOK THE CRÊPES

With a ladle or small measuring cup, quickly pour a small amount of batter into the pan. Immediately tilt and swirl the pan to spread the batter in a thin, even layer that just covers the bottom of the pan. Cook for a few minutes, and then check the doneness of a crêpe by carefully lifting one edge and looking underneath it for a golden color with specks of light brown. With a spatula, loosen the edge of the crêpe from the pan, turn, and cook on the other side until golden.

MAKING CRÊPES IN ADVANCE

Crêpes are easily made in advance. Cool them completely on baking sheets lined with parchment or waxed paper, then stack the crêpes with parchment or waxed paper between each one. They can be wrapped well and refrigerated or frozen for later use.

4. Stack the crêpes to fill now, or refrigerate or freeze them and assemble later. If desired, divide the mushroom filling evenly among the crêpes.

Spicy Mushroom & Queso Fresco Filling

MAKES 2 CUPS

*T*HE MUSHROOMS need to be added to the pan in a single layer to brown properly, so sauté them in two batches.

2 tablespoons olive oil, divided use

½ cup minced onion, divided use

1½ teaspoons minced garlic, divided use

4 cups sliced mushrooms, divided use

2 teaspoons minced serrano chiles, divided use

2 tablespoons lime juice

¾ teaspoon epazote

¾ teaspoon salt

¼ teaspoon ground black pepper

¾ cup crumbled queso fresco

1. Heat 1 tablespoon of the olive oil in a sauté pan over medium-high heat. Add half of the onion and half of the garlic to the oil and sauté, stirring frequently, until the onion is tender and translucent, 2–3 minutes.

2. Increase the heat to high. Add half the sliced mushrooms and half the serrano chiles. Sauté the mushrooms without stirring until they are browned on one side, 3–4 minutes. Stir the mixture and continue to cook over medium heat until the liquid given off by the mushrooms cooks away. Transfer to a bowl and reserve. Repeat to cook the remaining mushrooms.

3. Return the reserved mushroom mixture to the pan and sauté until the mushrooms are very hot, 1–2 minutes. Add the lime juice, epazote, salt, and pepper.

4. The completed mushroom filling can now be spooned onto each crêpe over the crumbled queso fresco, or the cheese can be mixed into the warm mushroom mixture before filling.

LEFT TO RIGHT *Ladle the batter into the pan and tilt it up to swirl the batter evenly around the pan; make the thickness as uniform as possible, so the crêpe will cook more evenly. The edges of the crêpe will turn golden brown and signal that one side of the crêpe is properly cooked; use a spatula to check the color of the crêpe before turning it over. If using a filling, spoon a small amount down the center of each crêpe, then carefully fold over the two sides to cover the filling.*

Apple-Filled Crêpes *with Cinnamon Sauce*

MAKES 8 SERVINGS

*T*RY THE topping for the Dutch Baby (page 132) as an alternative to the apple filling we've suggested here.

24 Crêpes (page 124)

1½ cups Apple Filling (page 103)

⅔ cup heavy cream

2 tablespoons sugar

2 cups Cinnamon Sauce (recipe follows)

Lemon zest for garnish

1. Make the crêpes and apple filling. These can be made ahead. Let the crêpes and filling return to room temperature if they have been refrigerated or frozen.

2. Combine the cream and the sugar and whip to soft peaks. Fill each crêpe with 2 tablespoons of the apple filling. Top with 3 tablespoons of the sauce and 2 tablespoons whipped cream. Garnish the crêpes with lemon zest.

Cinnamon Sauce

MAKES 2 CUPS

*S*ERVE THIS cinnamon sauce with the Apple-Filled Crêpes, or try it over French toast or as a topping for ice cream.

1 tablespoon cornstarch

¾ cup apple juice, divided use

¾ cup water

½ cup sugar

¼ cup orange juice

¼ cup light rum

2 tablespoons lemon juice, about 1 lemon

1 teaspoon ground cinnamon

1 tablespoon butter

1. Combine the cornstarch with ¼ cup of the apple juice in a small bowl and stir until the cornstarch is completely dissolved.

2. Combine the remaining apple juice, water, sugar, orange juice, rum, lemon juice, and cinnamon in a saucepan; bring to a boil over high heat, stirring until the sugar is dissolved. Add the dissolved cornstarch and return the mixture to a boil, stirring constantly, until thickened and smooth, about 2 minutes.

3. Remove the sauce from the heat and stir in the butter until it melts and is evenly blended. The sauce is ready to serve hot now, or transfer it to a bowl set in an ice bath and cool, stirring from time to time. Once the sauce has cooled, it is ready to store in a covered container in the refrigerator for up to 4 days.

Cheese Blintzes *with Mixed Berry Sauce*

MAKES 8 SERVINGS

You CAN bake the blintzes instead of cooking them in a skillet, as we've done here. Coat a baking dish liberally with some of the butter and drizzle the rest over the tops of the blintzes. Bake at 400°F for about 15 minutes, or until bubbly and golden brown.

24 Crêpes (page 124)

2 cups Mixed Berry Sauce (recipe follows)

1 cup farmer or pot cheese

1 cup whole-milk ricotta cheese

1 cup cream cheese, softened

¼ cup sugar

3 large eggs

¼ teaspoon vanilla extract

¼ teaspoon salt

4 tablespoons butter, or as needed

1. Make the crêpes and the berry sauce. These can be made ahead. Let the crêpes return to room temperature while you make the filling if they have been refrigerated or frozen. Warm the sauce.

2. Combine the cheeses and sugar and beat with a wooden spoon until thoroughly blended. Add the eggs, vanilla, and salt and stir until smooth.

3. To assemble the blintzes spoon 2–3 tablespoons filling on the lower third of each blintz. Fold the bottom of the blintz over the filling then fold each of the remaining sides over to make a little package. Repeat with the remaining blintzes.

4. Melt 1 tablespoon butter in a skillet over medium-low heat. Arrange 6 blintzes at a time seam side down in the skillet and sauté until faintly brown and crisp, about 2 minutes. Turn the blintzes and brown on the second side, another 2 minutes.

Repeat with remaining blintzes, adding another tablespoon of butter for each batch, and serve with the warm berry sauce.

Mixed Berry Sauce

MAKES 2 CUPS

You CAN make this sauce with one type of berry or a combination. If you have a surplus of berries on hand, make a double, triple, or even quadruple batch and freeze the sauce to enjoy a taste of summer in the heart of winter.

1½ cups fresh or frozen raspberries, divided use

1½ cups fresh or frozen sliced strawberries, divided use

1 cup fresh or frozen blueberries, divided use

¾–1 cup sugar, or to taste

1–2 tablespoons freshly squeezed lemon juice, or to taste

1. Combine 1 cup of the raspberries, 1 cup of the strawberries, ¾ cup of the blueberries, ¾ cup of the sugar, and 1 tablespoon of the lemon juice in a saucepan and bring to a simmer over medium heat.

2. Simmer until the sugar has dissolved, about 10 minutes. Taste the mixture and, if necessary, add more sugar. Continue to heat until any additional sugar is dissolved.

3. Puree the sauce with a blender or push it through a wire-mesh sieve. Return the sauce to a simmer and adjust the flavor by adding additional lemon juice if necessary. Add the remaining ½ cup raspberries, ½ cup strawberries, and ¼ cup blueberries and simmer until the sauce is very hot.

4. The sauce can be served hot or cold; it will thicken slightly when stored in the refrigerator, and keeps for up to 10 days.

Crêpes Suzette

CRÊPES SUZETTE is a classic dessert, one often prepared at the table so that you can enjoy the dramatic flaming presentation. Warm the Grand Marnier and brandy to make them easier to ignite. And, if pyrotechnics in the morning seems a little too dramatic, you can simply let the sauce simmer without setting it aflame.

3 tablespoons sugar

1 cup butter, cubed

3 tablespoons orange zest

¼ cup orange juice

24 Crêpes (page 124)

3 tablespoons Grand Marnier

3 tablespoons brandy or cognac

Orange zest for garnish

1. Preheat a small sauté pan over medium heat. Sprinkle the sugar evenly over the bottom of the pan. As the sugar begins to caramelize, 2–3 minutes, add the butter to the outside edges of the pan and gently shake the pan; this allows the butter to evenly blend with the sugar.

2. Add the orange zest and shake the pan gently to thoroughly blend all the ingredients and let the sauce become a light orange caramel color, 1–2 minutes. Pour the orange juice on the outside edges of the pan slowly, allowing it to blend with the sugar. Shake the pan gently, incorporating all the ingredients and simmer until the sauce begins to thicken.

3. Place one crêpe at a time in the sauce, coating both sides, and remove. Repeat with the remaining crêpes, moving quickly so the sauce does not become too thick.

4. Remove the pan from the heat and add the Grand Marnier, being careful not to allow the liquor to flame. Return the pan to the heat and stir gently until sauce is hot.

5. Remove the pan, add the brandy, and tip the pan slightly to collect the liquid on one side. Use a lit match to set the brandy on fire. Shake the pan until the flame dies.

6. Fold each crêpe into fourths; place 3 on each plate, slightly overlapping, and coat with sauce. Garnish with orange zest.

Dutch Baby *with Spiced Fruit*

MAKES 6–8 SERVINGS

*F*EEL FREE to substitute sour cream or yogurt for the whipped cream, if you prefer. For the spiced fruit, experiment with other fruits or combinations of fruits such as bananas, raspberries, apples, or strawberries.

½ cup all-purpose flour

½ teaspoon salt

2 large eggs

½ cup milk

¼ cup butter, melted, divided use

2¾ cups peeled and sliced peaches

1 teaspoon ground cinnamon

2 tablespoons packed brown sugar

1 tablespoon lemon juice

Powdered sugar, as needed

¼ cup heavy cream, whipped to soft peaks

1 teaspoon lemon zest

1. Preheat the oven to 450°F.

2. Sift the flour and salt together into a small bowl. Make a well in the center of the dry ingredients.

3. Put the eggs in a blender and blend at low speed. Add the flour mixture and the milk alternately, in thirds. Scrape down the sides of the blender and continue to blend until smooth. Blend in 2 tablespoons of the melted butter.

4. Pour the batter into a nonstick skillet, a well-greased 10-inch cast-iron skillet, or ovenproof sauté pan. Bake for 20 minutes without opening the oven door. Reduce the heat to 350°F and bake 10 minutes longer.

5. While the Dutch baby is baking, prepare the spiced fruit. Heat the remaining 2 tablespoons melted butter in a medium sauté pan over high heat. Add the peaches, cinnamon, and brown sugar. Continue to cook until the peaches are browned, 5–6 minutes.

6. Remove the Dutch baby from the oven. Drizzle with the lemon juice and sprinkle with the powdered sugar. Fill the center of the Dutch baby with the hot fruit mixture. Top with the whipped cream and lemon zest. Serve at once.

French Toast with Orange Sauce (Torrijas)

MAKES 8 SERVINGS

YOU CAN opt to serve this French toast with maple syrup or butter without the topping of cream and orange sauce, but this delicious orange sauce gives a familiar breakfast and brunch favorite a delightful Spanish flair for something a little out of the ordinary.

5 cups orange juice

1½ cups sugar, divided use

3 cinnamon sticks

5 lemons, zested

12 large eggs

4 teaspoons orange zest

½ cup clarified butter or canola oil for frying, as needed

24 slices Challah (page 89), about 1½ loaves

1½ cups heavy cream

2½ cups oranges, broken into segments
    or cut into suprêmes

1. For the sauce, combine the orange juice, 1 cup of the sugar, the cinnamon, and lemon zest in a saucepan over medium heat. Simmer the mixture until slightly thickened, about 20 minutes. Strain the sauce and reserve hot.

2. Whisk together the eggs and orange zest. Place a large sauté pan over medium heat until hot. For each batch of French toast, add 1 tablespoon clarified butter or oil to the pan. Dip 2 or 3 slices of challah into the egg mixture. Sauté until golden brown, about 2 minutes on each side. Repeat until all of the French toast is cooked, adding more oil or butter to the pan as necessary. Hold the French toast warm until needed.

3. To serve, carefully spoon 1 tablespoon of heavy cream over each piece of French toast. Sprinkle about 1 teaspoon of sugar on top and place under the broiler until the sugar is lightly caramelized, about 2 minutes. Serve 3 pieces of French toast per serving, top with ¼ cup orange sauce, and garnish with 3 orange segments.

Swedish Pancake Torta

MAKES 8 SERVINGS

*I*F YOU can't find lingonberry preserves, substitute another good-quality jam or preserve in its place.

4 large eggs

4½ cups milk

1½ cups flour

½ cup butter, melted

½ teaspoon salt

½ teaspoon vanilla extract

½ cup lingonberry preserves

⅔ cup heavy cream, whipped to medium peaks

¼ cup mint leaves for garnish

1. Beat the eggs well in a blender or food processor. Then add the milk, flour, butter, salt, and vanilla and blend for 30 seconds more.

2. Heat a crêpe pan or small sauté pan over medium-high heat without any oil or fat. Pour ¼ cup batter into the pan spreading evenly. Brown the pancake on each side, 30–60 seconds per side.

3. Spread lingonberry preserves between each pancake and stack four together. Garnish the tops of each stack with whipped cream and mint leaves.

Making Waffles

Waffles, made on a special griddle, are no more difficult to make than any other pancake as long as you take a few minutes to get familiar with your waffle iron. We've included several tips for making and enjoying waffles.

Waffle irons are essential if you want to make waffles. Belgian waffles are thicker than standard waffles, so if you enjoy them, be sure your iron is one that can make them. You can find waffle irons that make heart-shaped, round, square, or rectangular waffles. Each waffle iron has its own idiosyncrasies.

PREHEATING THE WAFFLE IRON

Clean the waffle iron before you start, to remove any debris that might make your waffles stick.

Allow the waffle iron plenty of time to heat up. Some models may take 10 minutes or longer.

Position the waffle iron so that it is stable and well away from the usual traffic flow. The outside of a waffle iron will be extremely hot once it is fully preheated.

Very lightly rub the iron with a little oil or shortening, even if your waffle iron is nonstick.

ADDING THE BATTER AND ADJUSTING THE HEAT

Make a sample waffle or two, until you determine how much batter you need to completely fill the iron and make a good-sized waffle.

Adjust the temperature on your waffle iron and, again, make a note about what setting made the best waffle.

The time it takes to cook a waffle will vary according to how thick or thin your waffles are. Make a note of the time it takes on your machine for future reference.

CLEANUP

Let the waffle iron cool completely before cleaning and storing it.

Waffles *with Hot Raspberry Syrup*

MAKES 8 SERVINGS

WE MADE these waffles in a round waffle iron. Your yield may be slightly different if your waffle iron makes rectangular or square waffles.

3½ cups all-purpose flour

2 teaspoons salt

½ cup sugar

2 tablespoons baking powder

8 large eggs, separated

3 cups milk

1 cup butter, melted

2 cups Hot Raspberry Syrup (recipe follows)

1. Sift together the flour, salt, sugar, and baking powder into a large mixing bowl. Make a well in the center of the dry ingredients.

2. Whisk together the egg yolks, milk, and melted butter in a separate bowl. Pour the wet ingredients into the well of the dry ingredients, stirring until just combined. The batter will be slightly lumpy. Do not overmix.

3. Preheat the waffle iron.

4. Whip the egg whites to soft peaks and fold into the batter in 2 additions. Ladle about ¾ cup batter into the waffle iron. Cook the waffles until they are crisp, golden, and cooked through, 3–6 minutes per waffle. Serve at once. Pass the raspberry syrup on the side.

Hot Raspberry Syrup

MAKES 2 CUPS

YOU CAN substitute good-quality vanilla extract for the vanilla bean. Add the extract to the syrup after it has reduced and you've taken it from the heat.

7 cups raspberries, fresh or frozen (thaw slightly)

1¾ cups sugar

2¼ cups water

½ vanilla bean, split and scraped or 1 teaspoon vanilla extract

¾ cup lemon juice

1. Combine the raspberries, sugar, and water in a saucepan and bring to a simmer over medium heat. Simmer until raspberries are soft, about 15 minutes. *(recipe continues on page 138)*

1. Ladle the batter into the center of the waffle iron so that the batter will spread evenly.

2. Remove the waffle using a fork or other utensil; if the waffle iron was greased properly, the waffle should not stick.

2. Strain the raspberry mixture through a fine-mesh sieve, pressing against the solids with the back of a ladle.

3. Discard the seeds and pour the extracted juices into a saucepan; add the vanilla bean, its seeds, and the lemon juice to the saucepan. Simmer until reduced by one-half over medium-low heat or to the consistency of syrup, 20–25 minutes.

4. The syrup is ready to serve now, or it can be cooled and stored in a container in the refrigerator for up to 10 days.

Four-Grain Waffles

MAKES 8 SERVINGS

*I*F YOU can't find oat flour or don't want to make it yourself, simply increase the amount of all-purpose flour to 1¼ cups. Waffles will stay warm and crisp for a little while in a low oven (about 200°F.). They also are perfect to freeze after they have cooled off. Put them in zip-close bags and pop them into a toaster or toaster oven straight from the freezer.

1 cup all-purpose flour

⅔ cup whole-wheat flour

⅔ cup oat flour

⅓ cup cornmeal

4 teaspoons baking powder

2 tablespoons sugar

2 cups buttermilk

2 large eggs

¼ cup vegetable oil plus extra for greasing

1. Preheat a waffle iron to medium heat.

2. Combine the flours, cornmeal, baking powder, and sugar. Make a well in the center of the dry ingredients.

3. In a separate bowl combine the buttermilk, eggs, and oil and whisk just until evenly blended. Add the wet ingredients to the dry ingredients and mix by hand with a wooden spoon just until the batter is evenly moistened.

4. Lightly brush the preheated waffle iron with vegetable oil. Ladle ¾ cup of the batter into the waffle iron and cook until the waffles are golden brown, 3–6 minutes per waffle. Serve at once.

Raised Waffles

MAKES 8 SERVINGS

S INCE THIS batter needs time to rise, it's a perfect choice to mix the night before. Ale gives the waffles extra lightness.

2 teaspoons instant dry yeast

1 cup water, warmed to 110°F

2½ cups milk, warmed to 110°F

1 cup butter, melted

1½ teaspoons salt

2 teaspoons sugar

4 cups all-purpose flour

8 large eggs, lightly beaten

½ teaspoon baking soda

½ cup brown ale

1. Dissolve yeast with warm water in a large bowl and let sit for 5 minutes. Add milk, butter, salt, sugar, and flour to yeast mixture and blend until batter is smooth. Cover with plastic wrap and let sit overnight at room temperature.

2. When ready to serve, whisk together the eggs, baking soda, and ale and add to the yeast mixture. Stir just until all ingredients are incorporated. Do not overmix.

3. Preheat the waffle iron.

4. Pour about ¾ cup batter into the waffle iron and cook the waffles until they are crisp, golden, and cooked through, 3–6 minutes per waffle. Serve at once.

Oatmeal Waffles

MAKES 8 SERVINGS

L EMON CURD (page 71) makes a wonderful topping for these crisp, light waffles.

3⅓ cups all-purpose flour

1⅓ cups quick-cooking oatmeal or rolled oats

½ cup granulated sugar

2 tablespoons plus 2 teaspoons baking powder

1 teaspoon baking soda

1 teaspoon salt

1 teaspoon ground cinnamon

¼ teaspoon ground nutmeg

Pinch ground cloves

7 large eggs

1 quart buttermilk

½ cup butter, melted

1. In a large bowl mix together the flour, oatmeal, sugar, baking powder, baking soda, salt, cinnamon, nutmeg, and cloves and make a well in the center.

2. In a separate bowl combine the eggs with the buttermilk and mix well. Pour the egg mixture into the center of the dry ingredients. Stir the mixture until the dry ingredients are about ¾ moistened. Add the butter and stir only until the butter is worked in. Do not overmix. The batter is ready to use now, or it may be refrigerated for up to 12 hours.

3. Preheat the waffle iron to medium-high. Pour about ¾ cup batter into the waffle iron and cook the waffles until they are crisp, golden, and cooked through, 3–6 minutes per waffle. Serve at once.

Chapter Six

EGGS

E GGS ARE ONE of the most popular of all breakfast foods and certainly the most versatile. This chapter includes recipes for such familiar favorites as fried and scrambled eggs as well as some contemporary offerings: Breakfast Burritos (page 164) or Breakfast Pizza (page 165). The classic brunch dish, Eggs Benedict (page 155), is sure to impress your guests. Eggs baked in a ramekin (page 152) with or without a savory garnish make it easy to prepare brunch or breakfast without a last-minute rush in the kitchen.

About Eggs

Eggs are graded on the basis of external appearance and freshness. The top grade, AA, indicates that an egg is fresh, with a white that will not spread too much once the egg is broken and a yolk that sits high on the white's surface.

SELECTING EGGS

Buy eggs from a refrigerated case. Look at the packaging to be sure it is not dented or ripped. Inspect the eggs. The eggshells should be clean, without cracks, holes, or leaks. To keep eggs wholesome at home, store them in the carton in the coldest part of the refrigerator. As long as the shells remain unbroken, your eggs will keep for 3 to 5 weeks held at 40°F or less.

Once eggs are taken out of the shell, store them in clean containers, well covered, and use them within 2 days.

Pasteurized eggs may be used in preparations such as salad dressings, desserts, and eggnog for which the traditional recipe calls for raw eggs. You can buy them in the dairy case, near the other eggs, sold in cartons or as pasteurized eggs in the shell. For health reasons, many cooks use egg substitutes that are either entirely egg-free or produced from egg whites with dairy or vegetable products substituted for the yolks. These substitutes are valuable for people who must follow a reduced-cholesterol diet.

SEPARATING EGGS

Eggs separate most easily when they are cold, so keep them in the refrigerator until you are ready. You'll need a clean bowl to break each egg into, as well as bowls to hold the whites and yolks separately, and also a container to hold any eggs that don't separate cleanly.

Crack each egg's shell and carefully pull apart the halves. Gently pour the egg yolk back and forth from one half to the other, allowing the egg white to fall into the empty bowl. Drop the egg yolk into another bowl.

Examine the white in the first bowl to be sure that it contains no bits of yolk. If it is clean, transfer it to the egg white bowl. If you see drops of yolk in the egg white, however, it cannot be used for whipping. Save it for another dish such as scrambled eggs or to use as egg wash for baked goods, and wash out the bowl before separating the next egg.

Frying Eggs

From cheerful sunny-side-up eggs with bacon to richly layered Huevos Rancheros, fried eggs are an essential part of breakfast for many of us.

Use the freshest eggs possible for fewer broken yolks and find a smooth-surfaced skillet or griddle that is heavy enough to cook evenly. Break each egg separately into a small bowl.

Heat the skillet or griddle over medium heat. Even if you are using a nonstick pan, add a small amount of flavorful fat, oil, or butter to give

good flavor and a crisp-edged texture to the eggs. Wait until the cooking fat is hot and then slide the eggs into the skillet.

Lower the heat to medium-low. Egg whites become opaque quickly, but the yolk determines an egg's doneness. Leave them soft and runny for sunny-side up, or cook until firm or very firm ("medium" or "hard"). For over-easy, over-medium, or over-hard eggs, turn the eggs carefully with a spatula and cook for 30 seconds to 2 minutes more.

Fried Eggs

MAKES 8 SERVINGS

*Y*OUR EGGS will look the most attractive if you fry them one serving at a time. If you like the egg yolks set and firm, you can baste the tops with some of the butter or oil or you can sprinkle a few drops of water into the skillet, cover tightly, and "steam" for about 30 seconds.

½ cup clarified butter or olive oil

16 large eggs

2 teaspoons salt, or as needed

1 teaspoon freshly ground black pepper

1. Break 2 eggs per portion into a clean cup or small bowl.

2. To make eggs sunny–side up, heat 1 tablespoon of butter in a small sauté pan over medium heat and carefully slide the eggs into the pan.

3. When the egg whites are set, after about 2 minutes, tilt the pan, allowing the fat to collect at the side of the pan, and baste the egg whites with the fat as they cook. To make eggs over–easy, –medium, or –hard, turn the eggs near the end of their cooking time with a spatula and cook them on the second side, 20–30 seconds for over–easy, 1 minute for over–medium, 2½ minutes for over–hard.

4. Season the eggs with salt and pepper and serve at once on heated plates. Be careful not to break the yolks while sliding the eggs onto the plate.

1. These eggs have been fried to the sunny–side-up stage; note that the egg whites have fully cooked but the egg yolks have not. 2. The eggs have been flipped and fried to the over–medium stage. It is difficult to judge the doneness just by looking at the eggs, so we advise using a timer for the first few tries at making fried eggs. Over time, you may be able to judge the doneness of the eggs by touch.

Huevos Rancheros *with Salsa Fresca*

MAKES 8 SERVINGS

HUEVOS RANCHEROS are a hearty breakfast of fried eggs over refried beans on a corn tortilla topped with cheese, avocado, and salsa. If you prefer, you can make this dish with Poached Eggs (page 153), instead of frying them.

Eight 6-inch corn tortillas

2 cups Refried Beans (page 189)

¼ cup unsalted butter or vegetable oil

16 large eggs

Salt and freshly ground pepper

1 cup grated Monterey Jack cheese

2 avocados

4 teaspoons fresh lime juice, juice of half a lime

1 cup Salsa Fresca (recipe follows) or prepared salsa

½ cup sour cream, as needed for garnish

8 cilantro sprigs for garnish

1. Preheat the broiler.

2. Heat the tortillas by toasting them one at a time in a dry cast-iron skillet or directly over a gas flame until lightly toasted. Place on a baking sheet; spread each tortilla with ¼ cup refried beans and cover to keep warm.

3. Working in batches as needed, heat the butter in a large skillet over medium-high heat until it is very hot but not smoking and the foaming has subsided. Crack the eggs directly into the hot butter and reduce the heat to medium-low or low. Fry the eggs, shaking the pan occasionally to keep the eggs from sticking. Season the eggs with salt and pepper. Fry about 2 minutes for "sunny-side up," 3 minutes for medium yolks, and 3½–4 minutes for hard yolks.

4. Top each prepared tortilla with 2 fried eggs and 2 tablespoons of the grated cheese. Slide the tortillas under the broiler to melt the cheese.

5. Meanwhile, dice the avocados and toss with the lime juice to prevent the avocados from discoloring. Divide the avocados among the tortillas. Top each serving with 2 tablespoons salsa and 2 tablespoons sour cream. Garnish each serving with a sprig of cilantro and serve.

Salsa Fresca

MAKES 2 CUPS

THIS SALSA is easy to put together from ingredients that are usually on hand. Unlike jarred, store-bought salsas, this salsa is at its best for only a brief period. Keep it chilled and use it within a day. You can use as much or as little of the jalapeño as you like. Try other chiles as well, including the smoky-hot canned chipotles with a little of their sauce (known as adobo) either instead of or in addition to the jalapeño. Other additions you might try include black beans, red peppers, or cucumbers.

1 cup seeded and diced tomatoes

¼ cup minced onion

2 tablespoons small-dice green bell pepper

1 tablespoon minced jalapeño

1 tablespoon extra virgin olive oil

1 garlic clove, minced

2 teaspoons chopped cilantro

½ teaspoon chopped oregano

1 tablespoon fresh lime juice

½ teaspoon salt

⅛ teaspoon freshly ground black pepper

1. Combine the tomatoes, onion, green pepper, jalapeño, olive oil, garlic, cilantro, and oregano. Add lime juice, salt, and pepper to taste.

2. Let the salsa rest in a covered container in the refrigerator at least 30 minutes before serving.

Scrambled Eggs

*T*HIS RECIPE is simple to make in smaller amounts. Plan on two or three eggs per person and use enough oil or butter to liberally coat the pan.

24 large eggs

½ cup whole milk

2 teaspoons salt

1 teaspoon pepper

¼ cup clarified butter or canola oil

1. Whisk eggs and milk in a bowl and season with the salt and pepper.

2. Heat 2 tablespoons butter or oil in a large sauté pan over medium-high heat until almost smoking. Add half of the eggs to the pan and stir until they are soft and creamy, about 1½ minutes for soft scrambled or 2 minutes for hard scrambled eggs.

3. Remove the eggs from the heat when fully cooked but still moist, and serve at once on heated plates. Repeat with the remaining butter or oil and eggs to make the second batch. *See photo on page 197.*

Making Scrambled Eggs

Scrambled eggs are perfect to make in large batches, but they cook so quickly you can easily make them to order.

MIXING THE EGGS

For best flavor, you should crack and blend the eggs just before cooking if possible, but if you need to streamline breakfast or brunch, you can crack and blend the eggs up to 12 hours in advance.

Season the eggs well with salt and pepper. If you like, blend them with a small amount of water, broth, milk, or cream for a more tender texture. The eggs should have an even color and consistency after you blend them.

SCRAMBLING EGGS

Since scrambled eggs lose their heat quickly once they come out of the pan, be sure to have heated plates or platters ready to serve them. If the entire crowd isn't on hand and ready to eat, you can make smaller batches rather than one big batch. Use a 4-ounce ladle or a ½-cup measure for each serving you want to prepare.

Heat a nonstick omelet pan or small skillet over high heat and add oil, butter, or a combination of both. Determining when the pan and fat are properly heated is key. Oil should shimmer but not smoke, while butter should melt and foam but not turn brown or black. Water droplets should skitter over the pan but not cook away instantly. Tilt the pan to coat its entire surface.

Add the beaten eggs and use one hand to swirl the pan on the burner and the other to stir the eggs in the opposite direction, using a fork or heat-resistant rubber spatula. Once the eggs set into smooth, small curds and lose their glossy look, they are ready to serve.

Egg & Sausage Breakfast Sandwiches

MAKES 8 SANDWICHES

THESE DELICIOUS but slightly messy sandwiches are the perfect thing for breakfast when you need to get everyone out the door and on with their day. If you prefer, use Kaiser rolls instead of bagels.

½ cup clarified butter or canola oil, divided use

¾ pound sliced mushrooms

4 cups thinly sliced onions

1 tablespoon salt, divided use

2 teaspoons freshly ground black pepper, divided use

¾ pound Breakfast Sausage (page 211)

16 large eggs

1 cup grated cheddar cheese

8 toasted bagels

1. Heat 2 tablespoons of the butter or oil in a sauté pan over medium-high heat until almost smoking. Add the mushrooms and sauté until lightly caramelized, 5–6 minutes, stirring occasionally. Remove the mushrooms from the pan, reserve.

2. Heat another 2 tablespoons butter or oil in the same sauté pan over medium-high heat. Add the onions and sauté until lightly caramelized, 5–7 minutes. Return the mushrooms to the sauté pan and season with 1 teaspoon salt and ½ teaspoon of pepper, or to taste. Reserve warm until needed.

3. Divide the sausage into 8 equal portions and shape into patties about the size of a bagel. Sauté them in batches over medium-high heat until golden brown and cooked thoroughly, 3–5 minutes on each side. Drain on paper toweling and reserve warm until needed.

4. Whisk eggs in a bowl and season with salt and pepper. Heat 2 tablespoons butter or oil in a large sauté pan over medium-high heat until almost smoking. Add the eggs to the pan and stir until they are soft and creamy, 1½ minutes for soft scrambled or 2 minutes for hard scrambled eggs. Remove the eggs from the heat when fully cooked but still moist.

5. Press the eggs into a thin layer in the sauté pan and sprinkle the cheese over the eggs.

6. For each sandwich, place 1 sausage patty on a toasted bagel. Top with the eggs and the onion-mushroom mixture. Place the top of the bagel on the onion mixture and serve hot.

Rolled Omelet

*T*RY THE mushroom and Brie filling we've included in our savory turnover recipe on page 104 as a filling for your omelet. Other filling options include grated cheese, sautéed spinach, roasted peppers, feta cheese, or jelly.

24 large eggs

½ cup whole milk, divided use

2 teaspoons salt, divided use

1 teaspoon pepper, divided use

½ cup clarified butter or canola oil

1. For each portion, whisk 3 eggs and 1 tablespoon of milk together and season with about ¼ teaspoon salt and ⅛ teaspoon pepper.

2. Heat a nonstick omelet pan over medium-high heat and heat the butter or oil until almost smoking, tilting the pan to coat the entire surface of the pan.

3. Pour the egg mixture into the pan and scramble it with a heatproof rubber spatula or a wooden spoon. Move the pan and utensil at the same time until the egg mixture has coagulated slightly, about 15–20 seconds. Smooth out the eggs into an even layer by spreading with a wooden spoon or shaking the pan. Let the egg mixture nearly finish cooking without stirring, 45 seconds to 1 minute. Tilt the pan and slide the spatula around the lip of the pan under the omelet to be sure it is not sticking. Slide the omelet to the front of the pan and use a fork or a wooden spoon to fold it inside to the center.

4. Turn the pan upside down, rolling the omelet onto the plate. The finished omelet should be oval shaped.

NOTE: *To make an American-style omelet, simply fold the eggs in half once they have finished cooking and slide the omelet onto a plate.*

1. Keep the eggs in motion until soft curds begin to form. 2. Add the garnish to the omelet, as desired. If you are using cheese, spread it around the eggs in an even layer to give it a chance to melt. Other garnishes, like ham or mushrooms, should be placed in the center of the omelet in a line.

Making Rolled Omelets

Rolled omelets, also known as French-style omelets, are a classic test of an aspiring chef's skills. They require perfectly fresh and flavorful ingredients, the right equipment, and a deft touch.

START TO COOK THE EGGS

Cook the eggs as you would to prepare Scrambled Eggs (page 146), but instead of continuing to cook the eggs until they are done, stop when they look like very soft, moist curds. Use the back of a fork or a heatproof spatula to lightly press the eggs into an even layer.

ADD THE FILLING

If you are adding a filling, add it now in an even layer down the center of the omelet. Continue to cook without stirring for another minute or two to set the omelet.

ROLLING THE OMELET

Place one edge of the omelet pan on a work surface next to a serving plate and lift up the handle so that gravity can help roll your omelet. Using a rubber spatula or wooden spoon, lift the highest side of the omelet free of the pan and fold it over toward the center. Keep rolling the omelet over on itself until it is nearly out of the pan.

Tilt the pan over the plate and push or roll the omelet out of the pan and onto a plate. Alternatively, simply fold the omelet in half to make a half-moon and slide it onto the plate. Rub or brush the top of the warm omelet with a pat of butter to give it an attractive sheen.

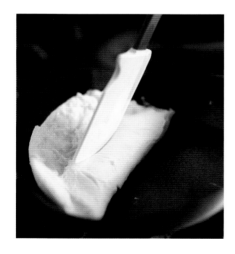

3. Use a spatula to gently lift one side of the omelet and fold it toward the center of the pan. If you are using a garnish, fold over enough egg to enclose the garnish. 4. Use the pan to help roll the omelet onto the plate.

Frittata

MAKES 8 SERVINGS

A FRITTATA IS an Italian-style flat omelet. You can substitute cooked pasta for the potatoes if you have some on hand.

12 ounces lean bacon, diced

2 cups minced onions

2 cups diced and cooked Yukon Gold potatoes

16 large eggs

½ teaspoon salt

¼ teaspoon freshly ground black pepper

1. Preheat the broiler.

2. Cook the bacon in a large skillet over medium heat until crisp, 10–15 minutes. Pour off any excess fat, leaving about 1 tablespoon in the skillet. Add the onions and sauté them for 1 minute. Add the potatoes and continue to sauté them until they are lightly brown, 12–15 minutes.

3. Beat the eggs and season with the salt and pepper. Pour the egg mixture over the onion-potato mixture in the skillet and stir gently to combine.

4. Reduce the heat to low, cover the skillet, and cook until the eggs are nearly set, about 5 minutes.

5. Remove the cover and place the skillet under a broiler to brown the eggs lightly, 1–2 minutes. Cut the frittata into wedges and serve immediately.

Tortilla Española *(Spanish-style Potato Omelet)*

MAKES 8 SERVINGS

THE SPANISH *tortilla* indicates a flat cake, not the Mexican flour or corn tortillas used to make tacos, burritos, or enchiladas. This version of a tortilla is quite similar to a frittata. At a tapas bar, the tortilla would be cut into pieces and pierced with a wooden toothpick to offer as hors d'oeuvres.

¼ cup olive oil, divided use

1½ cups minced onions

¾ cup small-diced green bell peppers

2 cups medium-diced Idaho potatoes

1½ teaspoons salt

16 large eggs

2 tablespoons chopped cilantro

1. In a large nonstick pan, heat 2 tablespoons of the olive oil. Add the onions and bell peppers and cook over medium heat until translucent, 3–5 minutes. Stir in the potatoes and mix well. Add salt and cover. Cook over low heat until the potatoes are tender, 12–15 minutes. Stir the ingredients every 3–4 minutes to prevent sticking. Once the potato mixture is cooked, remove it from the heat and cool for 5 minutes.

2. In a large bowl, whisk the eggs with the cilantro. Add the vegetable mixture and stir until combined.

3. Add the remaining oil to the pan and heat until smoking. Add the egg mixture to the pan, lower the heat, and cook without stirring until the eggs begin to set. When the omelet starts to turn golden brown on the bottom, turn the omelet over. Cook until the second side develops the same color. If necessary, divide the oil and egg mixture between two pans.

4. Serve very hot, warm, or at room temperature.

Eggs en Cocotte

MAKES 8 SERVINGS

ADD GARNISHES to the bottom of the ramekin (about 2 tablespoons per ramekin) before putting in the eggs. Be sure the garnish is hot before you add it. Some options include stewed or braised beans or lentils, diced ham, or the sautéed mushrooms served with the steak on page 196.

¼ cup butter, room temperature

16 large eggs

1 teaspoon salt, or to taste

½ teaspoon freshly ground pepper, or to taste

1. Preheat the oven to 350°F. Bring a kettle or pot of water to a boil.

2. Butter the inside of eight 4-ounce ceramic soufflé dishes or ramekins and set them in a large baking pan. Break 2 eggs into each ramekin, season with salt and pepper, and top with ½ teaspoon butter.

3. Place the pan in the oven and add about ½-inch of boiling water to the pan. Cover loosely with aluminum foil. Cook until the egg whites are opaque and firm and the yolks are set, about 20 minutes. Serve in the ramekins.

Poached Eggs

MAKES 8 SERVINGS

USE THE freshest eggs possible for poaching, as they will have a more centered yolk and more compact white and a cleaner edge. Use enough water to permit the egg to cook in the classic teardrop shape.

3 quarts water, or as needed

2 teaspoons salt

4 teaspoons distilled white vinegar

16 large eggs

1. Combine the water, salt, and vinegar in a deep pan and bring to a bare simmer.

2. Break each egg into a clean cup, reserving any with broken yolks for another use.

3. Carefully slide each egg into the poaching water. Cook for about 3 minutes or until the whites are set and opaque.

4. Remove the eggs from the water with a slotted spoon, blot them on absorbent toweling, and trim the edges if desired. The eggs are ready to serve now, or they may be properly chilled and held for later service.

5. Serve the hot eggs at once on heated plates. *See photo on page 154.*

Making Poached Eggs

Eggs should be poached in about 3 inches of water. Adding salt and a small amount of vinegar to the water prevents the whites from spreading too much and helps the egg proteins set faster.

HEAT THE POACHING LIQUID

Bring the seasoned water to a gentle simmer, about 160° to 170°F. The water should appear effervescent, with tiny bubbles collecting on the sides of the pan and breaking evenly over the surface. Adjust the heat to prevent a boil, as larger bubbles would break the egg.

CRACK THE EGGS

Crack the egg first into a small cup or bowl and then gently slide the egg into the poaching liquid. As the egg drops to the bottom of the pot, the whites will set in a teardrop shape around the yolk. Work in small batches without crowding. Too many eggs will cause the temperature of the water to drop, extend the cooking time, and make the eggs more difficult to handle.

DRAIN THE EGGS

After 3 to 4 minutes, lift the eggs out with a slotted spoon and drain on a clean towel to remove excess water. The whites should be set and opaque, while the yolks should be done to your liking. Trim away ragged edges on the egg whites with a paring knife or kitchen shears to form a compact oval shape.

MAKING POACHED EGGS IN ADVANCE

If you are preparing eggs in advance, transfer them to a bowl filled with cold or ice water. Once they are chilled, lift them from the water, blot dry, and store in the refrigerator in a tightly covered container. To reheat the eggs, lower them into gently simmering water for 1 minute.

Eggs Benedict

ALTHOUGH THIS is one of the most complex egg recipes we offer, you can simplify things by poaching your eggs in advance, making the hollandaise sauce ahead of time and keeping it warm over simmering water, and toasting the muffins under the broiler. Serving eggs Benedict on your own freshly made English muffins makes a wonderful difference, but they are still great served on store-bought English muffins.

16 slices Canadian bacon

16 Poached Eggs (page 153)

8 English Muffins (page 81), split, toasted, and buttered

2 cups Hollandaise Sauce (recipe follows), warm

1. Heat a sauté pan over medium-low heat. Add the Canadian bacon, working in batches, and sauté on both sides until heated through, about 1–2 minutes on each side.

2. If the eggs have been poached in advance, reheat them in simmering water until warmed through. Blot them on toweling and shape if necessary. Top each English muffin half with a Canadian bacon slice and a poached egg. Spoon 2 tablespoons warm hollandaise over each egg.

3. Serve immediately.

Hollandaise Sauce

YOU CAN use either fresh or pasteurized eggs to make this classic sauce. If you need to make the sauce ahead of time, try holding it in a thermos.

½ teaspoon cracked peppercorns

¼ cup white-wine or cider vinegar

¼ cup water, or as needed

4 large egg yolks, fresh or pasteurized

1½ cups melted or clarified butter, warm

2 teaspoons lemon juice, or as needed

2 teaspoons salt, or as needed

Pinch ground white pepper

Pinch cayenne (optional)

1. Combine the peppercorns and the vinegar in a small pan and reduce over medium heat until nearly dry, about 5 minutes. Add the water to the vinegar reduction. Strain this liquid into a stainless-steel bowl.

2. Add the egg yolks to the reduction and set the bowl over a pot of simmering water. Whisking constantly, cook the mixture until the yolks triple in volume and fall in ribbons from the whisk. Remove the bowl from the simmering water and set it on a clean kitchen towel to keep the bowl stationary.

3. Gradually ladle the warm butter into the egg mixture, whisking constantly. As the butter is blended into the yolks, the sauce will thicken. If it becomes too thick and the butter is not blending in easily, add a little water or lemon juice to thin the egg mixture enough to whisk in the remaining butter. Season the hollandaise with lemon juice, salt, pepper, and cayenne if desired.

4. The sauce is ready to serve at this point, or it may be finished as desired. The sauce should be held warm over a hot water bath or it can be held sealed in a thermos.

Orange & Cherry Bread-and-Butter Pudding

THIS RECIPE is a great way to use up any leftover challah or brioche you might have.

2 tablespoons butter, softened

½ cup dried cherries

½ cup rum, or as needed

11 slices Challah or Brioche Loaf (pages 88–89), about 1 inch thick

¼ cup butter, melted

4½ cups milk

1 cup sugar, divided use

6 large eggs, beaten

3 large egg yolks, beaten

3 teaspoons vanilla extract

2 tablespoons orange zest

1 teaspoon ground cinnamon

½ teaspoon salt

1. Preheat the oven to 350°F. Generously brush a large, shallow baking dish with softened butter.

2. Place the cherries in a bowl and add enough rum just to moisten. Cut the bread into 1-inch cubes. Arrange the bread cubes in a single layer on a baking sheet, drizzle with the melted butter, and toast in the oven, stirring once or twice, until golden brown, 8–10 minutes.

3. To make the custard, bring the milk and half of the sugar to a boil in a medium saucepan. Whisk together the eggs, egg yolks, vanilla, and remaining half of the sugar in a medium bowl. Gradually add about one-third of the hot milk mixture to the eggs, stirring constantly with a wooden spoon. Add the egg mixture to the remaining hot milk. Reduce the heat to low and simmer, stirring constantly, until the custard coats the back of the spoon. Remove from the heat and strain the custard through a fine-mesh sieve. Chill the custard in an ice bath until cooled, at least 1 hour.

4. Stir the orange zest, cinnamon, and salt into the cooled custard. Drain the cherries and add them to the custard along with the toasted bread cubes. Let this mixture set until the bread cubes have soaked up the custard and softened.

5. Ladle the custard mixture into the prepared baking dish. Bake in a water bath for 65–70 minutes. Remove the dish from the water bath, wipe down the sides and bottoms of the baking dish, and place on a cooling rack for at least 1 hour. Serve warm or refrigerate until fully cooled before serving.

Quiche Lorraine

*T*HIS SIMPLE quiche is rich and delicious. To create your own quiche, try other cheeses or even a blend of cheeses. Replace the bacon with diced ham or prosciutto, or try adding some sautéed domestic or exotic mushrooms.

1 tablespoon butter

1 cup minced onion

3 large eggs

1½ cups heavy cream

½ teaspoon salt

¼ teaspoon freshly ground black pepper

¾ cup grated Gruyère cheese

8 slices bacon, cooked and crumbled

One 9-inch Pie Crust (recipe follows), prebaked

1. Preheat the oven to 325°F.

2. Heat the butter in a sauté pan over medium heat. Add the onion and sauté until golden, about 8 minutes. Remove from the pan and reserve.

3. Combine the eggs, heavy cream, salt, and pepper in a mixing bowl and whisk until evenly blended. Stir the cheese, bacon, and reserved onion into the egg mixture. Spread the egg mixture evenly over the pie crust.

4. Set the quiche pan on a baking sheet and bake until a knife blade inserted in the center comes out clean, 40–45 minutes. If the pie crust begins to overbrown, cover the edges of the crust with strips of aluminum foil or pie shields. Remove the quiche from the oven and cool on a wire rack. Let the quiche rest at least 20 minutes before cutting in pieces.

Pie Crust

*I*F THE filling for your pie crust is very moist or wet, you need the relatively sturdy crust made by the technique described in this recipe. For a flakier crust that you can use with

Working with Pie Dough

ROLLING OUT DOUGH

Working with one piece of the dough at a time, unwrap the dough and place it on a lightly floured work surface and scatter a little flour over the top. Use the least possible amount of flour to prevent the dough from sticking as you work.

Lightly flour your rolling pin. Use a back-and-forth motion to roll the dough and give the dough a quarter turn periodically to maintain a round shape.

Lift the dough periodically and dust the work surface if necessary to keep the dough from sticking. The dough should be between ⅛ and ¹⁄₁₆ inch thick, depending upon your recipe.

LINING THE PAN WITH DOUGH

Pie dough can be used to line pans of various sizes. The pie dough should remain cool to the touch while you are working with it. If it begins to get too warm, refrigerate it briefly until it firms up again.

For large crusts, roll the pastry loosely around the rolling pin to lift it to the pan. Let the pastry roll off the pin and into the pan. Smaller pieces can be carefully lifted and set into the tartlet pan. Ease the dough into the pan, making sure that the sides and the rim are evenly covered. Press the dough gently against the sides and bottom.

Trim the overhanging dough to ¼ to ½ inch for pie pans, depending upon the size of the pan. In general, the larger your pan, the more over-

fruit filling, cut the butter in only until the pieces are about the size of a lentil.

2¾ cups all-purpose flour, plus extra as needed

1 teaspoon salt

1 cup diced cold butter (or ½ cup diced cold butter and
   ½ cup diced cold shortening)

½ cup ice cold water

1. Combine the flour and salt in a bowl and stir with a fork to blend the salt evenly with the flour.

2. Cut the butter into the flour using a food processor, pastry cutter, or 2 knives until the mixture looks like coarse meal. Drizzle a few tablespoons of the cold water over the flour mixture and quickly rub the water into the flour.

3. Continue to add the water a few tablespoons at a time until the dough is evenly moist although not wet and shaggy or rough in appearance. It should just hold together when you press a handful of it into a ball.

4. Turn the dough out onto a lightly floured work surface. Gather and press the dough into a ball. Divide the dough into 2 equal pieces for 1 double-crust or 2 single-crust pies, pat them into even disks, wrap well, and let chill in the refrigerator for 20 minutes before rolling and baking.

5. To prebake a pie crust, preheat the oven to 400°F. Prick the dough evenly over the bottom and sides with the tines of a table fork. Line the dough with a piece of parchment or waxed paper and fill about half-full with pie weights, dried beans, or rice. Bake until the crust is set and dry, 12–15 minutes.

6. Remove the pan from the oven and remove the paper and pie weights. Return the crust to the oven and bake until the crust is completely dry and a light golden brown, another 5–6 minutes. Let cool to room temperature before adding a filling.

hang you should have. Tuck the dough overhang under itself and flute the edges for a raised edge, such as that for a quiche. For tartlet pans (see the recipe for Sun-Dried Tomato and Goat Cheese Tartlets, page 236), trim the dough even with the edge of the pan. Return the pastry to the refrigerator to firm up before baking blind, about 15 minutes.

STORING DOUGH TO USE LATER

To store any leftover dough, pat the dough into flat disks or blocks and put them in a zip-close bag, pressing out as much air as possible before sealing the bag. It will hold 3–4 days in the refrigerator or up to 2 months in the freezer.

Another option for freezing the dough is to roll it out and fit it into a disposable aluminum pie pan. Crimp the edges as you would normally, then freeze the dough directly in the pie pan, well wrapped. To keep the crust well covered, line it with a piece of plastic wrap or waxed paper. Set a second pie plate inside the shell, and then wrap well with plastic wrap, using freezer tape or a zip-close bag to keep the wrap from coming loose.

Caramelized Onion Quiche

MAKES ONE 9-INCH QUICHE

OOKING ONIONS until they are soft, tender, and golden brown gives them a rich, caramel color and a surprisingly sweet flavor. Keep the heat low and stir frequently so that they develop a good even color with no scorching.

2 tablespoons extra virgin olive oil

2½ cups thinly sliced yellow onions

¾ cup heavy cream

¾ cup milk

3 large eggs

½ teaspoon salt

¼ teaspoon freshly ground black pepper

1¼ cups grated provolone cheese, divided use

One 9-inch Pie Crust (page 158), prebaked

1. Preheat the oven to 350°F.

2. Heat the olive oil in a sauté pan over medium heat. Add the onions and sauté, stirring frequently, until golden and very soft (caramelized), about 15 minutes. Remove the onions from the pan with a slotted spoon and reserve.

3. Whisk together the heavy cream, milk, eggs, salt, and pepper in medium bowl. Stir the reserved caramelized onions and 1 cup of the cheese into the egg mixture. Pour the egg mixture evenly into the pie crust. Sprinkle the remaining cheese evenly over the top of the quiche.

4. Set the quiche pan on a baking sheet and bake until a knife blade inserted in the center comes out clean, 40–45 minutes. If the pie crust begins to overbrown, cover edges of the pie crust with strips of aluminum foil or pie shields. Remove the quiche from the oven and cool on a wire rack. Let the quiche rest at least 20 minutes before cutting in pieces. Serve hot, warm, or room temperature.

Spinach & Goat Cheese Quiche

MAKES ONE 9-INCH QUICHE

CLEANING SPINACH used to be a time-consuming process. However, you can easily find "triple-washed" bagged spinach in the supermarket. Even though it has been washed already, you should still rinse and spin dry your spinach. If you find bunches of fresh spinach at the market, cut away the stems and rinse the spinach in several changes of cold water until you can't feel any traces of sand or grit in the rinse water.

2 tablespoons vegetable oil

½ cup minced onion

4 cups spinach leaves, blanched, squeezed dry, and chopped

½ teaspoon salt, divided use

¼ teaspoon freshly ground black pepper, divided use

¾ cup heavy cream

2 large eggs

⅓ cup fresh goat cheese, crumbled

¼ cup grated Parmesan cheese

2 tablespoons chopped sun-dried tomatoes (about 4)

One 9-inch Pie Crust (page 158), prebaked

1. Preheat the oven to 350°F.

2. Heat the oil in a large skillet over medium heat. Add the onion and sauté, stirring frequently, until translucent, 3–4 minutes. Add the spinach and sauté until very hot, about 4 minutes. Remove from the heat. Season with ¼ teaspoon of the salt and a pinch of the pepper.

3. Transfer to a colander and let the spinach drain and cool while preparing the custard.

4. Whisk together the cream and eggs. Stir in the goat cheese, Parmesan, sun-dried tomatoes, and reserved spinach. Season with the remaining salt and pepper. Spread the egg-spinach mixture evenly over the pie crust.

5. Set the quiche pan on a baking sheet and bake until a knife blade inserted in the center comes out clean, 40–45 minutes. If the pie crust begins to over brown, cover the edges of the pie crust with strips of aluminum foil or pie shields. Remove the quiche from the oven and cool on a wire rack. Let the quiche rest at least 20 minutes before cutting in pieces. Serve hot, warm, or room temperature.

Hard-Boiled Eggs

MAKES 8 SERVINGS

THE BEST way to prevent a green ring around the yolk is to avoid overcooking and to cool and peel the eggs as soon as possible.

3 quarts cold water, or as needed

16 large eggs

1. Fill a deep pot with enough water to hold the eggs comfortably. Lower the eggs gently into the pot so they don't crack.

Bring the water to a simmer and immediately pull the pot from the heat. Cover the pot and let the eggs finish cooking in the hot water for 20 minutes.

2. Place them under cold running water until they are cool enough to handle. Gently press down and roll the egg over a countertop to crack the shell before peeling. Peel the shell and membrane away with your fingers.

Deviled Eggs

MAKE 8 SERVINGS

PUSHING THE yolks through a wire mesh sieve gives the blended yolks a very smooth consistency, perfect for putting through a pastry bag. But you can always simply mash them with a table fork and spoon them into the hollows of the whites.

16 Hard-Boiled Eggs (page 162)

½ cup mayonnaise

2 teaspoons prepared mustard

½ teaspoon salt

½ teaspoon freshly ground black pepper

1. Slice the eggs in half lengthwise, carefully scoop out the yolks and place yolks in a medium-mesh sieve. Reserve the whites separately.

2. Press the yolks through the sieve with the back of a spoon into a medium bowl. Add the mayonnaise, mustard, salt, and pepper and mix well to combine.

3. Fill a pastry bag fitted with a plain pastry tip with the yolk mixture. Pipe the yolk mixture into the empty cavity of each egg white. Serve immediately or store refrigerated in an airtight container for up to 2 hours.

Deviled Egg Variations

There are numerous ways to change the flavor and color of your deviled eggs. Stir the garnishes we've suggested below into the yolks along with the mayonnaise, as directed in the recipe for Deviled Eggs. If the garnishes are too large to fit through the tip of your pastry bag, use a spoon to fill the whites.

TOMATO, GARLIC, AND BASIL DEVILED EGGS

Sauté the following ingredients in a tablespoon of olive oil until very hot and tender. Most of the liquid should cook away from the tomato. Let the mixture cool before adding it to the yolks and other ingredients.

3 garlic cloves, minced

2 plum tomatoes, peeled, seeded, and minced

5 large basil leaves, minced

DEVILED EGGS WITH SPINACH

Add ½ cup blanched minced spinach to the yolk mixture. If you wish, you can use thawed and squeezed, chopped frozen spinach.

PARMESAN DEVILED EGGS

Add 2 tablespoons grated Parmesan cheese to the yolk mixture.

Egg Salad

MAKES 8 SERVINGS

SERVE THIS egg salad in lettuce cups or on pumpernickel bread. If you have an egg slicer, you can use it to quickly chop hard-boiled eggs.

16 Hard-Boiled Eggs (page 162), chopped

1 cup mayonnaise, or as needed

¾ cup chopped celery

¼ cup thinly sliced scallions

1 teaspoon salt

¼ teaspoon ground black pepper

Combine the eggs, mayonnaise, celery, and scallions. Add salt and pepper to taste and mix well. Add more mayonnaise if necessary for a smooth, light texture.

Scotch Eggs

MAKES 8 SERVINGS

SCOTCH EGGS are often fried instead of baked, as we do here. If you want to make them on the stovetop, add about 2 inches of oil to a deep-sided skillet or Dutch oven and heat it until a pinch of breadcrumbs sizzle and crackle. If you decide to fry your Scotch eggs, don't omit the breadcrumbs. Add the eggs to about 1 inch of hot oil and fry, turning to brown evenly, until the coating is golden brown and crunchy and the sausage is completely cooked.

8 Hard-Boiled Eggs (page 162)

1 pound Breakfast Sausage (page 211)

All-purpose flour for dusting, as needed

1 cup plain breadcrumbs, optional

1. Preheat the oven to 375°F.
2. Peel the eggs, blot dry on paper toweling, and dust lightly with flour.
3. Divide the sausage into 8 equal portions. Press a portion of sausage evenly around each egg. Roll in breadcrumbs if desired.
4. Place the sausage-covered eggs on a rack in a baking dish and bake until the sausage is thoroughly cooked and the exterior is nicely browned, 12–15 minutes.
5. Cut the eggs into halves or quarters and serve very hot.

Breakfast Burrito

MAKES 8 SERVINGS

BURRITOS MAKE a great walk-away breakfast. You can change the fillings to use up any tasty leftovers you might have on hand, such as very thinly sliced grilled steak or chicken, cooked corn kernels, or roasted peppers. Try whole beans instead of refried beans or diced fresh tomatoes instead of the salsa. As long as you can wrap your tortilla around it, you're good to go!

3 cups water

½ teaspoon salt

1½ cups medium-grain rice

2 teaspoons canola oil

¾ pound Mexican Chorizo (page 211)

16 large eggs, beaten

Eight 10-inch flour tortillas

4 cups Refried Beans (page 189)

8 green onions, sliced thinly on the bias

1½ cups grated cheddar cheese

1 cup Salsa Fresca (page 145)

1 cup sour cream

1. Bring the water and salt to a boil in a medium saucepan and add the rice. Bring to a simmer, cover, and reduce the heat to medium-low. Cook until the rice is tender, about 16–18 minutes.
2. Heat the oil in a sauté pan over medium-high heat. Add the chorizo and sauté until cooked, about 4 minutes. Reduce the heat to medium and add the eggs. Cook until scrambled, stirring frequently, about 3 minutes.
3. Preheat a griddle and warm the flour tortillas. Spread ½ cup of the refried beans on each tortilla. Top with ¾ cup scrambled egg and ½ cup rice. Sprinkle with 1 tablespoon green onion and 1 tablespoon cheese. Garnish with 2 tablespoons salsa and 2 tablespoons sour cream. Fold the sides in about 1 inch, then roll up the burrito to completely enclose the filling.

Chorizo & Egg Breakfast Pizza

MAKES 8 SERVINGS

BAKING STONES or tiles give pizzas a wonderfully textured crust. Chefs use a "peel," essentially a large, flat wooden paddle used to "shovel" the pizza into the oven. Scatter the peel with some cornmeal so the pizza won't stick to it. Some baking sheets have edges on only 2 or 3 sides. These sheets can be used as a peel if you want to bake the pizza on tiles or a baking stone. Use a quick, jerking motion and a flick of the wrist to slide the pizza from the peel or pan onto the tiles.

1 pound Semolina Pizza Dough (recipe follows)

½ pound Mexican Chorizo (page 211)

½ cup cooked or canned black beans, rinsed and drained

1 red bell pepper, roasted, peeled, seeded, and cut into strips

3 tablespoons chopped cilantro

½ teaspoon salt, or as needed

¼ teaspoon freshly ground black pepper, or as needed

4 large eggs

1 cup shredded Manchego cheese or sharp cheddar

1. Preheat the oven to 425°F. Spray a jelly roll pan or a round pizza pan with cooking spray or scatter it lightly with cornmeal.

2. Stretch or roll the pizza dough to fit the jelly roll or pizza pan. Let it rest at room temperature while preparing the toppings for the pizza.

3. In a large sauté pan over medium heat, sauté the chorizo, stirring frequently, until cooked, about 5 minutes. Remove the chorizo from the pan with a slotted spoon and drain on paper toweling. Sprinkle the chorizo over the pizza, followed by the black beans, red pepper, and cilantro. Season with salt and pepper.

4. In a small bowl mix the eggs together with a fork and pour evenly over the pizza, being careful not to pour the eggs too near the edges. Top with the cheese. Bake the pizza until the edges are golden and the eggs are fully cooked, 15–18 minutes. Cut into squares or wedges and serve hot or warm.

Semolina Pizza Dough

MAKES TWO 12-INCH PIZZAS OR
1 LARGE RECTANGULAR PIZZA

ADDING A bit of semolina to the pizza dough makes a crust that has a great crisp texture and a wonderful flavor. If time is running short, however, try picking up a ball of dough at your favorite pizza parlor.

3½ cups bread flour

½ cup semolina or durum flour

1½ tsp active dry yeast

1½ cups water

3 Tbsp olive oil

2 tsp salt

1. Combine the flours and yeast. Add the water, olive oil, and salt; mix on low speed for 2 minutes and on medium speed until the dough has good gluten development, but is still a little sticky, another 4 minutes.

2. Transfer the dough to a clean bowl, rub the surface with oil, cover with plastic wrap or damp towels, and let rise until nearly doubled, about 30 minutes. Fold the dough gently and allow it to relax another 30 minutes before cutting it into pieces.

3. Rest the dough, covered, until relaxed, 15–20 minutes. Scatter a thin layer of cornmeal on a baking sheet.

4. To shape pizza dough, press the dough into a disk, stretching and turning the dough as you work. *(recipe continues on page 166)*

You may finish stretching the dough by flipping it: With the dough resting on the backs of your hands, simultaneously spin the dough and toss it into the air. As it falls back down, catch it on the backs of your hands once more. Continue until the crust is evenly thick, about ⅛ to ¼ inch. If you prefer, you can pull and stretch the dough directly on a lightly floured work surface until it is an even thickness.

5. Transfer the pizza to a prepared baking sheet. Top the dough as directed, leaving the outer rim or the crust ungarnished.

Soft-Boiled Eggs

MAKES 8 SERVINGS

EGG CUPS are perfect for serving soft-boiled eggs. Have plenty of hot buttered toast on hand for dipping into the creamy yolks. Egg scissors cut through the shell, but you can use a spoon to crack the shell and lift it away from the top fourth of the egg and then scoop out the cooked egg.

3 quarts cold water, or as needed

16 large eggs

1. Fill a deep pot with enough water to hold the eggs comfortably. Bring the water to a simmer. Lower the eggs gently into the pot so they don't crack. After the water returns to a simmer, cook the eggs for 3 minutes.

2. Serve very hot, still in the shell.

Chapter Seven

GRAINS
& LEGUMES

*G*RAINS AND LEGUMES are simple and sustaining foods. Preparing them with care and attention is an excellent way to get back to basics in the kitchen. Both grains and legumes carry other flavors well, making them perfect candidates to pair with small amounts of intensely flavored foods, just as we do when we top nutty buckwheat kasha with toasted and caramelized pecans. This chapter introduces techniques and recipes for making familiar hot breakfast cereals like steel-cut oats and grits and our versions of popular cold cereal dishes: granola and muesli. To add variety to your brunch menu, try one of the great salads, like Mixed Bean Salad (page 187) or Warm Black-eyed Pea Salad (page 191).

Selecting and Preparing Grains

Nutritionists and chefs alike have been exploring and heralding the importance of grains in any meal. The grains that have the greatest "staying" power and that have the most intriguing flavors and textures are whole or minimally processed grains. You no longer have to seek out specialty stores in order to stock your pantry with exciting and flavorful grains like quinoa or steel-cut oats. Many of our recipes can be prepared with other grains as well. For instance, try substituting pearl or Scotch barley, oat groats, rye or wheat berries, cracked wheat, colored rices (black, brown, or red), teff, or Job's tears in the pilaf recipe on page 182.

When purchasing grains keep in mind that grains have a long but not unlimited shelf life. Grains that are older take longer to cook and require more liquid as they cook. Their flavors may turn musty or stale. Whole grains with the bran and germ intact may become rancid if they aren't properly stored since their natural oils are likely to oxidize if they become too warm or if they are exposed to air for too long. Use the following simple guidelines to keep your whole, cracked grains, cereals, and meals fresh and flavorful:

- *Look for stores with a good turnover of inventory especially if you prefer to purchase in small quantities from bulk bins.*

- *Keep whole grains in the refrigerator or freezer if you won't be using them within a few weeks of purchase.*

Most grains cook in less than 30 minutes. Some, notably bulgur, cook in 10 minutes or less. Other whole grains like groats or berries may take significantly longer and benefit from soaking prior to cooking.

To cook whole grains by the simmering method, you should bring the recommended amount of liquid and a bit of salt to a boil, then stir in the grain. Stir well to separate the grains and continue to stir from time to time while the grain cooks.

Keep the heat relatively low to avoid scorching the grain. If necessary, add a bit more liquid if the grain looks too dry before it is fully cooked. Properly cooked grains are tender to the bite.

Amaranth To cook 1 cup of grain, you will need 1 cup cooking liquid. Simmer for 12–17 minutes. This makes 1½ cups of cooked grain. Add salt after cooking rather than during. Optional: Toast amaranth until it begins to pop or crackle before adding the cooking liquid.

Buckwheat groats (kasha) To cook 1 cup of grain, you will need 1½ to 2 cups cooking liquid. Simmer for 12–20 minutes. This makes 2 cups of cooked kasha.

Farro To cook 1 cup of grain, you will need 2 cups of cooking liquid. Simmer for 20–25 minutes. This makes 2½ cups of cooked farro.

Job's tears To cook 1 cup of grain, you will need 2 cups cooking liquid. Simmer for 1 hour. This makes 3 cups of cooked Job's tears. Optional: Toast Job's tears until they begin to pop or crackle before adding the liquid and cooking.

Kamut Soak whole kamut overnight in cold water and drain before cooking; use the soaking water as cooking liquid. To cook 1 cup of grain, you will need 1½ cups cooking liquid. Simmer for 1 hour. This makes 2 cups of cooked kamut. Optional: Toast whole kamut until it begins to pop or crackle before adding the liquid and cooking.

Millet To cook 1 cup of grain, you will need 2 cups of cooking liquid. Simmer for 30–35 minutes. This makes 3 cups of cooked millet.

Quinoa To cook 1 cup of grain, you will need 1½ to 2 cups cooking liquid. Simmer for 10 to 12 minutes. This makes 3½ to 4 cups of cooked quinoa. To prepare quinoa for cooking, place it in a bowl and cover with cold water. Rub the grain between your palms for several seconds. Drain the water and repeat until the water is nearly clear.

Spelt Soak spelt overnight in cold water and drain before cooking; use the soaking water as cooking liquid. To cook 1 cup of grain, you will need 1½ cups cooking liquid. Simmer for 45 minutes. This makes 2 cups of cooked spelt.

Teff To cook 1 cup of grain, you will need 1 cup cooking liquid. Simmer for 7 minutes. This makes 1½ cups of cooked grain.

Triticale Soak triticale overnight in cold water and drain before cooking; use the soaking water as cooking liquid. Add salt after cooking rather than during. To cook 1 cup of grain, you will need 3 cups cooking liquid. Simmer for 75 minutes. This makes 2½ cups of cooked triticale.

Wild rice To cook 1 cup of wild rice, you will need 3 cups cooking liquid. Simmer for 30–45 minutes. This makes 4 cups of cooked wild rice.

PREPARING CEREALS AND MEALS

Oatmeal, polenta, grits, and farina are prepared by simmering and stirring cereal grains and meals in water, broth, or milk. Bring the liquid up to a full boil first, along with any desired seasonings or aromatics. Use one hand to add the measured cereal a little at a time or pour it slowly and gradually into the simmering liquid. Whisk or stir constantly with the other hand as you add the cereal, to keep it from clumping together.

Once you have added all the cereal, continue to cook over medium to low heat, stirring often. The more you stir, the creamier the finished dish will be.

The cereal thickens while it cooks and craterlike bubbles break the surface. When they are fully cooked, some cereals start to pull away from the sides of the pot as you stir. Serve soft and smooth directly from the pot.

Garlic Cheese Grits

MAKES 8 SERVINGS

THESE GRITS get a great garlic flavor from just a little bit of garlic, and they are jam-packed with cheese and butter, just the way they should be. The Tabasco and the cayenne give them a little kick. You may opt to leave out the eggs and milk for soft grits that don't have to be baked. Just stir the remaining cheese and seasonings into the hot grits right before serving.

2 teaspoons salt, divided use

1 quart water

1 cup regular grits

¾ cup butter

2½ cups grated sharp cheddar cheese, divided use

1 cup milk

2 large eggs

1½ cloves garlic, minced

½ teaspoon Worcestershire sauce

¼ teaspoon Tabasco sauce

⅛ teaspoon cayenne pepper

¼ teaspoon freshly ground black pepper, or to taste

1. Preheat the oven to 350°F. Butter a shallow baking dish.

2. Add 1½ teaspoons salt to the water and bring to a rolling boil. Stir the grits into the water and simmer until thick, 10–12 minutes. Remove from the heat and stir in butter and 1½ cups cheese until melted and thoroughly combined.

3. Whisk together the milk, eggs, garlic, Worcestershire, Tabasco, and cayenne in a mixing bowl. Stir the egg mixture into grits until well combined. Add the remaining ½ teaspoon salt and the black pepper.

4. Pour the grits into the buttered dish. Bake until firm, about 1 hour. Top with remaining grated cheese and place under the broiler until the cheese has melted and browned slightly, about 3 minutes. Serve the grits very hot on heated plates.

LEFT TO RIGHT *Pour the grits into the simmering water while stirring constantly; the mixture should be fairly thin and free of clumps. Cook the mixture until it thickens and the grits have absorbed the liquid; the grits will need to be stirred more frequently as they cook so that they don't stick to the bottom of the pan. Stir in the butter and cheese to provide a smooth and creamy base for the custard mixture. The finished grits should be rich and velvety. They are shown here with Poached Eggs (page 153) and Breakfast Sausage (page 211).*

Polenta *with Mushroom Ragout*

MAKES 8 SERVINGS

*I*F YOUR store doesn't stock something that is labeled polenta, simply choose a coarse-grain yellow cornmeal for this dish. If you can find cornmeal that has been stone-ground, it will add a wonderful flavor to the dish.

1 quart vegetable broth or water

1½ teaspoons salt, or as needed

1 cup polenta

¼ teaspoon freshly ground black pepper, or as needed

4 cups Mushroom Ragout (recipe follows)

1. Preheat the oven to 350°F. Butter a shallow baking dish.

2. Combine the water and salt in a large saucepan and bring to a rolling boil. Slowly pour the polenta into the water, stirring constantly with a wooden spoon. Reduce the heat and simmer, stirring constantly, until thick, 10–12 minutes. Remove from the heat and stir in additional salt and the pepper to taste.

3. Serve the polenta very hot in a heated serving bowl or individual pasta plates. Top each serving with ½ cup of the mushroom ragout.

Mushroom Ragout

MAKES 4 CUPS

*U*SE THIS ragout as a topping for polenta, a filling for an omelet (page 148), or for eggs en cocotte (page 152). You can also use it as a bed for poached eggs (page 153) or use as a savory filling for crêpes (page 124) or turnovers (page 104). When you find a good buy on mushrooms, make a double or triple batch. It will last up to 2 months in your freezer. Add a bit more fresh herbs and season it well once you reheat it for a great fresh flavor with relatively little fuss.

3 tablespoons olive oil

1½ cups small-diced onion

1 tablespoon minced garlic

¼ cup minced jalapeño

Two 10-ounce packages white mushrooms, sliced

2½ cups small-diced plum tomatoes

⅓ cup heavy cream

¾ cup chopped cilantro

¾ teaspoon salt, or to taste

½ teaspoon ground black pepper, or to taste

1. Heat the olive oil in a large sauté pan over medium-high heat. Add the onion and sauté, stirring frequently, until they are tender and translucent, about 3 minutes. Add the garlic and continue to sauté until the garlic is very fragrant, another minute.

2. Add the jalapeños and sauté until they are translucent, about 2 minutes. Increase the heat to high and add the sliced mushrooms. Stir to coat evenly with the olive oil and sauté until tender, 6–8 minutes.

3. Add the tomatoes and cook over medium heat until the tomatoes are very hot, about 2 minutes. Add the heavy cream and simmer until the ragout is slightly thickened and very flavorful, 4–5 minutes. Stir in the cilantro and add salt and pepper to taste.

4. The ragout is ready to serve now, or it can be cooled and stored in the refrigerator for up to 3 days. Reheat the ragout over low heat or in the microwave before serving and adjust the seasoning with additional salt and pepper if necessary.

Steel-Cut Oats

S TEEL-CUT OATS are sometimes labeled as Scotch or Irish oatmeal. They have a great texture and a nutty flavor. Keep the cooking speed low and stir often for a creamy consistency.

1½ quarts water or milk

1 ¾ cups steel-cut oats

⅔ cup dried fruits (such as cherries, blueberries, currants, cranberries, apricots, dates, figs, raisins, prunes, or a combination, diced if necessary)

¾ teaspoon ground cinnamon

¼ teaspoon salt

4 teaspoons honey

1. Bring the water to a boil in a large saucepan. If using milk, heat to a bare simmer over low heat. Gradually add the oats, stirring constantly. Simmer the oats over very low heat for about 20 minutes, stirring frequently.

2. Stir the dried fruits, cinnamon, and salt into the oats and continue to simmer until the oatmeal has absorbed the liquid, about 15 minutes.

3. Place 1 cup of oatmeal in a heated bowl for each serving and drizzle with ½ teaspoon honey.

Cream of Wheat *with Oranges & Pistachios*

W ORK OVER a bowl to catch any juices that come from the oranges as you cut them. The juice is a delicious extra for the cook—a real chef's bonus.

5 medium oranges

8 cups water

1½ teaspoons salt

1¾ cups cream of wheat

⅓ cup honey, or as needed

3 tablespoons butter

4 teaspoons orange zest

½ cup chopped toasted pistachio nuts

1. Cut the peel away from each orange, cutting just into the orange flesh with a sharp paring knife. Cut individual segments from the orange by slicing along both sides of the membrane that separates the segments. Reserve the orange segments.

2. Bring the water and salt to a boil in a heavy-bottomed pot. Add the cream of wheat in a slow, steady stream, stirring constantly with a wooden spoon.

3. Cook the cream of wheat, stirring constantly, about 3 minutes, or until it has thickened slightly and the grains are tender.

4. Remove the pan from the heat, stir in the honey, butter, orange zest, and half the reserved orange segments.

5. Garnish with the pistachio nuts and remaining orange segments. Serve immediately.

Kasha *with Spicy Maple Pecans*

COOKING THE kasha with an egg white before you add the broth keeps the buckwheat groats from sticking together after they are cooked.

1 cup kasha (buckwheat groats)

1 large egg white, lightly beaten

2 cups chicken broth or vegetable broth

1 tablespoon butter

½ teaspoon salt, or as needed

1 cup pecans, toasted and chopped

¼ cup maple syrup

¼ teaspoon cayenne pepper, or to taste

2 tablespoons minced or sliced chives for garnish

1. Combine the kasha and the egg white in a saucepan and cook over low heat, stirring constantly, for 2 minutes. Add the broth, butter, and salt to the kasha and bring to a boil over high heat. Reduce the heat to low and simmer covered for about 15 minutes.

2. Remove the kasha from the heat and let it steam for 5 minutes. Uncover and fluff the kasha by lifting it gently with 2 forks to remove any lumps.

3. While the kasha steams, place the pecans, maple syrup, and cayenne in a small skillet. Cook over low heat, stirring occasionally, until the pecans are well coated and the maple syrup has reduced to a very thick consistency, about 6–8 minutes.

4. Sprinkle the spiced pecans over the kasha. Serve very hot garnished with the chives.

Wild & Brown Rice with Cranberries

MAKES 6–8 SERVINGS

TRY OTHER dried fruit or a combination of dried fruits in this delicious and unusual breakfast or brunch dish. Other garnish options you might try include finely diced smoked ham or turkey. This dish is excellent with pan-fried fish or as an accompaniment to roast chicken or turkey, as shown here.

¼ cup sweetened dried cranberries

½ cup apple cider

2¾ cups chicken or vegetable broth, divided use

¼ cup minced yellow onion

½ cup wild rice

½ cup long-grain brown rice

1. Preheat the oven to 350°F.

2. Combine the cranberries with the apple cider in a microwave-safe dish. Cover and heat in a microwave oven on full power for 40 seconds. Drain the cider from the cranberries, reserving both the cider and the cranberries separately.

3. In an ovenproof saucepan, heat ¼ cup of the broth over medium heat. Add the onion and cook them for about 2 minutes, or until translucent and tender. Add the wild and brown rice, the remaining broth, and the reserved apple cider; bring to a simmer. Cover and bake until the rice has absorbed the moisture and is just tender to the bite, 45–50 minutes.

4. Fluff the rice with a fork and fold in the reserved cranberries. Serve hot.

Couscous Salad *with Curried Vegetables*

MAKES 8 SERVINGS

Couscous is not a grain; it is actually a pasta. To make a steaming setup for the couscous, put about 2 inches of water in a pot with a tight-fitting lid and bring it to a simmer. Line a colander with rinsed cheesecloth to keep the couscous from falling through the holes. Put it over the simmering water, not directly in it. Cover the pot again and steam until the couscous swells and is very tender.

1½ bunches medium asparagus, cut on the bias into 2-inch pieces

2 cups cauliflower florets

1¾ cups julienned fennel bulb

⅔ cup cooked or canned chickpeas, drained and rinsed

½ cup Curry Vinaigrette (recipe follows)

½ teaspoon salt

¼ freshly ground black pepper

1½ cups dry couscous

One 3-inch cinnamon stick

¼ cup toasted slivered almonds

3 tablespoons flat-leaf parsley leaves, whole or chiffonade

3 tablespoons dry currants, plumped in warm water

1¼ cups grape or cherry tomatoes, cut in half

½ cup Harissa (recipe follows)

1. Steam or boil the asparagus, cauliflower, and fennel separately until tender. Drain well; combine the vegetables and chickpeas with the curry vinaigrette while the vegetables are still hot. Season with salt and pepper. Cover and marinate in the refrigerator for at least 30 minutes and up to 3 days before serving.

2. Steam the couscous with the cinnamon stick until hot, fluffy, and tender, 10–12 minutes. Fluff the couscous to break up any lumps and fold in the almonds, parsley, and currants. Top with the marinated vegetables and tomatoes. Serve with the harissa sauce spooned over the vegetables or passed on the side.

Curry Vinaigrette

MAKES 2 CUPS

To give your curry vinaigrette an intense aroma, you can infuse the oil with the curry powder as follows: Combine the oil and the curry powder in a small saucepot over low heat and warm the oil until the mixture has a good aroma. The oil should not get much hotter than 160°F. Remove the oil from the heat and let the oil cool before continuing to make the vinaigrette.

6 tablespoons cider vinegar

4 teaspoons lemon juice

1 tablespoon orange juice

1 tablespoon honey

1 tablespoon minced fresh ginger

1 tablespoon finely minced lemongrass

2 teaspoons curry powder

1¼ cups canola or sunflower oil

¾ teaspoon salt, or to taste

½ teaspoon ground black pepper, or to taste

1. Whisk together the vinegar, lemon juice, orange juice, honey, ginger, lemongrass, and curry powder.

2. Whisk in the oil gradually until the vinaigrette is slightly thickened and evenly blended. Adjust the seasoning with the salt and pepper. *The recipe for Harissa follows on page 182.*

Harissa

*T*HIS SAUCE. a traditional accompaniment to couscous in Tunisia, is fiery, so use it with discretion.

5 roasted jalapeños, peeled and seeded

2 roasted red peppers, peeled and seeded

3 tablespoons hot Hungarian paprika

1½ teaspoons toasted cumin seeds

1 tablespoon minced garlic

1 teaspoon cayenne pepper

¾ cup olive oil

3 tablespoons fresh lemon juice, or to taste

½ teaspoon salt, or to taste

1. Combine the jalapeños, peppers, paprika, cumin, garlic, and cayenne in a blender. Grind to a pastelike consistency.

2. Transfer the jalapeño mixture to a bowl and slowly whisk in the oil to create a smooth sauce. Add the lemon juice and salt to taste. The harissa is ready to serve now, or it can be transferred to a clean storage container and kept in the refrigerator for up to 2 weeks.

Quinoa Pilaf *with Red & Yellow Bell Peppers*

*Q*UINOA (PRONOUNCED "KEEN-wah") is an ancient grain grown in the New World. When properly cooked, quinoa is a light, fluffy grain with a subtle flavor. Most quinoa sold in this country has already been cleansed of its saponin, the resinous, bitter coating that protects quinoa from birds. You need to rinse it thoroughly to remove any powdery residue of saponin, however.

2 teaspoons canola oil

2 tablespoons minced shallots

1 garlic clove, minced

1 cup quinoa, rinsed and drained

2 cups chicken broth

1 bay leaf

1 sprig thyme

½ teaspoon salt

¼ teaspoon freshly ground black pepper

¼ cup diced roasted red bell pepper

¼ cup diced roasted yellow bell pepper

1. Heat the oil in a heavy saucepan over medium heat. Add the shallots and garlic and cook over medium heat until translucent, about 2 minutes. Add the quinoa and sauté, stirring frequently, until coated with the oil and heated through, about 2 minutes.

2. Add the broth to the quinoa and bring to a boil. Reduce the heat to a simmer, stirring once or twice to prevent the quinoa from clumping together or sticking to the bottom of the saucepan.

3. Add the bay leaf, thyme, salt, and pepper.

4. Cover the pot and cook until the grains are tender, 10–12 minutes. Grains should have an opaque rim but not be falling apart. Remove from the heat and fold in the roasted peppers. Season with additional salt and pepper, if desired.

Rice Pudding

MAKE 8 SERVINGS

RICE PUDDING is a homey, delicious dessert, but you can also enjoy it as a breakfast or brunch dish. Serve the pudding warm instead of cold for a sustaining dish on chilly days.

3 cups milk

1½ cinnamon sticks

1 orange slice, ¼ inch thick

5 tablespoons sugar, divided use

½ cup long-grain white rice, rinsed

1 tablespoon cornstarch

2 large eggs

1 teaspoon vanilla extract

1. Combine the milk, cinnamon sticks, orange, and 2 tablespoons of the sugar in a medium saucepan and bring to a boil. Add the rice and simmer over low heat, covered, until tender, about 30 minutes.

2. Just as the rice finishes cooking, combine the cornstarch with the remaining 3 tablespoons sugar in a medium mixing bowl. Add the eggs to the cornstarch mixture, stirring with a wire whip until the mixture is completely smooth.

3. Add about one-third of the hot milk-rice mixture to the egg mixture, stirring constantly with a wooden spoon. Return the egg mixture to the remaining hot milk in the saucepan.

4. Continue cooking, stirring constantly, until the pudding comes to a boil. Remove from the heat and remove the cinnamon sticks and orange slice. Blend in the vanilla extract.

5. Pour the rice pudding into individual dishes or a single large bowl. Cover and refrigerate until fully chilled.

Muesli

MAKES 8 SERVINGS

MUESLI IS a popular Swiss-style cold cereal. It requires no cooking at all. You simply combine the oats with the milk and let the muesli soak up the liquid. Use other fresh fruits when they are in season, such as plums, apricots, or peaches. We've gilded the lily by folding in some whipped cream.

⅓ cup milk

4 teaspoons granulated sugar

4 teaspoons lemon juice, about 1 lemon

½ cup old-fashioned oats

1 cup small-diced pears

1 cup small-diced apples

¾ cup seedless grapes, halved

¾ cup sliced bananas

¼ cup heavy cream, whipped to medium peaks

½ cup chopped almonds, toasted

1. Combine the milk, sugar, and lemon juice in a medium bowl. Add the oats to the milk mixture, cover, and refrigerate for a minimum of 2 hours or overnight.

2. Combine the pears, apples, grapes, and bananas; stir into the oat mixture. Fold the whipped cream into the mixture.

3. To serve, place ½ cup of the muesli in a small bowl or glass and top with 1 tablespoon toasted almonds.

Granola Parfait

*T*HESE PARFAITS are easy to prepare. You can assemble them 3 or 4 hours ahead of time, so they're great for both busy weekdays as well as leisurely brunches. Use whatever fruit is in season. Bananas, apples, and oranges are wonderful in the winter, while this berry parfait is a perfect summertime dish.

1¼ cups blueberries

1¼ cups raspberries

1¼ cups quartered or sliced strawberries

4 cups plain yogurt

4 cups Granola (recipe follows)

1. Combine the berries in a bowl and toss together.

2. Add a layer of the berries to each parfait glass, then a layer of yogurt, followed by a layer of granola. Add a second layer of berries, followed by additional layers of granola and yogurt. Top the parfait with berries.

3. Serve at once or keep refrigerated for up to 4 hours.

Granola

*G*RANOLA IS a great cold cereal that you can make in large amounts. Feel free to double or triple this recipe. Pack the extra granola in zip-close bags or tightly sealed jars. Bring a bag along to work or school for a midmorning or late afternoon snack that's packed with flavor and fiber.

1½ cups rolled oats

¼ cup canola oil

½ cup turbinado or light brown sugar

2 teaspoons ground cinnamon

½ cup sunflower seeds

½ cup packed sweetened shredded coconut

¼ cup wheat germ

¼ cup sesame seeds

¼ cup chopped almonds

¼ cup chopped walnuts

½ cup raisins

1. Preheat the oven to 300°F.

2. Combine the oats, oil, sugar, and cinnamon. Spread the oat mixture in an even layer on a baking sheet and bake, stirring occasionally, until it is fragrant and lightly toasted, about 20 minutes.

3. Add the sunflower seeds, coconut, wheat germ, sesame seeds, almonds, and walnuts to the mixture in the pan. Stir together and spread into an even layer on the pan and bake until golden brown, about 15 minutes. Add the raisins and cool completely.

4. Store in an airtight container in a cool, dry place.

Green Lentil Salad

LTHOUGH YOU can use brown lentils for this salad, it really is worth the effort to seek out green lentils, also known as lentilles du Puy or French lentils. They hold their shape better and have a wonderful flavor. Add other vegetables to the cooked lentils. Try minced celery, minced or grated radish, or small-diced cucumber.

2 cups green lentils

1 medium onion

2 tablespoons finely minced shallots

2 whole cloves

1 small bay leaf

DRESSING

2 teaspoons Dijon mustard

2 tablespoons red wine vinegar

½ teaspoon salt, or as needed

¼ teaspoon ground black pepper, or as needed

2 tablespoons extra virgin olive oil

⅓ cup chopped flat-leaf parsley

1. Sort and rinse the lentils; drain well. Combine the lentils, onion, shallots, cloves, and bay leaf in a medium pot and add enough cold water to cover the lentils by about 2 inches.

2. Bring to a boil over medium heat. Reduce the heat to low, cover, and simmer until the lentils are tender but still intact, about 35 minutes. The lentils should absorb the cooking liquid, but if there is still some liquid, drain the lentils in a sieve. Remove and discard the onion, cloves, and bay leaf.

3. To make the dressing, combine the mustard, vinegar, salt, and pepper. To this, slowly add the oil while continuously whisking. Taste the dressing and season with additional salt and pepper, if needed. Add the dressing to the warm lentils and shallots; mix well.

4. Add freshly chopped parsley and serve warm or at room temperature. Or, store the salad covered in the refrigerator for up to 2 days; let it return to room temperature for 15–20 minutes before serving.

Selecting and Preparing Legumes

As with grains, choose dried legumes from a store with high turnover. Beans, lentils, and dried peas can be stored in plastic bags or other airtight storage containers for a few months and don't require refrigeration.

Although it is fine to substitute one bean for another in many recipes, there is a noticeable difference in taste between favas and limas, black beans and kidney beans, and navy beans and black-eyed peas. If time is short, use canned beans instead of cooking dried beans from scratch.

SORTING AND RINSING

Pour the legumes onto a baking sheet and, working methodically from one end to the other, carefully sort through them, removing discolored or misshapen pieces. Submerge the sorted beans in cold water, then remove and discard any that float to the surface. Drain the legumes and rinse them well with cold running water.

SOAKING

Some chefs believe that soaking dried beans and other legumes before cooking gives a better texture. Place the sorted and rinsed legumes in a container and add enough cool water to cover them by a few inches, about four times the volume of water to beans. Let the legumes soak

Mixed Bean Salad

MAKES 8 SERVINGS

*F*EEL FREE to make your own version by using different beans or by replacing the olive oil with walnut or almond oil, or replacing the red wine vinegar with sherry vinegar. Add about ½ cup of steamed or blanched green beans or Romano beans that you have cut into 1-inch-long pieces for more color and crunch.

¾ cup cooked or canned black beans, drained and rinsed

¾ cup cooked or canned pinto beans, drained and rinsed

¾ cup cooked or canned chickpeas, drained and rinsed

¾ cup cooked or canned cannellini beans, drained and rinsed

1 cup small-diced red onion

½ cup minced celery

3 tablespoons minced flat-leaf parsley

½ teaspoon salt

¼ teaspoon freshly ground black pepper

VINAIGRETTE

4 teaspoons red wine vinegar

1 tablespoon fresh lemon juice

⅓ cup extra virgin olive oil

2 tablespoons canola oil

1 tablespoon minced flat-leaf parsley

1 teaspoon minced chives

½ teaspoon salt

¼ teaspoon freshly ground black pepper

1. Combine the black beans, pinto beans, chickpeas, cannellini beans, red onion, celery, and parsley. Season with salt and pepper and stir to combine.

2. To make the vinaigrette, combine the vinegar and lemon juice. Gradually whisk in the oils and add the herbs, salt, and pepper.

3. Gently toss the vinaigrette with the bean mixture. Cover and marinate in the refrigerator for at least 30 minutes and up to 3 days before serving.

in the refrigerator for at least 4 hours or overnight. For a quicker soak, place the sorted legumes in a pot and add enough water to cover by a few inches. Bring the water to a simmer. Remove the pot from the heat, cover, and let steep for 1 hour.

COOKING LEGUMES

Drain the soaked legumes, put in a large pot, and add enough water to cover the beans by about 2 inches. Bring the liquid to a full boil and then reduce the heat to maintain a simmer. Stir the beans occasionally as they cook and add more liquid if the level starts to drop. Most

recipes tell you when to add various seasonings and flavorings, but the general rule is to add salt and any other acidic flavoring ingredients, such as tomatoes, vinegar, or citrus juices, only after the beans are nearly tender to preserve their smooth, creamy consistency.

Braised Lentils *with Eggplant and Mushrooms*

MAKES 8 SERVINGS

*I*F YOU have any braised lentils left over, add them to the Eggs en Cocotte (page 152) or reheat and top with a poached or fried egg for a simple and hearty breakfast dish.

1¾ cups dry brown lentils

2 quarts plus 1 cup chicken broth or water

4 teaspoons extra virgin olive oil

1¼ cups diced onions

¾ tablespoon minced garlic

2½ cups peeled and chopped eggplant

1½ cups quartered mushrooms

½ teaspoon ground cinnamon

½ teaspoon ground turmeric or curry powder

½ teaspoon lemon zest

¾ teaspoon salt

½ teaspoon freshly ground black pepper

¾ cup bread crumbs

3 tablespoons butter, melted

1. Preheat the oven to 350° F.

2. Sort the lentils and rinse well with cold water. Cook the lentils in broth or water until barely tender, about 15–20 minutes. Drain the lentils. Reserve the cooking liquid.

3. Heat the olive oil over medium heat in a saucepot. Add the onions and sauté until tender and slightly browned, about 8 minutes. Add the garlic and sauté 1 minute more, stirring frequently. Add the eggplant, stirring to coat evenly with oil. Add the mushrooms, cinnamon, turmeric, lemon zest, salt, and pepper. Cook until mushrooms begin to release their juices.

4. Add the lentils and 2 cups of the reserved cooking liquid. Lentils should be moistened but need not be covered. Add more liquid if necessary. Cover the pot, place it in the oven, and braise until the eggplant and lentils are very tender, about 15 minutes. While the lentils are braising, combine the breadcrumbs and butter and reserve.

5. Transfer the cooked lentil mixture to a baking pan and sprinkle with the breadcrumb mixture. Bake until a crust has developed and is evenly browned, another 10–15 minutes.

Refried Beans

MAKES 8 SERVINGS

*I*F YOU are short on time or if tomatoes aren't in season when you make these beans, substitute canned diced tomatoes.

2 cups dried pinto beans

2½ quarts chicken broth or water

½ cup bacon fat or lard

1½ cups minced onion

1 garlic clove, minced

1 cup diced tomato, peeled and seeded

1½ teaspoons salt

¼ teaspoon freshly ground black pepper

½ teaspoon chili powder

¼ teaspoon ground cumin

1. Soak the beans overnight in cool water.

2. Drain the soaked beans and add them to the broth or water in a heavy saucepan and bring to a boil.

3. Lower the heat to medium-low and simmer, covered, for about 1 hour or until tender. Add heated broth or water as needed to keep the beans covered. Once the beans are tender, strain them, reserving the cooking liquid.

4. Heat the bacon fat in a sauté pan over medium heat until hot but not smoking. Sauté the onions and garlic until translucent, 3–4 minutes. Add the tomatoes and cook until the tomatoes have just softened, about 2 minutes. Add the cooked beans to the vegetables and stir thoroughly, mashing the beans with the back of the spoon as you stir. If desired, leave some of the beans whole to provide additional texture.

5. Season the beans with the salt, pepper, chili powder, and cumin. If the beans are too thick they can be thinned with a little of the reserved cooking liquid.

Lima Bean Spread

MAKES 2 CUPS

*W*HEN YOU make this delicious spread, double the recipe. Use the leftover spread to make a pasta sauce by adding enough of the reserved liquid (or broth or water) to the spread and simmering until you get a light, pourable consistency. Serve over hot tricolored pasta.

2 tablespoons extra virgin olive oil, divided use

½ cup minced onion

1 garlic clove, chopped

2 cups frozen lima beans, thawed

½ cup frozen peas, thawed

½ cup vegetable broth

½ teaspoon salt

2 teaspoons coarsely chopped flat-leaf parsley

2 teaspoons lemon juice

1 teaspoon chopped rosemary

½ teaspoon freshly ground black pepper

1 tablespoon grated Parmesan cheese

Coarse sea salt for garnish

1. Heat 1 tablespoon of the olive oil in a large sauté pan over medium heat. Add the onion and garlic and sauté until translucent, 3–5 minutes. Add the beans, peas, broth, and salt. Reduce the heat to low and simmer until heated through, about 5 minutes. Drain, reserving the remaining liquid.

2. While the mixture is still warm, puree in a food processor. Slowly drizzle in remaining olive oil while pureeing. Add the parsley, lemon juice, rosemary, and black pepper and continue to puree. Adjust the consistency with the reserved liquid, if needed; the spread should be thick but spreadable. Transfer to a bowl, add the cheese, and mix thoroughly.

3. Refrigerate at least 30 minutes before serving. Garnish with sea salt, if desired.

Warm Black-Eyed Pea Salad
with Lemon-Basil Vinaigrette

MAKES 8 SERVINGS

BLACK-EYED PEAS are one of the quickest-cooking dried beans. Substitute other herbs for the basil, if you wish. Some suggestions include thyme, oregano, or chives. Add a sprinkling of lemon zest to give additional color and appeal to the salad.

1 tablespoon olive oil

1 cup minced onion

2 garlic cloves, minced

1 tablespoon lemon zest

6 cups chicken broth, plus as needed

2 cups dried black-eyed peas, sorted and rinsed

2 sprigs rosemary

2 sprigs thyme

2 bay leaves

LEMON-BASIL VINAIGRETTE

½ cup extra virgin olive oil

¼ cup fresh lemon juice

½ cup basil, chiffonade

½ teaspoon salt

¼ teaspoon freshly ground black pepper

1. Heat the oil in a sauce pan over medium heat. Add the onions and sauté until translucent, about 5 minutes. Add the garlic and lemon zest and continue to sauté until aromatic, 2 minutes more.

2. Add the broth, black-eyed peas, rosemary, thyme, and bay leaves and bring to a boil. Reduce the heat and simmer until the peas are tender, about 1 hour. Add additional broth if necessary to keep the peas covered thoughout the cooking time.

3. While the peas are cooking, combine the olive oil, lemon juice, basil, salt, and pepper. Whisk to combine.

4. Drain the black-eyed peas in a colander. Remove and discard the rosemary, thyme, and bay leaves. Add the hot peas to the lemon basil vinaigrette and toss gently until evenly coated. Serve warm or at room temperature.

Chapter Eight

MEATS, FISH
& POTATOES

MEAT AND POTATOES are classic accompaniments to a plate of fried or scrambled eggs—hearty sirloin or ham steaks, crisp bacon, and sputtering-hot sausage are all favorite breakfast meats; perennially popular potato dishes include crisp, golden hash brown or O'Brien potatoes. Extend your menu with a roast turkey or baked ham, perfect for larger gatherings as well as for other meals throughout the week. Poached salmon can be served hot or cold with a variety of accompaniments. From flavorful Ginger Sesame Stir-Fried Scallops (page 198) to the elegant Stuffed Rösti Potatoes (page 219), we've gathered dishes here that will make your breakfast and brunch menus memorable.

Ham Steaks *with Redeye Gravy*

MAKES 8 SERVINGS

IF YOUR ham steaks are large enough, you may want to cut them into portions before you cook them. Spoon the redeye gravy over the cooked steaks, and serve very hot. Traditional accompaniments are scrambled, fried, or poached eggs (pages 146–153) or grits (page 172).

3 pounds ham steaks (cut into 8 portions, if desired)

⅔ cup very strong coffee

1. Heat a large cast-iron skillet over medium heat. Place the ham steaks in the skillet and cook until they develop a deep brown color, 4–5 minutes.

2. Turn the steaks and continue to cook until browned on the second side, another 4 minutes. Adjust the heat as necessary as the steaks cook. Transfer the steaks to a heatproof platter or dish and keep warm. Repeat until all of the steaks have been cooked.

3. Return the skillet to medium heat. Add the coffee, stirring to dissolve the drippings and simmer until very flavorful, about 3 minutes.

4. Serve the steaks at once on a heated platter or plates with the gravy spooned over them.

1. Drippings from the ham steaks have caramelized on the pan, which will give the gravy a significant amount of flavor. 2. It is imperative that the pan is hot when you deglaze it with the coffee; the drippings release from a hot pan more easily.

Broiled Sirloin Steak *with Sautéed Mushrooms*

MAKES 8 SERVINGS

BREAKFAST STEAKS are usually smaller than those you might serve at dinner, though you can choose steaks of any size you like, from a diminutive 3-ounce piece of tenderloin to a hearty bone-in porterhouse. If you have lit the grill, use it to prepare the steaks instead of your broiler. This simple dish is best paired with a fine cut of beef where a rich beefy taste can shine. Use a variety of mushrooms—oyster, porcini, and shiitake, or others when they are available—to underscore the indulgence of this simple but singular dish.

2 tablespoons butter

¼ cup minced shallots

6 cups sliced white or exotic mushrooms

1½ teaspoons salt, divided use

½ teaspoon ground black pepper, divided use

½ cup dry white wine

8 sirloin steaks (about 5 ounces each)

2 tablespoons vegetable oil, or as needed

1. Heat the butter in a large heavy skillet over medium heat. Add the shallots and cook until they are translucent and soft, about 3 minutes.

2. Increase the heat to medium-high and add the mushrooms. Season with ½ teaspoon salt and ¼ teaspoon black pepper. Sauté until they develop a golden color, a rich aroma, and most of the liquid they release has cooked away, about 12–15 minutes.

3. Add the white wine, stirring to release the drippings in the pan. Simmer until the wine is reduced, about 3 minutes. Keep the mushrooms warm if you are broiling the steaks right away, or let them cool and keep refrigerated up to 2 days.

4. Preheat the broiler and the broiler pan.

5. Blot the steaks dry and season them with the remaining salt and pepper. Brush lightly with the oil.

6. Place the steaks on the broiler pan. Broil until browned on the first side, about 4 minutes. Turn the steaks and continue broiling to the desired doneness, about 5 more minutes for medium rare.

7. Serve the steaks on a heated platter or plates topped with hot sautéed mushrooms.

The Broiled Sirloin Steak is shown here with Scrambled Eggs (page 146) and Hash Brown Potatoes (page 214).

Ginger Sesame Stir-Fried Scallops
with Lo Mein Noodles

MAKES 8 SERVINGS

SCALLOPS HAVE a sweet flavor that's a perfect foil for the pungent marinade in this stir fry, but other seafood works well, too: shrimp (peeled and deveined first), swordfish cut into chunks, or monkfish cut into rounds.

1 pound sea scallops

5 tablespoons peanut oil, divided use

1 tablespoon rice wine vinegar

1 tablespoon soy or tamari sauce

1 tablespoon minced ginger

1 tablespoon dark sesame oil

1 tablespoon fermented black beans, optional

2 teaspoons minced garlic

1 teaspoon honey

1 teaspoon lemon juice

½ teaspoon salt, or to taste

¼ teaspoon ground black pepper, or to taste

1½ cups fine julienne carrots

2 cups sliced shiitake mushrooms caps

4 cups finely sliced bok choy or Savoy cabbage

2 packages lo mein noodles

½ cup thinly sliced scallions, cut on the bias

2 tablespoons toasted sesame seeds

1. Pull the muscle tabs from the scallops. Blot the scallops dry and set aside.

2. Combine 3 tablespoons of the peanut oil, the rice vinegar, soy sauce, ginger, sesame oil, fermented beans (if using), garlic, honey, lemon juice, salt, and pepper in a bowl and whisk until blended. Add the scallops and toss until evenly coated. Cover and marinate in the refrigerator at least 2 and up to 24 hours.

3. Bring a large pot of salted water to a rolling boil while you stir-fry the vegetables.

4. Heat a large wok or sauté pan over high heat. Add the remaining 2 tablespoons peanut oil. When the oil is very hot, add the carrots and mushrooms and stir-fry for 1 minute.

5. Add the cabbage and stir-fry until the cabbage is wilted, 3–4 minutes. *(recipe continues on page 200)*

1. Add the cabbage once the mushrooms have caramelized slightly and the carrots have started to soften. 2. Add the scallops once the cabbage has started to turn translucent and wilted slightly.

6. Add the scallops and their marinade to the vegetable mixture and stir-fry until the scallops are opaque and just cooked through, 3–4 minutes.

7. Add the lo mein noodles to the boiling water at the same time that you add the scallops to the wok. Stir once or twice with a fork or chopsticks to separate the strands. Boil the noodles until they are fully cooked and tender, about 3 minutes. Drain in a colander and keep hot.

8. To serve, place the noodles on a heated platter or individual plates and top with the scallops and vegetables. Sprinkle with the scallions and toasted sesame seeds.

Smoked-Fish Platter with Accompaniments

Smoked fish—salmon, trout, sturgeon, or whitefish—is easy on the cook. Buy the fish from a reputable source and keep it well-wrapped until you are ready to put your platter together.

SERVE ONE KIND OF FISH OR A VARIETY

Trout can be purchased whole. Cut the trout into pieces or present it as a whole "side." Smoked trout breaks easily into large flakes that you can mound or present in a bowl.

Smoked salmon is cured and then smoked; lox is a cured salmon that is not smoked. Both are usually cut into paper-thin slices. You can find packaged sliced smoked or cured salmon, but you may have a market or deli in your area that hand carves salmon. Good smoked salmon is smooth, silky, and supple. Shingle the slices or roll them into loose rosettes.

Experiment with other smoked fish, like sturgeon or whitefish. Some fish varieties tend toward flakiness; others are firmer and easier to slice.

Although you should hold smoked fish in the refrigerator, it is a good idea to give it some time to come to room temperature to bring out the best flavor and texture.

ARRANGE THE FISH AND ACCOMPANIMENTS

Some traditional accompaniments to smoked fish include pumpernickel or rye bread. Whole-grain breads and crackers are also good choices. Bagels, of course, are the classic choice to serve with lox. Add chopped red onions, Hard-Boiled Eggs (page 162), a dish of capers, and lemon wedges so that everyone can season and garnish to suit themselves. Cream cheese, plain or seasoned with dill or chives, makes a great spread and also helps hold the fish on your bagel, bread, or cracker.

Poached Salmon *with Hollandaise Sauce*

MAKES 8 SERVINGS

USE A wide, shallow pan to poach the salmon or a skillet with sides high enough to keep the salmon completely submerged as it cooks. To keep the salmon moist and prevent it from separating as it cooks, keep the court bouillon at a bare simmer. You should see tiny bubbles forming around the sides of the pan, but no big bubbles breaking on the surface. Cold poached salmon is delicious with a flavored mayonnaise.

2 quarts cold water

1½ cups white wine vinegar

1 medium onion, thinly sliced

1 carrot, thinly sliced

1 celery stalk, thinly sliced

6 parsley stems

1 sprig fresh thyme

1 bay leaf

2 teaspoons salt, divided use

¼ teaspoon whole black peppercorns

8 pieces salmon fillet (about 6 ounces each)

¼ teaspoon ground black pepper, or as needed

1½ cups Hollandaise Sauce (page 155)

1. To make a court bouillon for poaching the salmon, combine the water, vinegar, onion, carrot, celery, parsley stems, thyme, bay leaf, 1 teaspoon of the salt, and the peppercorns in a large pot. Bring to a simmer over high heat. Reduce the heat and simmer until flavorful, 20 minutes. Strain the court bouillon. (It is ready to use now or it may be properly cooled and stored for later use.)

2. Season the salmon with the remaining salt and ground pepper. Place the strained court bouillon in a wide saucepan or deep skillet and bring to a bare simmer. Add the salmon pieces using a slotted spoon or a poaching rack. Poach until the salmon is cooked through but still very moist, 8–10 minutes.

3. Lift the salmon from the court bouillon carefully and let drain briefly. Serve the salmon on heated plates with the warm Hollandaise sauce.

Roast Turkey Breast *with Pan Gravy & Chestnut Dressing*

MAKES 8 SERVINGS

ONE OF the great benefits of having a Sunday brunch is the opportunity it gives you to "cook big." Roast a turkey breast large enough to give you plenty of leftovers for sandwiches, soup, and salads. You could use the diced cooked meat in place of the chicken in the Chicken Pot Pie (page 213). A "rule of thumb" for roasting turkey is to allow about 20 minutes per pound; use this to calculate the approximate roasting time for birds larger than the one called for in this recipe.

One turkey breast, bone-in, about 7–8 pounds

1 bay leaf

1 large sprig fresh thyme

½ bunch fresh flat-leaf parsley

1–2 tablespoons fresh lemon juice

Salt and freshly ground pepper

¾ cup diced yellow onion

½ cup diced carrot

½ cup diced celery

5 cups chicken broth, divided use

⅓ cup cornstarch

⅓ cup cold water

6 cups Chestnut Dressing (recipe follows)

1. Preheat the oven to 450°F. Set a roasting rack in a large roasting pan.

2. Rinse the turkey in cool water and pat dry. Stuff the bay leaf, thyme, and parsley under the skin. Rub the lemon juice over the entire bird and season with salt and pepper.

3. Place the turkey skin side up on the rack in the roasting pan, transfer to the oven, and immediately reduce the oven temperature to 350°F. Roast, basting occasionally with the accumulated pan drippings, until an instant-read thermometer inserted in the thickest part of the turkey breast registers 170°F, about 2½–3 hours. Add the onion, carrot, and celery to the roasting pan during the final hour of roasting time. Remove the turkey from the oven and transfer it, still on its rack, to a baking sheet. Cover loosely with foil and let the turkey rest while preparing the pan gravy.

4. While the turkey is resting, prepare the pan gravy as follows: combine the pan drippings, onion, carrot, and celery in a saucepan. Add ½ cup of the broth to the roasting pan and stir to deglaze the pan, scraping up any browned bits. Add these drippings to the saucepan along with the remaining broth. Simmer over medium heat, skimming away any fat that rises to the surface, until slightly reduced and flavorful, 20–25 minutes.

5. Stir the cornstarch and water together to make a slurry. Gradually add the cornstarch slurry to the simmering broth, whisking constantly, until the gravy has a good consistency. Simmer 2 minutes more, strain, taste, and season with salt and pepper.

6. Carve the turkey into slices and serve with the gravy and the chestnut dressing.

Chestnut Dressing

MAKES 8 SERVINGS

DRY THE bread cubes in a low oven for 10 or 12 minutes for the best dressing. Using a parchment "lid" as we suggest here keeps the surface of the dressing from drying out too much as it bakes, but still lets it turn a good golden color.

8 cups bread cubes

3 bacon strips, minced

2 tablespoons water

½ cup minced onion

1 cup chestnuts, roasted and chopped

⅓ cup chicken broth, warmed

1 large egg, lightly beaten

3 tablespoons chopped parsley

½ teaspoon chopped sage

½ teaspoon ground black pepper, or to taste

1. Preheat the oven to 350°F. Butter a 2-quart baking dish or casserole. Cut a piece of parchment paper to use as a lid and butter it lightly.

2. Spread the bread cubes on baking sheets and place in the oven until dry, about 8–10 minutes. Transfer them to a large mixing bowl.

3. Heat a large skillet over medium heat. Add the minced bacon and water and cook slowly until the bacon is crisp. Remove the bacon with a slotted spoon and set aside. Add the onion and sauté, stirring frequently, until tender and translucent, about 5 minutes.

4. Remove from the heat and cool before adding to the bread cubes along with the reserved bacon, chestnuts, chicken broth, egg, parsley, sage, and pepper. Toss the ingredients together until evenly blended and moistened.

5. Place the stuffing in the baking dish and cover with the parchment paper. Bake the stuffing until the top and edges are browned and crisp, about 45 minutes. Serve the dressing very hot.

Baked Ham *with Mustard Sauce*

MAKES 8 SERVINGS

*I*F YOU think of baked ham only in terms of a shiny glazed roast with pineapple rings and maraschino cherries, this will be a revelation. The sauce has a delightful chunky texture. Its piquant flavors set off the smoky ham beautifully.

1 tablespoon vegetable oil

1 cup minced onion

1 tablespoon minced garlic

½ cup white wine vinegar

⅓ cup spicy brown mustard

2 tablespoons sugar

½ teaspoon celery seed

½ teaspoon salt

¼ teaspoon ground black pepper

3 pounds boneless ham roast

1. Preheat the oven to 350°F.

2. To make the mustard sauce, heat the oil in a medium sauté pan over medium heat. Add the onion and garlic and cook, stirring from time to time, until the onion becomes soft and translucent, about 5 minutes.

3. Add the white wine vinegar, mustard, sugar, and celery seed. Bring to a simmer over low heat, stirring to completely dissolve the sugar. Simmer until flavorful and very hot, about 3 minutes. Taste the sauce and season it with salt and pepper.

4. Score the ham with a wide crosshatch pattern, making incisions about ¼ inch deep. Set the ham on a rack in a roasting pan and spoon enough sauce over the ham to coat it evenly and lightly. Bake the ham, spooning a little additional sauce over the ham every 10–15 minutes, until it is heated through and the sauce forms a glaze, about 1 hour.

5. Allow the ham to rest for 5–10 minutes before slicing and serving. Return the remaining sauce to a simmer and serve it with the ham.

Horseradish-Marinated Chicken Wrap
with Creamy Black Peppercorn Dressing

MAKES 8 SERVINGS

THIS MARINADE is also excellent with beef. Substitute about 3 pounds of flank steak or London broil and grill to the doneness you like, and then carve the meat into thin slices at an angle.

8 boneless skinless chicken breasts

¼ cup prepared horseradish

¼ cup grated Vidalia onion

¼ cup balsamic vinegar

2 garlic cloves, minced

½ teaspoon juniper berries, crushed

1 teaspoon chopped rosemary

¼ cup olive oil, divided use

2 teaspoons salt

1 teaspoon ground black pepper

Eight 10-inch flour tortillas

4 cups mixed greens, rinsed and dried

1 cup Creamy Black Peppercorn Dressing (recipe follows)

1. Trim any visible fat from the chicken breasts, cut each breast in half lengthwise, and place in a shallow dish.

2. Puree the horseradish, onion, balsamic vinegar, garlic, juniper berries, and rosemary together with 2 tablespoons of the olive oil in a food processor. Pour the mixture over the chicken and turn each piece to coat. Cover and refrigerate for at least 4 and up to 12 hours, turning occasionally to keep the chicken evenly coated.

3. Preheat the grill to high. Remove the breasts from the marinade, shaking off any excess. Blot the chicken dry with absorbent paper toweling. Brush the chicken with some of the remaining oil and season with salt and pepper.

4. Grill the chicken on the first side until it is golden brown, 3–4 minutes. Turn the chicken and continue grilling until it is

cooked through and firm to the touch, another 3–4 minutes. Cut the chicken breasts on the bias into thin slices; reserve.

5. Warm the tortillas on the hot grill until they are flexible, about 15 seconds on each side.

6. Toss the greens with the dressing. For each tortilla wrap, place ½ cup of salad and a sliced chicken breast on the warmed tortilla. Wrap tightly and secure with a toothpick. Cut the wraps in half on the bias and serve at once.

Creamy Black Peppercorn Dressing

MAKES 1 CUP

THIS RECIPE makes just enough to use in our wrap recipe (above). However, it is great to have on hand, so double or triple the amounts called for here. It makes a great spread for sandwiches as well as a pungent dressing for salads. Try it instead of plain mayonnaise in a potato salad, if you like.

¾ cup mayonnaise

1 tablespoon Dijon mustard

1 tablespoon grated Parmesan cheese

2 teaspoons anchovy paste

1 teaspoon minced garlic

1 teaspoon salt

1 teaspoon coarsely ground black pepper

1. Combine all of the ingredients in a bowl and whisk together until thoroughly blended. The dressing is ready to use now, or you can store it under refrigeration for up to 1 week.

Grilled Quail *with Tomato, Avocado & Roasted Corn Salad*

MAKES 8 SERVINGS

*L*ong, slow roasting gives corn an intense flavor, since it essentially steams in its own juices while the husks darken and give the corn a satisfying deep gold color. If heirloom or specialty tomatoes are in season when you make this salad, select an array of shapes and colors to cut into slices or wedges.

4 ears corn on the cob with husks still attached

1 tablespoon salt, divided use

8 semi-boneless quail

2 tablespoons extra virgin olive oil

2 teaspoons freshly ground black pepper

6 cups mesclun lettuce mix, rinsed and dried

1 cup Chipotle-Sherry Vinaigrette (recipe follows), divided use

3 red beefsteak tomatoes, cut into ¼-inch-thick slices

2 avocados, cut into slices

1 medium red onion, thinly sliced

1 cup small-diced aged cheddar cheese

1. Preheat the oven to 400°F.

2. Roast unhusked ears of corn until tender, about 45 minutes. Check their doneness after about 45 minutes: Pull the husk partially away from the biggest of the ears. If you can pierce a kernel easily with a fork, it is done. Remove from the oven and cool completely.

3. Shuck the corn and cut the kernels from the cobs. Place the corn kernels in a mixing bowl and toss with 1 teaspoon of the salt. Keep the corn at room temperature if you are making the salad right away, or cover and refrigerate for up to 12 hours.

4. Preheat a grill to medium-high. Rinse the quail in cool water and pat dry with paper toweling. Lightly brush each quail with olive oil. Season generously with some of the remaining salt and pepper. Grill over medium-high heat until internal temperature reaches 165°F and meat springs back when pressed,

3–4 minutes per side. Be careful not to overcook the quail or they will become tough. Remove and keep warm.

5. Toss the mesclun mix with ½ cup of the vinaigrette. Mound the dressed mesclun on a chilled platter or individual plates. Arrange the tomato, avocado, and red onion slices over the mesclun. Sprinkle with cheese and the reserved corn. Top with the quail and drizzle with the remaining ½ cup dressing. Season with salt and pepper. Serve at once.

Chipotle-Sherry Vinaigrette

MAKES 1 CUP

*C*hipotle peppers are packed in a can with a rich sauce, known as adobo. Chipotles have a rich, deep flavor with noticeable but usually tolerable heat level. Add the chipotle gradually until the vinaigrette has the intensity you like. For a little extra kick, add some of the adobo sauce as well.

3 tablespoons sherry vinegar

1 tablespoon fresh lime juice

1 tablespoon minced shallots

1 tablespoon chopped fresh cilantro

1 teaspoon chopped fresh thyme

1 tablespoon chopped fresh parsley

2 canned chipotle peppers, drained and minced

1 garlic clove, minced

1 teaspoon real maple syrup

¾ cup olive oil

In a medium bowl, combine all of the ingredients except the olive oil. Gradually whisk in the olive oil until the dressing is lightly thickened. Taste and adjust the seasoning.

Taco Salad

*y*OU CAN assemble the salads before you serve them, or let your guests layer their own salad, choosing from among separate bowls filled with savory beef, beans, lettuce, tomatoes, and grated cheese. Add more options if you like, including diced avocados, salsa (page 145), or kernels of corn cut from steamed or roasted ears (for more about roasting corn, see page 207).

2½ pounds lean ground beef

3 cups Taco Sauce, divided use (recipe follows)

½ teaspoon salt, or as needed

¼ teaspoon freshly ground black pepper, or as needed

1 cup cooked or canned black beans, drained and rinsed

1 medium head iceberg lettuce, cut into fine shreds

8 tortilla bowls (made from 10-inch flour tortillas, see below)

½ cup diced tomato

½ cup diced red onion

1 cup Salsa Fresca (page 145)

½ cup sour cream

2 cups shredded cheddar or Monterey Jack cheese

20 pitted black olives

½ cup sliced scallions, cut thin on the bias

1. Heat a large skillet over medium heat. Add the ground beef and cook, stirring and breaking up the meat, until it is fully cooked and no longer pink. Remove the meat from the pan with a slotted spoon and drain well in a colander or sieve. Transfer to a bowl and combine with about 2 cups of the taco sauce. The meat mixture should hold together and be moist. Season with salt and pepper and keep warm. Heat the beans over low heat or in the microwave and keep warm.

2. Place a layer of lettuce in the bottom of each tortilla bowl. Layer the beans, beef mixture, tomato, onion, salsa, sour cream, cheese, and olives. Sprinkle with scallions and serve.

Making Tortilla Bowls

You can buy tortillas already made into bowls, but they are a lot of fun to make on your own. The tortilla bowls can be fried (as we show them here) or baked.

TO FRY TORTILLA BOWLS

Pour about 4 inches of oil into a deep, wide pot. A Dutch oven is a good choice, or you can also use a wok. Heat the oil until it reaches 350°F on a frying or candy thermometer. Or, if you don't have a frying thermometer, add a 1-inch cube of bread. If the oil is at a good frying temperature, it will turn golden brown in about 30 seconds.

Lay one of the tortillas in a frying basket or a wire mesh sieve. Use the bowl of a metal ladle to hold the tortilla in place as you lower the sieve and the tortilla into the hot oil. Hold the tortilla under the sur-

face with the ladle. The tortilla will wrap around the ladle to create a bowl shape.

Fry until the tortilla is very crisp and a light golden color. Remove the tortilla from the hot oil, letting the oil drain back into the pot. Carefully turn the bowl so the oil captured inside it can drain back as well. Transfer to a wire rack and let it drain briefly upside down. The shells can be prepared in advance and held for a few hours at room temperature.

TO BAKE TORTILLA BOWLS

Preheat the oven to 450°F. Set a heatproof cup (like a custard cup or soufflé dish) upside down on a baking sheet and drape the tortilla over the cup. Bake until the tortilla is dry and crisp and holds a bowl shape. Repeat until you have enough bowls.

Taco Sauce

MAKES ABOUT 3 CUPS

¼ cup canola oil

½ cup minced onion

3 garlic cloves, minced

2 tablespoons ground cumin

4 teaspoons ground dried chiles

1 tablespoon dried oregano

¼ teaspoon garlic powder

Pinch of ground coriander

Pinch of ground cloves

1½ cups tomato puree

2 cups chicken broth

1 teaspoon salt, or as needed

½ teaspoon ground black pepper, or as needed

2 tablespoons cornstarch dissolved in 2 tablespoons cold water

1. To make the taco sauce, heat the oil in a medium pan over medium heat. Add the onion and sauté, stirring frequently, until tender, 6–7 minutes. Add the garlic and sauté until aromatic, another 1–2 minutes. Add the dried spices and sauté for 1 minute. Add the tomato puree and continue to cook, stirring frequently, until the mixture is thickened, 10–12 minutes. Add the broth and simmer for 15–20 minutes, or until the sauce is well flavored. Adjust the seasoning with salt and pepper.

2. Add enough dissolved cornstarch to the simmering sauce to thicken it (it should coat a spoon evenly). The sauce is ready to use now or it may be cooled and refrigerated for up to 2 weeks.

Using a Meat Grinder

We've included two sausage recipes in this chapter that call for a meat grinder. You can also purchase preground meats for the sausages, but the difference in flavor and texture is dramatic if you make the effort to grind them yourself.

CHILL THE INGREDIENTS AND THE GRINDER PARTS

If you are grinding your own meat, choose meats from the shoulder for their good flavor. Cut the meat into strips or cubes that will fit easily through the feed tube of your grinder. Add the salt to the meat now, if your recipe calls for it; salt plays a big role in developing a good flavor.

Clean and dry all the grinder parts before you begin and get them very cold. Leaving them in the freezer for about 15 minutes helps keep meats cool as you grind them to preserve freshness and flavor.

PUT THE GRINDER TOGETHER

If you are using the grinder attachment of your stand mixer, be sure that the pieces are tightly secured. Manual meat grinders often at-tach to the counter top with a clamp. Tighten it down well to keep the grinder stable. Use a medium grinding disk for sausages and hash.

GRIND THE MEAT AND SEASONINGS TOGETHER

Add any additional ingredients or seasonings to the meat now. Put a bowl under the opening of the grinder to catch the ground meat. Drop the meat through the feed tube gradually so that it doesn't get blocked.

CHILL THE GROUND MEAT FOR SAUSAGE ONCE AGAIN BEFORE MIXING

Sausages are mixed for a while. To counteract the heat that builds up when you mix the meat, chill it for about 15 minutes before you begin. Mix the chilled meat by hand with a wooden spoon or in a stand mixer with the paddle attachment.

MAKE A TEST

You can adjust the seasonings and saltiness of your sausage if necessary, but in order to tell, you need to make a test. Take about 2 tablespoons and shape into a small patty. Sauté over low to medium heat until cooked through and browned. Taste the sausage and then add more salt, pepper, or other seasonings to your taste.

Mexican Chorizo

MAKES 2 POUNDS

*T*HIS IS a spicy sausage with just enough heat. A touch of cinnamon completes the flavor profile. Try any dried chiles you enjoy. Thai bird chiles are very hot; dried New Mexican chiles or dried chipotles are less intensely hot. We've given a recipe that makes 2 pounds; freeze any of the chorizo you don't need right away to enjoy as a topping on pizza or to cook and crumble over a plain cheese quesadilla.

2 pounds ground pork, chilled

2 tablespoons ground dried chiles

1 tablespoon salt

1 tablespoon minced garlic, sautéed and cooled

4½ teaspoons Spanish paprika

1 teaspoon ground cinnamon

1 teaspoon ground oregano

1 teaspoon ground thyme

1 teaspoon ground cumin

1 teaspoon ground black pepper

½ teaspoon ground cloves

½ teaspoon ground ginger

½ teaspoon ground nutmeg

½ teaspoon ground coriander seed

½ teaspoon ground bay leaf

2 tablespoons red wine vinegar

1. Mix the ground pork and the seasonings by hand with a wooden spoon or on low speed with the paddle attachment until evenly blended, about 1 minute. Mix for an additional minute, gradually adding the red wine vinegar.

2. Mix on medium speed for 15–20 seconds, or until the sausage mixture is sticky to the touch.

3. Make a patty with about 2 tablespoons of the mixture and sauté in a small skillet over low to medium heat until cooked through and browned. Taste and then adjust seasoning and consistency before shaping into patties.

4. The sausage is ready to prepare now or transfer it to storage containers, cover tightly, and refrigerate for up to 3 days or freeze for up to 2 months.

Breakfast Sausage

MAKES 2 POUNDS

*W*E USED this simple sausage to prepare Scotch Eggs (page 164) and, of course, the Egg and Sausage Breakfast Sandwiches (page 147). It's also wonderful as a pizza topping or made into patties to serve with your morning eggs.

2 pounds ground pork, chilled

1 tablespoon salt

1¾ teaspoons ground white pepper

1½ teaspoons poultry seasoning

⅓ cup ice-cold water

1. Mix the ground pork, salt, pepper, and poultry seasoning by hand with a wooden spoon or on low speed with the paddle attachment until evenly blended, about 1 minute.

2. Mix for an additional minute, gradually adding the cold water.

3. Mix on medium speed for 15–20 seconds, or until the sausage mixture is sticky to the touch.

4. Make a patty with about 2 tablespoons of the mixture and sauté in a small skillet over low to medium heat until cooked through and browned. Taste and then adjust seasoning and consistency before shaping into patties.

5. The sausage is ready to prepare now or transfer it to storage containers, cover tightly, and refrigerate for up to 3 days or freeze for up to 2 months.

Corned Beef Hash

MAKES 8 SERVINGS

*I*NSTEAD OF making individual patties, you can make one large hash cake to cut into wedges to serve. Heat the oil in a large skillet, add the corned beef mixture all at once, and lightly press into an even layer. To flip the hash after the first side browns, put a plate or platter upside down on top of the skillet. Hold the plate firmly in place as you lift and invert the skillet. The hash will fall out onto the plate. Return the skillet to the heat, slide the hash back into the skillet, and finish cooking.

2¼ pounds cooked corned beef, diced

2½ cups diced peeled potatoes

1½ cups diced onions

1 cup diced parsnips

½ cup diced carrots

¼ cup vegetable oil, divided use

½ teaspoon salt

¼ teaspoon ground black pepper

2 tablespoons tomato puree

1. Preheat the oven to 375°F.

2. Combine the corned beef, potatoes, onions, parsnips, and carrots in a large bowl. Drizzle 2 tablespoons of the oil over the mixture, add the salt and pepper, and toss until evenly coated. Transfer to a baking pan, cover with foil, and cook until the vegetables are tender, about 1 hour. Remove the foil and stir in the tomato puree. Return the pan to the oven and continue to bake until the mixture is browned and has a sweet aroma, another 15 minutes. Let this mixture cool while setting up a meat grinder with the coarse plate.

3. Grind the mixture through the meat grinder. Form into 16 patties by hand or using a circular mold. The patties are ready to pan fry now, or store them in a covered container in the refrigerator for up to 24 hours.

4. Heat the remaining 2 tablespoons oil in a heavy sauté pan or cast-iron skillet over medium high heat. Add the patties, working in batches so the pan doesn't become crowded. Cook until very crisp on the bottom, 2–3 minutes. Turn the patties and continue to cook until the second side is crisp and the corned beef is very hot all the way through, another 2–3 minutes.

Chicken Pot Pie

MAKES 8 SERVINGS

YOU CAN make one large pot pie, as we have done here, or prepare the pies in individual dishes. Make a few decorations with any scraps of dough you have left over after rolling it out and fitting it to your dish. Use a bit of egg wash to "glue" the decorations to the crust, and then brush the tops of the decorations before baking for glossy, golden crust.

1 pound Blitz Puff Pastry (page 96)

2 tablespoons butter or vegetable oil

2¾ cups diced onion

2 cups peeled and diced Yukon gold potatoes

1½ cups diced carrots

¾ cup diced celery

3 garlic cloves, minced

3 tablespoons flour

3 cups chicken broth, heated

4 cups diced cooked chicken

1 cup green peas, fresh or frozen

2 tablespoons chopped flat-leaf parsley

½ teaspoon salt

⅛ teaspoon freshly ground black pepper

Egg wash of 1 egg whisked with 2 tablespoons cream or milk

1. Preheat the oven to 350°F. Lightly grease a shallow casserole dish.

2. Roll out the puff pastry and cut it to fit the top of the casserole dish, allowing for a ½-inch overhang. Return the pastry to the refrigerator while you prepare the filling.

3. Heat the butter or oil in a saucepan over medium heat. Add the onion, potatoes, carrots, celery, and garlic. Sauté, stirring occasionally, until the onion is tender and translucent, about 10–12 minutes. Add the flour and cook, stirring constantly, until the mixture is evenly blended and has a slightly nutty aroma, 3 minutes. Gradually add the broth, stirring well to work out any lumps. Bring the broth to a simmer and cook over low heat, stirring frequently, until the vegetables are tender, about 15 minutes. The sauce will thicken as it simmers.

4. Remove the pan from the heat and stir the chicken, peas, and parsley into the vegetable mixture. Adjust the seasoning with salt and pepper. Pour into the prepared casserole.

5. Brush the rim of the casserole lightly with a bit of egg wash. Transfer the pastry to the dish and press it down onto the casserole so that the crust sticks to the dish. Cut a vent hole in the pastry. Brush lightly with egg wash.

6. Bake the pot pie until the crust is fully baked and golden brown, about 40 minutes. Serve at once.

Hash Brown Potatoes

*I*NSTEAD OF cubing the potatoes, as we do in this recipe, you can opt to grate the potatoes and then shape them into cakes before pan frying.

6 large Yukon gold potatoes

1½ teaspoons salt, divided use

2 tablespoons vegetable oil

2 tablespoons chopped parsley

¼ teaspoon ground black pepper, or to taste

1. Scrub and peel the potatoes. Put them in a large pot with enough cold water to completely submerge them. Place the pot over medium-high heat and bring to a simmer. Add 1 teaspoon of the salt to the water and cook the potatoes until you can easily insert a skewer or paring knife about halfway into the potatoes, about 20 minutes. Drain the potatoes and return them to the pot. Cook them over low heat until they stop giving off steam, about 5 minutes.

2. Remove the potatoes from the pot. As soon as they are cool enough to handle, cut into medium dice. Set aside.

3. Heat the oil in a large skillet over medium heat. Add the potatoes; they should be in a single layer, so work in batches if necessary. Cook until the potatoes are browned on the exterior and very tender on the interior, turning the potatoes occasionally with a spatula, about 10–12 minutes. Transfer to a bowl or platter and keep warm while cooking the remaining potatoes. Stir in the parsley, adjust the seasoning with the remaining salt and the pepper, and serve while very hot.

About Potatoes

Potatoes are easy to keep on hand as a pantry staple. They pair well with a wide range of flavors, and the dishes we've suggested here show their versatility.

SELECT THE RIGHT POTATO FOR THE DISH

Baking potatoes, sometimes known as russets or Idahos, are starchy enough to stick together; choose them for pancakes, rösti, and other dishes where you want the potatoes to hold together in a cake. Yukon Golds, red potatoes, and white potatoes hold their shape well after cooking. Try other varieties if they are available in your area, especially fingerlings, banana, and blue potatoes, for something out of the ordinary.

KEEP POTATOES WHITE

When you peel potatoes, they start to discolor if they are left exposed to the air. Before you start peeling, fill your pot about halfway with cold water. Scrub the potatoes well and remove any eyes, green spots, or blemishes with a paring knife. A peeler or a sharp paring knife is the right tool to cut away just the skin. As soon as the potato is peeled, *drop it into the cold water. If you know your time is limited, you can peel potatoes ahead of time and keep them in the refrigerator up to 8 hours before you cook them.*

SIMMER POTATOES, DON'T BOIL THEM HARD

A gentle simmer cooks potatoes evenly, and they'll be less likely to fall apart. Add salt to the water as it comes up to a simmer. There should be enough salt so that the water has a slightly salty taste. This assures a great potato flavor; you'll most likely be adding more salt to the dish as you finish it.

BAKE POTATOES PROPERLY FOR A GREAT TEXTURE

Baked potatoes are transformed into a classic potato cake in the Macaire Potatoes (page 217). Scrub potatoes well before you bake them and be sure to pierce them in a few places. This lets the steam escape so you don't end up with potatoes exploding in your oven. Chefs suggest rubbing a little salt on the outside of the potatoes to draw out the moisture and give the baked potatoes a dry, fluffy texture.

O'Brien Potatoes

MAKES 8 SERVINGS

O'BRIEN POTATOES make a colorful addition to any breakfast. Even though it's not traditional, you could add some corn kernels and replace the chives with cilantro to make a great side dish for Huevos Rancheros (page 145).

6 large white or red potatoes

1½ teaspoons salt, divided use

4 bacon strips, chopped

2 tablespoons water

¾ cup medium-diced onion

¾ cup medium-diced red pepper

¾ cup medium-diced green pepper

2 tablespoons minced or sliced chives or scallions

¼ teaspoon ground black pepper

1. Scrub and peel the potatoes. Put them in a large pot with enough cold water to completely submerge them. Place the pot over medium high heat and bring to a simmer. Add 1 teaspoon salt to the water and cook the potatoes until you can easily insert a skewer or paring knife about halfway into the potatoes, about 20 minutes. Drain the potatoes and return them to the pot. Cook them over low heat until they stop giving off steam, about 5 minutes.

2. Remove the potatoes from the pot. As soon as they are cool enough to handle, cut into medium dice. Set aside.

3. Heat a large skillet over low heat. Add the chopped bacon and water and cook slowly until the bacon is crisp and the fat is melted. Remove the bacon with a slotted spoon and set aside.

4. Increase the heat under the skillet to medium. Add the onion and sauté, stirring frequently, until tender and translucent, about 5 minutes. Add the peppers and continue to sauté until very hot and tender, another 3 minutes. Lift the vegetables from the pan with a slotted spoon, letting the fat drain back into the pan, and combine with the reserved bacon.

5. Increase the heat under the skillet to medium-high. Add the diced potatoes; they should be in a single layer, so work in batches if necessary. Cook until the potatoes are browned on the exterior and very tender on the interior, turning the potatoes occasionally with a spatula, about 10–12 minutes. Transfer to a bowl or platter and keep warm while cooking the remaining potatoes. Stir in the sautéed vegetables and bacon with the chives or scallions. Adjust the seasoning with the remaining salt and the pepper and serve while very hot.

Potato Pancakes (Latkes)

MAKES 8 SERVINGS

THE CLASSIC accompaniments for these crisp, buttery potato pancakes are sour cream or applesauce.

4 large russet potatoes, peeled

1 large yellow onion, diced

1 tablespoon lemon juice

1 egg, lightly beaten

½ teaspoon salt

⅛ teaspoon ground black pepper

2 tablespoons bread flour

3 tablespoons matzo meal

2 cups vegetable oil for frying

1. Grind or grate the potatoes and onion together with a food processor or by hand. Transfer to a bowl and toss with the lemon juice to prevent discoloration. Transfer to a colander and squeeze out the liquid. Place in a stainless-steel bowl. Add the egg, salt, pepper, bread flour, and matzo meal. Stir together to combine evenly.

2. Heat ¼ inch of oil in a heavy cast-iron skillet over medium heat. Drop about ¼ cup of the potato batter into the hot oil for each pancake. When the pancakes are medium brown, and just beginning to crisp, turn them and brown the other side, about 3½ minutes per side.

3. Blot the pancakes briefly on paper toweling and serve at once on heated plates.

Lyonnaise Potatoes

MAKES 8 SERVINGS

GIVE THE onions plenty of time to cook slowly to a rich golden color. They'll develop a savory and sweet flavor that is a perfect accompaniment to the potatoes.

6 large white or red potatoes

1½ teaspoons salt, divided use

3 tablespoons vegetable oil

3 cups sliced onions

⅛ teaspoon ground black pepper

2 tablespoons chopped parsley

1. Scrub and peel the potatoes. Cut them into thin slices and put them in a large pot with enough cold water to completely submerge them. Place the pot over medium-high heat and bring the water to a simmer.

2. Add 1 teaspoon of the salt and cook the potatoes until partially cooked, 6–8 minutes. Drain the potatoes and return to the pot. Cook them over low heat until they stop giving off steam, about 5 minutes.

3. Heat the oil in a skillet over medium-high heat. Add the onions and cook, stirring frequently, until very tender and lightly browned, 12–15 minutes. Add the potatoes and season with the remaining salt and the pepper. Cook until the potatoes are browned on the exterior and very tender on the interior, turning the potatoes occasionally with a spatula, 5–7 minutes. Stir in the parsley, adjust the seasoning with salt and pepper, and serve while very hot.

Macaire Potatoes

MAKES 8 SERVINGS

WELL-SEASONED, SIMPLE, and delicious, especially when eaten piping hot. They are crispy on the outside and soft and moist on the inside.

8 medium baking potatoes

¼ cup butter

1 large egg, lightly beaten

2 teaspoons salt, as needed

½ teaspoon ground black pepper, as needed

½ cup canola oil, divided use

1. Preheat the oven to 425°F. Scrub the potatoes well and blot them dry. Pierce the skins in a few places with a paring knife or kitchen fork. Set them on a baking sheet.

2. Bake the potatoes until very tender and cooked through, about 1 hour. *(recipe continues next page)*

OPPOSITE AND LEFT *A skillet of savory Lyonnaise Potatoes. For the Macaire Potatoes, the potatoes should be just cooked through before you cut them and scoop the flesh out; make sure that the first side of the potato cake has a rich golden brown crust before flipping it, otherwise it may fall apart while it is being flipped.*

3. Remove the potatoes from the oven. Cut the potatoes in half. Hold the halved potatoes in a clean towel to protect your hands, if needed. Use a serving spoon to scoop the flesh from the potatoes into a heated mixing bowl. It is important to do this while the potatoes are very hot.

4. Add the butter, egg, salt, and pepper to the potatoes. Use a wooden spoon or a table fork to mash them into the potatoes until evenly blended. Shape the potato mixture into 16 equal-sized cakes, about ½ inch thick.

5. Heat 2 tablespoons of the oil in a large sauté pan over medium-high heat. Add the potato cakes to the pan in batches. They should not be touching one another. Sauté until golden and crisp on the first side, 2–3 minutes. Turn the cakes carefully and cook until golden and crisp on the second side, another 2–3 minutes. Repeat, adding more oil to the pan as necessary, until all of the cakes are sautéed. Serve the potato cakes very hot.

Sweet Potato Chips

MAKES 8 SERVINGS

SERVE THESE bright orange chips with the Horseradish-Marinated Chicken Wrap (page 205). Add a few drops of lime juice or a sprinkling of chili powder to the chips when you add the salt after they come from the pot.

3 sweet potatoes

2 cups vegetable oil, as needed

1¼ teaspoons salt, or to taste

1. Peel the sweet potatoes and slice them as thinly as possible with a slicer or a mandolin (ideally, about ¹⁄₁₆ inch thick).

2. Heat the vegetable oil in a deep pot to 325°F.

3. Working in batches, carefully add the potatoes to the oil. Fry, stirring frequently, until the potato chips are just starting to become crisp and turn a darker orange, 8–11 minutes. The timing will depend on the moisture level of the potatoes. Immediately remove the chips with a slotted spoon and transfer them to paper towels to drain. Season the sweet potato chips with salt while still very hot. Repeat this process to fry the rest of the potato slices.

4. Serve hot or at room temperature.

Stuffed Rösti Potatoes

MAKES 8 SERVINGS

RÖSTI IS a rich and buttery potato cake. We've taken this popular Swiss potato dish and made it into a main course event by adding a mushroom filling and a puff pastry crust.

6 tablespoons butter, divided use

1½ cups julienned leeks

1 shallot, minced

3 cups sliced mushrooms

3 tablespoons dry white wine

1½ cups heavy cream

1¾ teaspoons salt, divided use

½ teaspoon ground black pepper, divided use

Dash of ground nutmeg, optional

6 Yukon Gold potatoes

¼ cup chopped parsley

2 tablespoons chopped tarragon

4 ounces Blitz Puff Pastry (page 96)

Egg wash of 1 large egg blended with 1 tablespoon milk or cream

1. Heat 2 tablespoons of the butter in a sauté pan over medium heat. Add the leeks and shallot; sauté, stirring frequently, until soft, about 6 minutes. Add the mushrooms and continue to sauté until the liquid released by the mushrooms cooks away, 8–10 minutes. Add the wine and cook until almost dry, 2 minutes. Add the cream and simmer until the cream thickens, 8 minutes. Add ¼ teaspoon salt, ¼ teaspoon pepper, and the nutmeg (if using). The mushroom filling is ready to use now, or cool to room temperature and store in a covered container in the refrigerator for up to 2 days. Warm gently over low heat or in the microwave.

2. Preheat the oven to 375°F.

3. Scrub and peel the potatoes. Put them in a large pot with enough cold water to completely submerge them. Place the pot over medium-high heat and bring to a simmer. Add 1 teaspoon of the salt and cook the potatoes until you can easily insert a skewer or paring knife about halfway into the potatoes, about 20 minutes. Drain the potatoes and return them to the pot. Cook them over low heat until they stop giving off steam, about 5 minutes. When the potatoes are cool enough to handle, grate them using the widest opening on a box grater. Toss them together with the parsley and tarragon. Season with the remaining salt and pepper.

4. Heat the remaining 2 tablespoons of butter in a sauté pan with an ovenproof handle over medium heat. Add the grated potatoes to the pan in an even layer and press lightly. Dot the remaining 2 tablespoons of butter around the edge of the potatoes. Cook the potatoes until they are golden brown on the bottom, about 10 minutes.

5. Roll the puff pastry into a circle that will fit the pan. Spread the mushroom mixture in an even layer on top of the potatoes and top with the puff pastry. Brush the puff pastry with the egg wash and bake until golden brown, about 10–12 minutes. Cut into wedges and serve on heated plates.

Chapter Nine

Soups, Salads & Small Bites

A N ARRAY OF small dishes such as soups, salads, or hors d'oeuvres creates the effect of a celebratory banquet. French for "outside of the work," *hors d'oeuvre* refers to the bite-sized nibbles served to guests while they gather. At a brunch, you can serve them right along with the "main course." Most hors d'oeuvres are finger foods, small enough to eat in one or two bites, and require no plates or utensils.

Cold soups make an elegant but easy option at a brunch. You won't have any last minute work to do and will not need to worry about how to keep the soup hot. Serve cold soups in chilled cups or glasses. A touch of color or texture contrast adds a great deal to any soup.

Whether a plate of carefully composed vegetables or an informal toss of spring greens, a salad provides a pleasant counterpoint to the richer elements of a meal. Some salads are served as a starter, some are meant as accompaniments to other dishes. In either case, choose dishes that are suited to the weather or the season.

Select the most delicious raw materials you can find. This does not mean the most expensive. It is easy enough to purchase a big tin of beluga caviar and trim the crusts off little toast points. The real goal, however, is to bring out the very best from simple foods.

We've included little dishes that you can enjoy hot, cold, or at room temperature. No matter which recipes you choose, serve them at the proper temperature. Hot foods, like empanadas or crab cakes, should be very hot. Use skewers or picks for foods that are too hot to hold in your hand or make sure there are plates and forks on hand. Use chilled platters or bowls to serve cold foods. You can even nest a soup bowl filled with one of our chilled soups in a bed of crushed ice for an elegant presentation. Some of these dishes are best at room temperature. If you've made them ahead of time, take them out of the refrigerator a few hours before you want to serve them so they will lose their chill and their flavors can develop.

Season all little dishes like soups, salads, and starters with meticulous care. These flavorful little bites are meant to stimulate the appetite. Seasonings should be noticeable, but not overpowering.

Slice and shape tea sandwiches and other items properly. Each serving should be just large enough to please. Bite-sized items should be just right to pop into your mouth. Eating two or three pieces should leave you satisfied but not stuffed.

Be prepared with everything you and your guests need. Have tongs on hand for hot items, napkins for finger food, little plates and forks for hors d'oeuvres that are large enough to call for them. If there are likely to be shells, picks, or other uneaten items left after you've enjoyed the appetizer, set up a bowl or other container to hold them so you don't find them in unexpected places later on.

Pureeing Soups

A variety of techniques and tools can be used to puree soups and other preparations.

FOOD MILL

Food mills tend to make denser purees than blenders or food processors, as no air is whipped into the mixture. They will also strain out skins, seeds, and tougher fibers as they puree. If your food mill has more than one disk, fit it with a fine disk for a velvety smooth soup, or a coarse disk for a thicker, more textured puree. For the best consistency, pass the soup through the coarse disk first and then switch to the fine disk. (If you cannot change disks on your food mill, use the mill for the first pass and a blender for the second.) Work in batches, filling the food mill no more than halfway each time, and discard the accumulated solids between batches.

IMMERSION BLENDER

An immersion blender, also known as a stick blender, allows you to purée a soup or other preparations directly in the pot. First, remove

Chilled Potato Herb Soup with Lobster

MAKES 8 SERVINGS

THE ADDITION of lobster meat in this recipe takes a rustic soup straight to elegant. But chilled potato soup is wonderful even without the lobster. The soup will keep in the refrigerator for 3 or 4 days, as long as you haven't added the cream. Instead of blending the cream into the soup, you can swirl it into individual servings and scatter the herbs over the top. Or, try the soup hot on a cold day.

2 tablespoons butter

1 medium leek, medium dice

3 cups peeled and thinly sliced potatoes

1¾ quarts chicken or vegetable broth

1½ teaspoons salt, divided use

½ teaspoon ground white pepper, divided use

¾ cup heavy cream, cold

1 tablespoon dry sherry

2 tablespoons chopped chives

2 teaspoons chopped tarragon

2 teaspoons chopped flat-leaf parsley

1 cup diced cooked lobster meat

1. Heat the butter in a soup pot over medium heat. Add the leek and sauté, stirring frequently, until softened and translucent, 5–7 minutes. Add the potatoes, broth, 1 teaspoon of salt and ¼ teaspoon pepper. Bring to a boil and then reduce the heat so that soup simmers gently; simmer until the potatoes are tender and starting to fall apart, about 20 minutes.

2. Remove the soup pot from the heat. Puree the soup until smooth (see below). Season with the remaining salt and pepper to taste. Chill the soup at least 4 and up to 24 hours.

3. Add the cream, sherry, chives, tarragon, and parsley to the chilled soup. Taste and adjust the seasoning with the remaining salt and pepper if needed.

4. Serve the soup in chilled cups garnished with the cooked lobster.

any sachets, bay leaves, or other inedible ingredients. Stir the soup slowly with the blender while its motor is running. Keep the head completely submerged while the blades are turning to prevent splatters.

BLENDER OR FOOD PROCESSOR

You can use a blender or food processor to puree soups and other foods. It is safest to let the soup cool slightly before you puree it. Take the pot off the heat and let it sit for 10–12 minutes. Fill the blender or the bowl of the food processor no more than halfway to avoid making a mess, or worse, scalding yourself. Like immersion blenders, standing blenders and food processors produce a very fine, smoothly textured soup with just a small amount of air incorporated into the puree.

SIEVE AND SPOON

Rustic or home-style purees or puree soups can be relatively coarse and rely simply on pressing the cooked solids through a sieve using a wooden spoon. Work in several small batches and discard the solids frequently to keep the sieve's holes open. Using a circular motion, press firmly against the food with the rounded back of a wooden spoon. Be sure to collect the puree that clings to the outside of the sieve.

Chilled Cucumber Soup *with Shrimp & Dill*

*U*SING THE same broth to cook the shrimp and make the soup infuses this elegant soup with a bold shrimp flavor.

4 cups fish, chicken, or vegetable broth

¾ pound medium shrimp, peeled and deveined

2 tablespoons butter

1 cup chopped yellow onions

¾ cup diced celery

6 medium cucumbers, peeled, seeded, and chopped

2 teaspoons salt, divided use

½ teaspoon freshly ground white pepper, divided use

1½ teaspoons cornstarch dissolved in 2 teaspoons water

1½ cups sour cream

½ cup heavy cream

½ cup chopped dill

2 tablespoons lemon juice, or as needed

½ teaspoon Tabasco sauce, or as needed

½ cup small-diced cucumber for garnish

Dill sprigs for garnish

1. Heat the broth in a large stockpot until simmering. Add the shrimp and cook for 2–3 minutes, or just until they turn opaque. Remove the shrimp from the broth, cut in half lengthwise, refrigerate, and reserve for garnish. Reserve the broth.

2. Heat the butter in a soup pot over medium heat. Add the onions and celery and sauté, stirring frequently, until the onions are translucent, 5–7 minutes. Add the reserved broth and the cucumbers. Add 1 teaspoon of salt and ¼ teaspoon pepper. Bring to a boil, then reduce the heat so that the soup simmers gently. Simmer until the cucumbers are tender, about 10 minutes.

3. Remove the soup pot from the heat and let it cool slightly. Puree the soup until smooth. Return the soup to medium heat and bring to a simmer. Stir in the dissolved cornstarch and simmer, stirring constantly, until thickened, about 2 minutes. Chill the soup at least 4 and up to 24 hours.

4. Combine the sour cream, heavy cream, dill, lemon juice, and Tabasco in a small bowl and stir until evenly blended. Whisk the sour cream mixture into the chilled soup. Taste and adjust the seasoning with the remaining salt and pepper. Add additional lemon juice or Tabasco if needed.

5. Serve the soup in chilled cups garnished with the reserved shrimp and diced cucumbers. Top with a dill sprig.

Cold Strawberry Soup

*C*HOOSE THE reddest, most fragrant strawberries you can find for this cold soup. We've used Grand Marnier, but you could substitute other cordials or liqueurs. Chambord, a raspberry-flavored liqueur, or amaretto, an almond-flavored liqueur, would be good choices, too.

1 quart strawberries, hulled and quartered

⅓ cup sugar

¼ cup Grand Marnier or strawberry liqueur

3 cups heavy cream, cold

3 cups apple juice, cold

½ cup honey

1 teaspoon lemon juice

Strawberry slices for garnish

1. In a large nonreactive bowl, combine the quartered strawberries, sugar, and liqueur and refrigerate for at least 2 and up to 24 hours.

2. Puree the berries with their juices until smooth. Add the heavy cream, apple juice, honey, and lemon juice to the puree. Chill the soup at least 4 and up to 24 hours.

3. Serve the soup in chilled cups garnished with a slice of strawberry.

Cold Roasted Tomato & Basil Soup

ROASTING THE tomatoes before you make the soup intensifies their flavor and adds an additional level of complexity and sophistication to tomato soup.

12 plum tomatoes

4 tablespoons extra virgin olive oil, divided use

2 teaspoons salt, divided use

½ teaspoon freshly ground black pepper, divided use

1 cup small-diced onion

1 cup chopped celery

½ cup chopped leeks, white part only

4 garlic cloves, minced

4 cups vegetable broth

1 bay leaf

¼ cup chopped basil

Halved yellow pear tomatoes for garnish

Shredded basil leaves for garnish

1. Preheat the oven to 375°F.
2. Core the tomatoes and cut them in half lengthwise. Place the tomato halves on a baking sheet or in a baking dish large enough to accomodate them. Brush them with 3 tablespoons of the olive oil and season with ½ teaspoon of the salt and a pinch of the ground pepper. Roast the tomatoes until they are browned and have a rich, roasted aroma, approximately 1 hour. Set aside.

3. Heat the remaining olive oil in a soup pot over medium heat. Add the onion, celery, and leeks and sauté, stirring frequently, until the onion is translucent, 5–7 minutes. Add the garlic and sauté until aromatic, 2 minutes. Add the reserved tomatoes, broth, and bay leaf. Season with 1 teaspoon salt and ¼ teaspoon pepper. Bring to a boil, then reduce the heat so that the soup simmers gently; simmer until the vegetables are tender, about 30 minutes.

4. Remove the soup pot from the heat. Remove and discard the bay leaf. Add the chopped basil and puree the soup until smooth. Chill the soup at least 4 and up to 24 hours. Season with the remaining salt and pepper, if needed, just before serving.

5. Serve the soup in chilled cups garnished with yellow pear tomatoes and shredded basil.

Tropical Fruit Salad

TRY USING some of the more unusual tropical fruits in this salad, like passion fruit, guava, or pomegranates.

2 cups medium-diced mangos

2 cups medium-diced pineapple

2 cups medium-diced melon

2 cups medium-diced papaya

⅓ cup fresh orange juice

2 bananas, sliced

¾ cup unsweetened shredded coconut

1. In a medium bowl toss together the mango, pineapple, melon, and papaya with the orange juice; cover and refrigerate at least 2 and up to 12 hours.

2. Arrange the fruit salad on a chilled platter or individual plates and top with bananas. Sprinkle with coconut and serve.

Endive Salad *with Roquefort Cheese & Walnuts*

MAKES 8 SERVINGS

WALNUT OIL gives this salad a deep, heady aroma. We recommend you store walnut oil in the refrigerator to keep it fresh and flavorful. If you can't find walnut oil, use a good-quality extra virgin olive oil instead.

¼ cup lemon juice, about 2 lemons

⅓ cup walnut oil

1 tablespoon chopped tarragon

½ teaspoon salt

⅛ teaspoon freshly ground black pepper

2¼ pounds Belgian endive

1 cup toasted walnut halves

1 cup crumbled Roquefort cheese

1. To make the dressing, whisk the lemon juice, walnut oil, tarragon, salt, and pepper together in a small bowl and let stand about 30 minutes.

2. Separate the endive heads into individual leaves, rinse and dry them, and place them in a large bowl. Just before serving add the toasted walnuts and crumbled Roquefort cheese. Whisk the dressing to recombine it and add it to the endive. Toss gently until the salad is evenly coated. Serve at once.

Jícama & Sweet Red Pepper Salad

MAKES 8 SERVINGS

JÍCAMA MAY not look too promising when you buy it, but underneath its coarse skin lies a sweet, crunchy, refreshing vegetable.

3 tablespoons lime juice, about 2 limes

1 tablespoon sugar

1½ teaspoons salt

1 teaspoon Tabasco sauce

⅓ cup canola oil

1 medium jícama, peeled and julienned

1 large red bell pepper, julienned

2 garlic cloves, minced

2 tablespoons chopped cilantro

2 scallions, sliced thinly on the bias

1. To make the dressing, combine the lime juice, sugar, salt, and Tabasco sauce in a medium bowl. Add the oil in a steady stream, whisking constantly.

2. Add the jícama, bell pepper, garlic, cilantro, and scallions to the dressing and toss to combine.

3. Cover the salad and marinate in the refrigerator for at least 30 minutes and up to 3 days before serving. Serve the salad chilled or at room temperature.

Mushrooms, Beets, and Baby Greens
with Herb & Truffle Vinaigrette and Walnuts

MAKES 8 SERVINGS

YOU MAY be able to find golden or striped beets at your market. They are wonderful in this elegant salad. Be sure to cook golden beets separately from red beets, if you are planning to combine colors. Otherwise, your golden beets will be dyed by the red ones.

24 baguette slices, cut ¼ inch thick on the bias

½ cup extra virgin olive oil, divided use, or as needed

½ cup crumbled goat cheese

½ cup mascarpone

2 tablespoons salt, divided use

½ teaspoon ground black pepper, divided use

4 medium red beets, tops removed

3 cups halved white mushrooms

3 cups assorted exotic mushrooms (portabellas, shiitakes, porcini, oyster, morels, etc.)

1 cup Herb and Truffle Vinaigrette (recipe follows), divided use

1 head Belgian endive, cut into ribbons

1½ cups baby arugula

3 cups mesclun greens

1⅓ cups chopped toasted walnuts

4 teaspoons white truffle oil, as needed

1. Preheat the oven to 400°F.

2. To make croutons, brush each baguette slice on both sides with a little of the olive oil. Place them on a baking sheet, and bake until golden brown on the first side, about 2½ minutes. Turn the croutons over to brown opposite side, about 2½ minutes more. Remove from the oven.

3. Preheat the broiler.

4. Blend the goat cheese and mascarpone until smooth. Season with a little salt and pepper. Spread 1 tablespoon of the cheese mixture on one side of each crouton. Broil until the cheese is melted. Remove from the broiler and reserve.

5. Place the beets in a saucepot with enough cold water to cover them by about 2 inches. Add salt to taste. Bring the water to a simmer and cook the beets until they are tender enough to pierce easily with the tines of a fork, 30–40 minutes. Remove the beets from the water and let them cool until they can be handled easily. Slip the skins from the beets and cut them into medium dice. Place them in a bowl and drizzle 3 tablespoons of the olive oil over them. Add salt and pepper to taste, toss until evenly coated, and reserve.

6. Heat a large sauté pan over medium-high heat. Add 2 tablespoons of the remaining olive oil to the pan. Add the mushrooms to the pan in a single layer, working in batches to avoid overcrowding the pan. Sauté the mushrooms until golden brown and tender, 4–5 minutes. Continue until all of the mushrooms are sautéed. Transfer the mushrooms to a bowl, add ¾ cup of the vinaigrette, and toss until evenly coated.

7. Toss together the endive, arugula, and mesclun and toss with the remaining vinaigrette. Make a bed of the mushrooms and top with the greens. Scatter the beets around the greens and garnish with the walnuts and croutons. Drizzle with the truffle oil and serve at once.

Herb & Truffle Vinaigrette

MAKES 1 CUP

TRUFFLE OIL is a perfect way to get the unforgettable perfume of truffles into your dishes. It has become widely available over the past few years. Good-quality truffle oils are made by infusing either white *(recipe continues on page 230)*

or black truffles into olive oil without subjecting them to heat, gases, or chemicals. Keep truffle oil in the refrigerator to maintain the best flavor.

½ cup minced shallots

2 tablespoons sherry vinegar

2 tablespoons lemon juice

½ teaspoon minced garlic

½ teaspoon salt, as needed

¼ teaspoon ground black pepper, as needed

½ cup extra virgin olive oil

2 tablespoons truffle oil

3 tablespoons chopped marjoram

3 tablespoons chopped parsley

2 tablespoons chopped mint

1. Combine the shallots, sherry vinegar, lemon juice, garlic, salt, and pepper in a bowl and whisk until blended. Let this mixture rest for 5 minutes to allow the flavors to blend.

2. Add the oils to the vinegar mixture in a thin stream, whisking as you add it. Whisk in the herbs. Taste the dressing and add a little more salt or pepper if necessary. The vinaigrette is ready to use now or it can be stored in the refrigerator for up to 4 days.

Chilled Asparagus
with Mustard Herb Vinaigrette

MAKES 8 SERVINGS

YOU CAN cook and chill the asparagus the day before you want to serve this salad, but don't combine the asparagus and vinaigrette until you are ready to put it on the table to keep the best texture and color in the asparagus.

2 pounds asparagus

5 cups water

2 teaspoons salt

¼ cup Mustard Herb Vinaigrette (recipe follows)

1. Trim the asparagus to remove the white, fibrous ends. Cut the asparagus on the diagonal into 2-inch pieces.

2. Bring the water to a boil in a large pot and add the salt. Add about ½ of the asparagus and cook until the spears are bright green and just tender, 4–5 minutes. Lift the asparagus from the water with a slotted spoon or spider, transfer to a bowl filled halfway with ice water, and stir gently until the asparagus is cold. Drain the asparagus well. Cook the remaining asparagus in the same boiling water, chilling it in an ice bath and draining as directed above. Reserve the asparagus, covered, in the refrigerator, until needed.

3. Toss the chilled asparagus with the vinaigrette and serve immediately.

Mustard Herb Vinaigrette

MAKES 2 CUPS

A GOOD BASIC vinaigrette like this one is great to keep on hand for dressing salads, drizzling on cooked vegetables, or even using on a sandwich instead of mayonnaise. It will keep in your refrigerator for up to 4 days. As the vinaigrette ages, the fresh herbs can lose their color, although the flavor is still fine. You may prefer to add fresh herbs to small batches just before serving the vinaigrette for a great color.

½ cup white wine or cider vinegar

2 tablespoons Dijon mustard

1 tablespoon chopped flat-leaf parsley

2 teaspoons chopped tarragon leaves

2 teaspoons chopped thyme leaves

1 teaspoon sugar

½ teaspoon salt, or as needed

¼ teaspoon ground black pepper, or as needed

¼ teaspoon onion powder

Dash of garlic powder

1½ cups canola oil

1. Combine the vinegar, mustard, parsley, tarragon, thyme, sugar, salt, pepper, onion powder, and garlic powder in a bowl and whisk until blended. Let this mixture rest for 5 minutes to allow the flavors to blend.

2. Add the oil to the vinegar mixture in a thin stream, whisking as you add it. Taste the dressing and add a little more salt or pepper if necessary.

Wedge of Iceberg Lettuce
with Thousand Island Dressing

MAKES 8 SERVINGS

*I*CEBERG LETTUCE presented in wedges has a "retro" appeal that makes it a great choice for low-stress family brunches. Add as many or as few garnishes as you like and let everyone dress their own.

1 head iceberg lettuce, cleaned and cut into 8 wedges

1 pint cherry tomatoes, washed and halved or quartered

8 strips bacon, cooked until crisp and crumbled

1 cup Thousand Island Dressing (recipe follows)

Place each lettuce wedge on a chilled salad plate and garnish with tomatoes, bacon, and dressing.

Thousand Island Dressing

MAKES 2 CUPS

*T*HOUSAND ISLAND and Russian dressings are very similar. To make this into an "authentic" Russian dressing, stir in 2 or 3 tablespoons of salmon or other caviar.

1 cup mayonnaise

⅔ cup prepared chili sauce

3 tablespoons ketchup

2 tablespoons minced onion

2 tablespoons sweet pickle relish

2 teaspoons lemon juice

1 Hard-Boiled Egg (page 162), finely chopped

1 garlic clove, minced

Dash of Worcestershire sauce

Dash of Tabasco sauce

½ teaspoon salt

¼ teaspoon freshly ground black pepper

To make the dressing, combine all the ingredients together in a medium mixing bowl. Mix thoroughly. The dressing is ready to use now or it may be stored in a covered jar in the refrigerator for up to 4 days.

Hearts of Artichoke Salad

MAKES 8 SERVINGS

*Y*ou may be able to find baby artichokes at some times of the year. These tender little globes are easy to peel and prepare. Plan on about 2 or 3 baby artichokes for each person.

3 quarts water

3 tablespoons lemon juice

3 garlic cloves, peeled and left whole

3 parsley stems

1 sprig thyme

1 bay leaf

One 2-inch piece of celery

1 leek leaf

2 teaspoons salt, divided use

8 large artichokes

½ cup extra virgin olive oil

3 tablespoons balsamic vinegar

⅛ teaspoon freshly ground black pepper

3 tablespoons parsley leaves

18 kalamata olives, pitted

4 plum tomatoes, peeled, seeded, and quartered

1 medium red onion, sliced into thin rings

1. Place the water, lemon juice, garlic, parsley stems, thyme, bay leaf, celery, leek leaf, and 1½ teaspoons salt in a large pot.

2. Trim and clean the artichokes as directed below (leave about ½ inch of the stem attached). Add each artichoke to the pot as you finish with it so that it doesn't turn brown.

3. Set the pot over medium heat and bring the water to a simmer. Simmer until a knife pierces the base of an artichoke easily, 8–12 minutes. Remove the artichokes and set aside to cool.

4. In a bowl, whisk together the olive oil, vinegar, the remaining salt, and the pepper. Add the artichoke hearts, parsley leaves, olives, tomatoes, and onions to the bowl and stir to combine.

5. Cover the salad and marinate in the refrigerator for at least 30 minutes and up to 3 days before serving.

1. Cut away the tough tips of the leaves by slicing off the top half of the artichoke, just above the widest point. Make a cut into the artichoke that stops just outside of the yellow center. Roll the artichoke away from the knife as you cut around the center to trim away all of the outer leaves. 2. If using the stem, cut away the fibrous outside. 3. The center, or "choke," should be completely removed from mature artichokes. Scoop out all of the spiny purple-tipped hairs with a spoon.

Apple Sandwiches
with Curry Mayonnaise

TOASTING THE curry powder gives a boost to the flavor of the spread for this tea sandwich.

2 teaspoons curry powder

½ cup mayonnaise

½ teaspoon salt, or to taste

Pinch of ground black pepper, or to taste

16 thin slices fine-grain white sandwich bread

2⅔ cups thinly sliced Granny Smith apples, peeled if desired

¼ cup chopped toasted almonds or cashews, optional

1. Toast the curry powder in a small sauté pan over medium heat until fragrant, about 30 seconds, then stir into the mayonnaise and season the mixture with salt and pepper to taste.

2. Spread curry mayonnaise on the bread slices. Evenly divide the apples among 8 of the bread slices. Top with nuts, if desired. Top each sandwich with the remaining slices of bread. Trim the crusts, cut into shapes, and serve. The sandwiches can be made ahead and stored in an airtight container in the refrigerator for up to 2 hours.

Watercress Sandwiches
with Herbed Mayonnaise

MAKES 8 SERVINGS

WATERCRESS SANDWICHES are the ultimate tea sandwich—easy to assemble, attractive, and delicious.

½ cup mayonnaise

1 tablespoon finely minced chives

1 tablespoon finely minced parsley

1 tablespoon finely minced dill

½ teaspoon salt, or to taste

Pinch of ground black pepper, or to taste

16 slices fine-grain white sandwich bread

1 bunch watercress, rinsed and dried

1. Combine the mayonnaise, chives, parsley, and dill; add salt and pepper to taste.

2. Spread the herbed mayonnaise on the bread slices. Place a layer of watercress on 8 slices of bread. Top with the remaining slices of bread. Trim the crusts, cut into shapes, and serve. Sandwiches can be made ahead and stored in an airtight container in the refrigerator for up to 2 hours.

Cucumber Sandwiches

MAKES 8 SERVINGS

MARINATING THE red onions gives them a mellower flavor and a great texture. If the cucumbers you buy are waxed, remove the peel in thin strips before you make these sandwiches. *(recipe directions continue on page 236)*

1 tablespoon minced red onion

2 teaspoons salt, divided use

⅛ teaspoon sugar

1 tablespoon white wine vinegar

5 ounces cream cheese

2 teaspoons minced chives

2 teaspoons minced dill

3 tablespoons heavy cream, or as needed

Pinch of freshly ground black pepper, or to taste

16 slices fine-grain white sandwich bread

2 cups thinly sliced cucumber, about 1 medium

OPPOSITE *Apple Sandwiches with Curry Mayonnaise (rectangular), Watercress Sandwiches with Herbed Mayonnaise (triangles), and the Cucumber Sandwiches (rounds).*

1. Combine the red onion, ⅛ teaspoon of the salt, the sugar, and vinegar in a bowl and marinate at room temperature for at least 30 minutes.

2. Blend the cream cheese, chives, and dill. Add the heavy cream gradually, using just enough to get a smooth spreading consistency. Add salt and pepper to taste.

3. Spread the cream cheese mixture on the bread slices.

4. Evenly divide the cucumber slices among 8 of the bread slices and lay them evenly on top of the cream cheese mixture, overlapping them slightly. Sprinkle a little additional salt over the cucumber slices and top with the red onion mixture. Top each sandwich with the remaining slices of bread. Trim the crusts, cut into shapes, and serve. Sandwiches can be made ahead and stored in an airtight container in the refrigerator for up to 2 hours.

Sun-Dried Tomato & Goat Cheese Tartlets

MAKES 8 SERVINGS

*I*F YOU don't have little tartlet shells, you can use mini-muffin tins to bake the crust instead.

8 ounces Pie Crust (page 158), unbaked

1 large egg

¼ cup whole milk

1 tablespoon dry sherry

2 teaspoons chopped basil

1 garlic clove, minced

1½ teaspoons all-purpose flour

½ teaspoon ground white pepper

½ cup crumbled fresh goat cheese

3 tablespoons minced sun-dried tomatoes

1 tablespoon minced scallion

1. Preheat the oven to 350°F.

2. Roll out the pie dough ⅛ inch thick. Cut 30 rounds from the pie dough using a 2½-inch round cutter and press gently into 1¾-inch diameter tart molds. Make sure there are no air pockets under the dough. Prick the dough with the tines of a table fork.

3. Cover the dough in the molds with a small piece of foil or parchment paper and fill with dried beans or pie weights. Refrigerate for 5 minutes.

4. Bake the tartlet shells until baked through and dry, 20 minutes. Remove the foil and beans or weights and cool the tartlet shells completely.

5. Combine the egg, milk, sherry, basil, garlic, flour, and pepper in a bowl. Whisk until just evenly blended. Set aside.

6. Mix together the goat cheese, sun-dried tomatoes, and scallion in a separate bowl.

7. Place 1 teaspoon of the goat cheese mixture in each tartlet shell. Fill each tartlet nearly full with the egg mixture, about ¾ teaspoon per tartlet. Bake until the filling is set, 6–8 minutes. Serve immediately.

Black Bean Empanadas

MAKES 8 SERVINGS

*T*HESE EMPANADAS make great hors d'oeuvres. Serve with sour cream, Salsa Fresca (page 145), or guacamole. Assembled empanadas may be held refrigerated for up to 24 hours or frozen for up to 3 weeks.

EMPANADA FILLING

1 tablespoon olive oil

¼ cup small-diced onion

¾ teaspoon minced garlic clove

¼ teaspoon ground cumin

¼ teaspoon dried Mexican oregano

1½ cups cooked or canned black beans, drained and rinsed

1 teaspoon salt

¼ teaspoon freshly ground black pepper

3 tablespoons water, or as needed

¼ cup crumbled queso blanco or grated cheddar cheese

EMPANADA DOUGH

¾ cup all-purpose flour

½ cup masa harina

1½ teaspoons baking powder

¾ teaspoon salt

1 tablespoon canola oil or lard, melted and cooled

2 large eggs

2 tablespoons water

Egg wash of 1 large egg whisked with 1 tablespoon water

3 cups canola oil for frying, or as needed

Kosher salt for garnish

1. To make the filling, heat the olive oil in a medium sauté pan over medium-high heat. Add the onion and garlic and sauté, stirring frequently, until tender, 3–4 minutes. Stir in the cumin and oregano and cook for 30 seconds more. Add the beans to the onion mixture and season with the salt and pep-

per. Puree the bean mixture with 3 tablespoons water. If the beans are too stiff to puree easily, add additional water to thin them. Transfer the beans to a bowl and stir in the cheese. The filling is ready to use now, or it can be stored in a covered container in the refrigerator for up to 2 days.

2. To prepare the dough, combine the flour, masa harina, baking powder, and salt in a mixing bowl. Add the oil or lard and mix by hand with a wooden spoon until evenly distributed. In a small bowl, stir together the eggs and water. Add the egg mixture gradually to the flour mixture, stirring as you add. Knead the dough until it is pliable, about 3 minutes. Adjust the consistency of the dough with more flour or water if needed.

3. To assemble the empanadas, roll out the dough ¹⁄₁₆ inch thick. Using a 3-inch round cutter, cut the dough into circles, making 24 circles. Place 2½ teaspoons of the filling on each circle. Brush the edges of the dough with the egg wash, fold in half, and seal the edges by crimping with the tines of a fork. *(recipe continues on following page)*

4. Place the empanadas on parchment-lined baking sheets, cover, and refrigerate until ready to use. They may be held for up to 24 hours or frozen for up to 3 weeks.

5. Heat the oil in a deep fryer or deep skillet to 350°F. Add the empanadas to the hot oil and fry until golden brown and crisp, turning if necessary to brown both sides evenly, 3–4 minutes. Drain briefly on paper toweling. Sprinkle with a little kosher salt and serve very hot.

Potato Crêpes
with Smoked Salmon & Caviar

MAKES 8 SERVINGS

S ALMON CAVIAR would be an excellent choice for this elegant dish.

3 medium potatoes, peeled, boiled, and mashed

⅓ cup all-purpose flour

3 large eggs

4 large egg whites

¼ cup heavy cream

½ teaspoon salt

⅛ teaspoon ground white pepper

Pinch of freshly grated nutmeg

2 tablespoons canola oil

5 ounces thinly sliced smoked salmon

½ cup crème fraîche or sour cream

4 tablespoons caviar

24 dill sprigs for garnish

1. Place potatoes in mixer with a paddle attachment. Add the flour gradually to the mashed potatoes, mixing on low speed. Mix in the eggs one at a time, then the egg whites, mixing thoroughly between each addition. Adjust the consistency of the potato mixture with the heavy cream until it has a pancake batter consistency. Season the batter with salt, pepper, and nutmeg.

2. Coat a large sauté pan lightly with oil and place over medium heat. Drop about 2 tablespoons of batter into the pan for each crêpe and cook until bubbles appear on the surface and the underside is golden brown, about 2 minutes. Turn the crêpe over in the pan and cook until the other side is golden brown, about 2 more minutes. Keep finished crêpes warm in a 150°F oven until you have made them all.

3. Serve topped with smoked salmon and crème fraîche and garnished with caviar and dill.

Shrimp & Avocado Quesadillas

MAKES 8 SERVINGS

T OMATILLOS HAVE a bright, almost citrusy flavor. Charring them in an open gas flame or over a hot grill gives them a rich, smoky taste. Sautéing the onion gives the tomatillo mixture a touch of sweetness for a perfect counterpart to the heat from the chipotles.

¼ cup olive oil, divided use

1½ cups diced onion

7 medium tomatillos, charred, husks removed

2 cups diced avocado

3 tablespoons chopped cilantro

1 tablespoon cumin seeds, toasted

½ teaspoon salt, or as needed

⅛ teaspoon freshly ground black pepper, or as needed

Eight 6-inch flour tortillas

2 cups shredded Monterey Jack cheese, divided use

1½ teaspoons minced garlic

1 teaspoon minced chipotles, optional

24 extra-large shrimp, peeled and deveined

1 bunch watercress, washed and dried

½ cup Orange Vinaigrette (recipe follows)

1. Heat 1 tablespoon of the olive oil in a large skillet over medium-high heat. Add the onion and sauté, stirring frequently, until golden and tender, 5–7 minutes. Transfer the sautéed onion to a mixing bowl and let cool.

2. Finely chop the tomatillos and add to the cooled onion along with the diced avocado. Use a wooden spoon or a potato masher to work the mixture into a coarse paste. Stir in the cilantro and cumin and season with salt and pepper.

3. Spread the avocado mixture on one side of each tortilla, top with 2 tablespoons cheese, and fold the tortilla in half, pressing lightly to close them. Continue until all 8 quesadillas are filled. This may be done up to 1 hour in advance.

4. Heat 1 tablespoon of the olive oil in a large skillet over medium heat. Add the garlic and chipotles, if using, and sauté until golden, about 2 minutes. Increase the heat to medium-high. Add the shrimp and sauté until opaque and completely cooked through, 4–5 minutes. Keep warm.

5. Just before cooking the quesadillas, toss the watercress with the vinaigrette and set aside.

6. Brush both sides of the quesadillas with the remaining olive oil. Heat a large sauté pan over medium heat. Add the oiled quesadillas in batches and cook until golden brown on the first side, about 3 minutes. Turn and complete cooking on the second side, another 2–3 minutes.

7. Cut the quesadillas in half and serve them very hot, garnished with 3 shrimp and a little of the watercress.

Orange Vinaigrette

MAKES 2 CUPS

*I*F YOU roast the garlic for this dressing, you'll be rewarded with a savory, sweet flavor. You can roast a head of garlic anytime you have the oven or the grill going. Put an entire head in a small pan or baking dish. Drizzle with a little oil, cover loosely with foil, and bake until the juices are browned and the entire head feels soft. *(recipe continues on following page)*

The roasted garlic now squeezes easily from the peel and is soft enough to puree with the back of a spoon.

¾ cup orange juice

2 teaspoons lemon juice

1 teaspoon balsamic vinegar

½ teaspoon prepared Creole mustard

½ teaspoon finely minced garlic

1 cup canola oil

¼ cup extra virgin olive oil

¾ teaspoon salt, or to taste

¼ teaspoon freshly ground black pepper, or to taste

Combine the orange and lemon juices, vinegar, mustard, and garlic. Gradually whisk the oils into the orange mixture. Adjust seasoning with salt and pepper. The vinaigrette is ready to use now or can be covered and held in the refrigerator for up to 3 days.

Gougères

MAKES ABOUT 50 PIECES

*I*N ADDITION to being a great snack item, these Gruyère cheese puffs, made from a pâte à choux batter, lend texture to cream or pureed soups. They are best when served warm from the oven, but they can also be cooled, held in an airtight container, and served at room temperature. This recipe makes a large amount because it is difficult to make a smaller quantity of dough, but you can freeze any that you won't eat within a few days. To reheat, defrost at room temperature for 10 minutes, then crisp in a 350°F oven for 5–10 minutes.

1 cup water

6 tablespoons olive oil

½ teaspoon salt

1 cup all-purpose flour, sifted

4 large eggs

¾ cup grated Gruyère cheese

¼ teaspoon ground black pepper, or to taste

1. Preheat the oven to 400°F. Line baking sheets with parchment paper.

2. Combine the water, olive oil, and salt in a saucepan over high heat and bring to a boil. Add the sifted flour all at once and stir in well. Cook, stirring constantly, until the dough begins to come away from the sides of the pan, about 5 minutes.

3. Immediately transfer the dough to the bowl of a stand mixer with the paddle attachment and beat on medium speed to cool to room temperature. Add the eggs one at a time, beating well after each addition, to achieve a stiff but pliable texture. Add the cheese and the pepper. Continue mixing for 1 minute.

4. Transfer the dough to a pastry bag with a plain round tip and pipe 1-inch-diameter balls (or other shapes as desired) about 2 inches apart onto the prepared baking sheets. Alternatively, use a spoon to drop the dough onto the baking sheets.

5. Bake until golden brown and puffed, about 5 minutes, then reduce the oven temperature to 325°F and continue to bake until cooked through, 20–25 minutes more. Serve warm.

Index

onions/scallions
    Caramelized Onion Quiche, 160, 161
    Cheddar and Onion Rye Rolls, 93
    Corn & Scallion Pancakes, 121
oranges
    Cranberry Orange Muffins, 45
    Cream of Wheat with Oranges & Pista-
        chios, 175
    Mimosa, 29
    Orange & Cherry Bread-and-Butter
        Pudding, 156–57
    Orange Biscotti, 109
    Orange Sauce (Torrijas), 134
    Orange Vinaigrette, 239–40
ovens, 77